Causes and Consequences
of Global Migration

Causes and Consequences of Global Migration

Joakim Ruist

ANTHEM PRESS

Anthem Press
An imprint of Wimbledon Publishing Company
www.anthempress.com

This edition first published in UK and USA 2022
by ANTHEM PRESS
75–76 Blackfriars Road, London SE1 8HA, UK
or PO Box 9779, London SW19 7ZG, UK
and
244 Madison Ave #116, New York, NY 10016, USA

First published in the UK and USA by Anthem Press in 2021

British Library Cataloguing-in-Publication Data
A catalogue record for this book is available from the British Library.

Library of Congress Control Number: 2020952826

ISBN-13: 978-1-83998-538-6 (Pbk)
ISBN-10: 1-83998-538-0 (Pbk)

Cover image: Rebekah Zemansky/Shutterstock.com

This title is also available as an e-book.

CONTENTS

FIGURES

TABLES

Chapter 1

WHAT AND WHY

The world currently has around 260 million international migrants, that is, people who live in a country different from the one in which they were born. Out of these, around 90 million have moved to the richer Western world (Europe, North America, Australia, New Zealand) from the mostly poorer rest of the world. This corresponds to approximately 1.5 percent of the population in the part of the world they have left, and about 10 percent in the part to which they have moved. Each year over the last few decades, their number has increased on average by around two million.[1]

This book is about this migration. Some of it happens because people are forced to flee from war or persecution in their home country, or for family reasons. Yet most migrants move for predominantly economic reasons. They move to enhance their living standards, or at least for an opportunity to do so. Roughly estimated, an average migrant from the rest of the world has increased their annual income by more than US$10,000 by migrating to the West (see Chapter 7). Multiplied by 90 million migrants, this implies a considerable increase in global living standards. A part of this income is also sent to relatives in the migrants' home countries, contributing to improved living standards there as well.

The vast economic consequences of migration for people who were born in low- and middle-income countries are thus evident. They are commonly seen as mostly positive, although there are also fears that some of these countries may have lost too many of their most talented and educated people, whom they would have needed for creating better economic development at home.

Yet in the receiving countries, migration leads to more far-reaching and polarizing conflicts than perhaps any other political issue of today. Many feel warmly about migration, because it gives others possibilities to improve their lot through their own sacrifices and hard work, or allows them to escape war and persecution. Many others worry about how migration impacts labor market opportunities for those who have already been hit by decades of

---

[1] Source: United Nations Global Migration Database.

deindustrialization, automation and increasing demands on workforce skills; about migration draining public finances; harming national identity, cohesion, community, trust or communication and understanding between people— ultimately about the risk of migration harming the very foundation of society, which is people's shared willingness to constitute one.

Since the United States and Canada enacted more restrictive immigration laws gradually about a hundred years ago, and since the United Kingdom terminated its free immigration from Commonwealth countries in 1962, all migration from poorer countries to the West has been strictly regulated. According to polls that have been conducted across the world by Gallup, the 90 million migrants who exist correspond to only a small fraction of the number of people who say they too would migrate to the West "if they had the opportunity." Many also try to do this, even in situations where it is forbidden and dangerous. Today, the United States has a wall erected and tight patrolling along almost the entire stretch of the Mexican border that does not comprise the Rio Grande. Spanish Ceuta and Melilla, which share the European Union's (EU's) only land borders with Africa, are surrounded by triple six-meter-high patrolled barbed fences with heat sensors, to keep migrants out. But the willingness to migrate is too strong among too many, for all of this to succeed in bringing illegal migration to a halt. And the humanitarian consequences are grave. Thousands die each year during their attempts to reach Europe or the United States, and many more suffer gravely.[2]

At the same time, large shares of the population of nearly all Western countries say that they think the immigration policy in their country is too generous, while typically very small shares say it is not generous enough. This has also been the case for decades (see Chapter 6). In other words, a—mostly silent— majority has long opposed the way immigration policy has been conducted. Occasionally this opposition has been ignited, and there have been stronger demands for change. But the general pattern has persisted.

This has changed quite spectacularly in the past few years. Three far-reaching political events have shaken the Western world and its political landscape: the United Kingdom voted to leave the EU in 2016; Donald Trump was elected president of the United States in the same year; the refugee crisis brought the EU's ability to cooperate and compromise more or less to a collapse. Of these three events, the last was entirely due to popular resistance to immigration. Of the former two, cautious interpretations would say that resistance to immigration was one among several major causes. Yet it is

---

[2] The NGO network *UNITED for Intercultural Action* has documented over 40,000 deaths among refugees attempting to travel to Europe since 1993 at: http://www. unitedagainstracism.org (accessed on November 17, 2020).

also undeniably true that neither the British leave-EU campaign nor Donald Trump's election campaign really took off before they began to focus more on immigration than what each of them had done initially.

How they choose to handle issues of how to regulate immigration thus appears crucial for the future development of Western societies. Considering this, and considering the many strong opinions on these matters, actual popular knowledge about the consequences of higher or lower migration is surprisingly low. This is not just a personal opinion. In fact most people, at least in Europe, appear to think they know too little. In April–June 2018, the EU Commission reported results from its Eurobarometer surveys, where immigration was the political issue that the highest share of the population of the EU, 38 percent, identified as the most important for the Union. It was followed by terrorism, which is also partly linked to immigration, at 29 percent. Yet at the same time, only 37 percent said they considered themselves well-informed about immigration and integration-related matters, while 61 percent said they did not.[3]

This book is written for anyone who wants to learn more about migration, that is, about why people migrate and the consequences of them doing so. It focuses on the migration, and deals with the questions about its consequences, which create the most important political tensions in the West today. Hence, the book focuses on migration from the, mostly poorer, rest of the world to the Western world, and not on migration between countries in either of these two large groups. It also primarily focuses on consequences in the receiving countries, while those in the sending countries are treated more briefly.

Migration from Eastern to Western Europe since the EU enlargements in 2004 and 2007 is a borderline case in the delimitation between the West and the rest. In many cases, I include the new EU member states in the "West" category. Yet several interesting things about migration from poorer to richer countries can be learned from this migration, which has been unique in modern history with respect to how easy it has been to move between countries whose income levels have been very different. Hence I also draw on insights from this migration in several sections of the book.

Chapter 2 of the book gives an overview of the migration of the last 180 years. Chapter 3 deals with the forces that create migration, that is, who migrate, and where and why. Chapter 4 describes patterns in migrants' economic performance, that is, their incomes, in receiving countries. Chapter 5 deals with the economic consequences of migration in receiving countries,

---

[3] Sources: Most important issues for the EU: Eurobarometer 89, the EU Commission. Well-informed about immigration and integration related matters: Eurobarometer 88.2, the EU Commission.

focusing mainly on wages, unemployment and public finances. Chapter 6 deals with the impact of migration on inequality, cultural heterogeneity, attitudes and social cohesion in receiving countries. Chapter 7 takes a look at two of the most widely discussed consequences of migration for the sending countries: the resulting inflows of migrants' remittances, that is, money sent mostly to the migrants' relatives, and the consequences of the emigration of very high shares of the most highly educated people in several countries. Finally, Chapter 8 deals with factors that are decisive for what future migration will look like: how driving forces for migration are likely to evolve, and what scope the receiving countries have to control their immigration.

The narrative account of Western immigration in Chapter 2 begins around 1840, when migration from Europe to America began taking off. The part of the chapter that deals with migration before 1970 is—in contrast to the rest of the book—not limited to migration from the rest of the world to the West. In this period, income differences were large also between countries in the West, and an important part of global migration from poorer to richer countries was between these.

The book reports many numbers and statistics and is generally much concerned with describing broad patterns at a high level of aggregation. Migration is very different in different cases. It is easy to find both examples that paint very bright pictures of it, and others that paint very dark ones. One can easily write a whole book that shows only one of these pictures (and some have done so). Yet to give a fairer account, it is important to show what things look like most often, or on average, and also the amount of variation around the averages.

I want to present these results in a way that makes them as accessible as possible to a wide readership. As this is most often not the primary ambition in the research articles on which much of our knowledge is based, numbers and illustrations in the book are seldom taken directly from such. More often I create new illustrations and complement these with references to research articles that contain similar and broader results. Thus, the empirical material presented is not always chosen for constituting in itself the highest quality or most convincing analysis. On the contrary, it is sometimes even quite simplistic. It is then chosen because it provides good illustrations of general patterns that have also been confirmed in more advanced analyses—to which references are also provided.

The conclusions I draw about the causes and consequences of migration are in most cases based primarily on empirical rather than theoretical results. We are sometimes in a fortunate situation where theoretical results are unambiguous, that is, where things could not reasonably be in more than one way. Yet, such cases are rare. More commonly, there are several different theories that are all reasonable, but which lead to very different conclusions. Then empirical results are needed to make any conclusions convincing. Furthermore, theory is most often capable only of predicting the direction of an effect, not its size. Yet, size is central. Too many discussions about the impact of migration focus too much on direction only, that is, on whether an effect is positive or negative, and too little on size. But if an effect is small anyway, it should not matter so much whether it is positive or negative.

However, it should be said already at this point that far from all questions about effect sizes are given exact and empirically well-founded answers in the book. It is difficult to produce completely trustworthy empirical results on the consequences of migration. The main reason for this is that if we are to credibly measure the impact of something, such as migration, we need *exogenous* variation in this something. This means variation that was not in turn caused by that something on which we want to measure effects (or by some third factor, which also impacts on that which we want to measure effects on, through some other mechanism than the one under study).

When we want to measure the impact of migration, we seldom or never have any such perfectly exogenous variation to study. On the contrary, the historical variation in migration between places and time periods has been strongly determined by the situations in the receiving countries, most often primarily the opportunities on their labor markets. Hence for example, we may want to find out the extent to which immigration increases unemployment, by comparing unemployment between places with higher immigration and places with lower immigration. Yet this typically does not work, because most migrants prefer moving to places where unemployment is low. Research on the consequences of migration is much about trying to find ways of getting around this problem (see further in Chapter 5). Yet on several central questions, the results are still not fully convincing.

Furthermore, several of the most important, perhaps *the* most important, consequences of migration concern how immigration affects peoples' thoughts and attitudes. And such effects are not predetermined. We may study empirical patterns and form pictures of what reactions to immigration commonly look like. But humans and societies can, at least in part, choose their reactions. Things do not necessarily have to turn out the way they usually do.

Hence there are difficult challenges to overcome in empirical migration research, of which there exists a lot, but of varying quality and reliability. There is much published research, the results of which few researchers actually believe in. The picture of which studies are more or less credible also differs between researchers. This makes it difficult to summarize the state of knowledge on several of the questions that are dealt with in this book, and it can be done in different ways. What is presented in this book is primarily my own assessment of what is most credible. When the picture is complicated, I try to be as clear as possible about on what assumptions or methodological reasoning the interpretations are based.

With this clarity, I also hope to give readers some competence of their own in assessing research results, which I think would be valuable. Public discussions should not have to cede the task of interpreting research results from the social sciences to researchers only the way it most often does. The central methodological questions are seldom too advanced to not be accessible to anyone, who may then form their own conclusions and not rely only on others' claims about what is "proved" or not.

Also, almost nothing is entirely "proved" in social science. We are seldom— or should at least seldom be—entirely convinced. The question is rather how strong we find the indications that matters are in one way or another. Yet although we are most often not certain, we are seldom fully ignorant either. Existing indications favor some conclusions over others. And the margins of uncertainty are often narrow enough for us to be able to rule out at least some of the more extreme claims of very positive or negative consequences of migration that are sometimes (of often) voiced publicly.

Several people have contributed importantly to this book, by reading and giving valuable comments to all or parts of its contents. I am grateful for the help from Andreas Bergh, Arne Bigsten, Bernt Bratsberg, Martin Dribe, Anthony Edo, Jakob Enlund, Robert Erikson, Karin Jonnergård, Stefan Sandström, Gabriella Stjärnborg, Jan Stuhler and Ulf Waltré.

Chapter 2

180 YEARS OF MIGRATION

Most people prefer not to move long distances. We appreciate living in the place and the social context in which we grew up. Examples abound of geographical regions where unemployment has been high for decades and which are situated only a few hundred kilometers from other regions, within the same country, where opportunities to find work have consistently been greater. Neither high monetary costs nor linguistic or cultural differences make it difficult for people to move between these regions. Yet too few do, for the important differences in unemployment to level out even over a time span of several decades.

It thus evidently takes quite a lot to make many of us move even to familiar and nearby places. And of course it takes even more to make us move to places of which we know little, to where the move is costly and risky, and where we would find ourselves among foreign language and customs. In most instances we prefer to avoid this, if we can.

Yet over and over throughout history, many have found themselves in situations where they have thought it worthwhile to move to faraway places. After the earliest of our *Homo sapiens* ancestors left Africa, it took only a few ten thousand years before their descendants had colonized most corners of the Earth, even including islands that are situated thousands of kilometers into the Pacific Ocean. What most certainly drove them were possibilities to find more secure livelihoods. Resources were scarce where they were, and if they took the risk of venturing into the lesser known, they saw a chance of obtaining greater abundance. With all certainty, many such risk-takers failed. But consistently some succeeded, and kept pushing the frontiers.[1]

Later, when numerous Europeans began moving to America by the middle of the nineteenth century, we know that it was primarily for reasons of finding secure basic livelihoods. Many among the earliest movers knew almost nothing about America. But they had heard that it was easier to survive there, for those who were lucky enough to survive the voyage and get there at all. And their

---

[1] Goldin, Cameron and Balarajan (2011).

subsistence at home was so insecure that they thought trying this alternative was worth all the costs and all the risks.[2]

Today's migration to the West is both similar to and different from that of 180 years ago. In the Internet age, destinations are often better known to prospective migrants. The decision to migrate is thus more often a well-informed one than what it once was. Many still move to escape poverty, or conflict. Many others are at no risk of poverty in the home country, but they still hope that a move to the West may substantially improve their living standards. High shares of Western immigrants today are highly educated. Today's migration is diverse. It cannot be justly summarized in a few sentences, or one grand theory.

In this chapter, I want to convey a basic understanding of what the phenomenon of migration in the West has looked like over the last 180 years: its directions and magnitudes and how it has been a component of important economic, social and political events that have shaped this part of the world to what it is today—including what unites and what separates migration between different places and time periods. The chapter aims to provide a basic overview before the rest of the book deals with migration topic by topic in more detail.

Background and migration before 1840

The main cause of the great migration from Europe to America that took off considerably by the middle of the nineteenth century was the big income differences between the two continents. America's economic development was strong, and huge land areas were also sparsely populated. Both industry and commercial agriculture experienced shortages of labor, and large regions had almost no agriculture at all. America thus generally offered better economic conditions than Europe, for wage labor as well as for subsistence agriculture.[3]

From the middle of the nineteenth century large numbers of Europeans began to afford one-way tickets across the Atlantic. They could thus begin to make use of these opportunities and meet America's—most of all the United States'—great demand for labor. This had not previously been the case. In the eighteenth and first half of the nineteenth centuries, voluntary migration had been far from sufficiently high to meet the demand for labor on the American continent, in particular, on the big plantations in the US South, the Caribbean and Brazil.[4]

---

[2] Gould (1979); Hatton and Williamson (1998).

[3] Hatton and Williamson (1998).

[4] Goldin, Cameron and Balarajan (2011).

The solution to these labor shortages had therefore become involuntary migration. Until 1888, when Brazil became the last country in the Americas to abolish slavery, around ten million people in total were shipped from Africa to America for slave labor, of which around nine million were shipped during the peak years of 1700–1860.[5] Before 1820, more than three-fourths of all migration to the American continent was involuntary, and it was not until the 1880s that accumulated voluntary migration since Columbus would catch up with involuntary.[6] In 1835, the last year in which involuntary migration was higher than voluntary, the population of African descent—almost all of them slaves, former slaves or descendants of slaves—had accumulated to a full one-fourth of the continent's total population.[7] This average masks substantially higher shares in the plantation regions.

Accumulated migration of non-slaves before 1820 amounted to about 2.6 million people, mostly from the colonial powers of England, Spain and Portugal. Around 75 percent of these migrants paid for the voyage by their own financial means, 5 percent were convicts and 20 percent were indentured workers, that is, workers whose employers paid for their voyages in return for the workers committing to work for them, typically for several years.[8]

Slavery persisted into the 1860s in the United States, where its abolishment required a civil war, and into the 1880s in Brazil, in spite of the political ideas of freedom, equality, brotherhood and democracy that became widespread in the West already in the late eighteenth century and of decades of widespread abolition campaigns. Slavery was simply too economically important to be easily done away with. And when abolition finally managed to prevail, its importance had been reduced, precisely because voluntary migration had begun to increase.

1840–1930: Migration to America

Voluntary migration from Europe to North America increased gradually in the first decades of the nineteenth century and took off considerably toward the middle of the century. Central to the gradual increase were rising incomes in larger shares of the European population, which meant that more people could afford one-way tickets across the Atlantic.[9] Most migrants came from the countryside, where most Europeans still lived.[10] Yet many of the good income

---

[5] Goldin, Cameron and Balarajan (2011).
[6] Eltis (1983).
[7] Eltis (1983).
[8] Hatton and Williamson (2005).
[9] Hatton and Williamson (2005).
[10] Hatton and Williamson (2005).

opportunities, most of all in the United States, were in the fast-growing cities. According to the census taken in 1860, 17 percent of the native population of the United States, but a full 51 percent of its European immigrants, lived in cities.[11]

However, Europeans often constituted more visible shares of total populations in the western territories that were being settled in the same period. In these territories, the US government sold "unused" land (meaning that it was not used by non-Indians) at very low prices to anyone intending to make productive use of it. After 1862, the land was even given away for free. Europeans made use of this opportunity to a higher degree than natives. This settlement of new lands also enabled strong geographic concentration of immigrants of the same nationality, or even from the same village.

Migration from Europe to the United States kept increasing consistently decade by decade. Several factors contributed to gradually making it easier for more people to emigrate, and more and more people did so, until several countries and regions had lost considerable shares of their total populations. One of these factors was the continued process of industrialization in Europe. While the increased employment opportunities that came with industrialization would in themselves provide more reasons *not* to emigrate, they also gave more people high-enough incomes to afford emigration. (We will see more in Chapter 3 of how increasing incomes may affect migration in different directions.) Another migration-enhancing factor was the introduction of transatlantic steamboat traffic in the 1860s. This did not importantly affect the monetary cost of the voyage. Yet it reduced the travel time to around 10 days from previously in the worst cases (the wind direction was never known in advance) being several months. Thus it also brought an end to the high mortality that was previously associated with transatlantic travel. Railroad expansion in Europe also facilitated emigration by making the journey to the port cities easier and cheaper.[12]

The vast majority of European emigrants went for the United States. The gradual increase in migration from Europe to the United States between the 1820s and the First World War can be seen in Figure 2.1. The war, and after that gradually more restrictive immigration laws, subsequently reduced immigration from seven and a half million in 1900–1909 to only two and a half million in 1920–29. Finally, the depression of the early 1930s brought an end to the almost a hundred-year long period of high migration from Europe to the United States. In the 1930s and the 1940s, migration was below half

---

[11] Source: Own calculations using data from the US census in 1860, from Ruggles et al. (2015).

[12] Gould (1979).

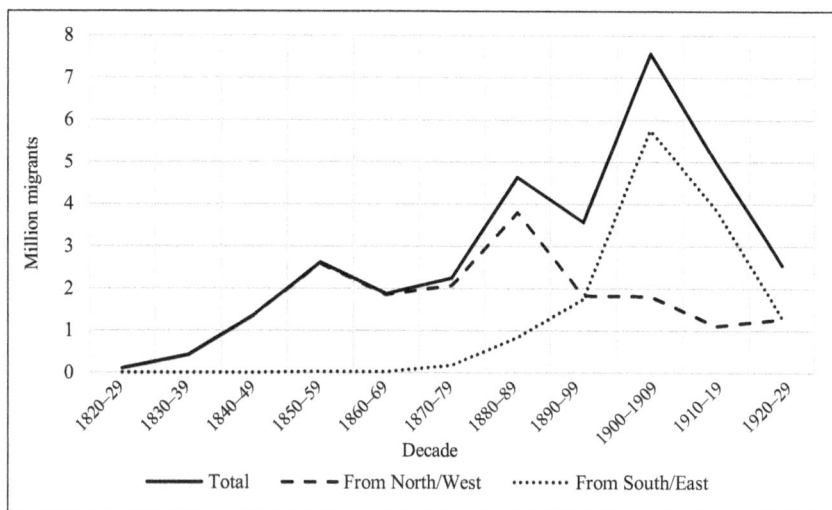

Figure 2.1 Migration (million migrants) from Europe to the United States per decade. "North/West" refers to Belgium, Denmark, France, Germany, Ireland, the Netherlands, Norway, Sweden, Switzerland and the United Kingdom. "South/East" refers to all other European countries (including Russia).

Source: US Department of Homeland Security (2016).

a million per decade, and it has never again reached above one and a half million.[13]

First Northern and Western, then Southern and Eastern Europe. The economic and technological developments that contributed to increasing migration to a large degree happened at different times in different parts of Europe: earlier in its northern and western and later in its southern and eastern parts. Hence, as Figure 2.1 also shows, this long period of high European emigration consists of two quite different sub-periods.

Before 1890, almost all migration to the United States originated in Northern and Western Europe. Before 1880, it is almost impossible to distinguish migration from that region from total migration in Figure 2.1. The numerically most important emigration country in this period was Ireland. Already in the early nineteenth century, Ireland had stood out with a substantially higher share of the population emigrating compared with other European countries. And in spite of being fairly small, Ireland was the single

---

[13] Source: US Department of Homeland Security (2016).

most important country of origin for migration to the United States in both the 1820s and the 1830s.[14]

However, one of the explanations for this appears to be that the Irish population at the time was not as small relative to those of other countries, or not even in absolute numbers, as it is today. According to the census of 1841, the population of Ireland (including current Northern Ireland) was around eight million. Today it is only slightly above six million. (The population of the rest of Europe, on the other hand, is more than twice as large today as it was in 1841.)

Ireland was thus crowded in the first half of the nineteenth century. It was poor, and its food production could barely sustain its population. As Ireland was situated far to the west and was English-speaking and also part of the British empire, North America probably also felt less distant seen from there compared with from continental Europe or Scandinavia. All these factors probably contributed to the high propensity of the Irish to emigrate.

The difficulties with producing enough food probably also contributed to the fact that the poor people in Ireland relied to such a large extent on growing potatoes, which give comparably high yields per cultivated area. And because they did, Ireland was hit extremely hard when potato blight struck Europe by the middle of the 1840s. The Irish famine of 1845–52 killed around one million people, and kick-started Irish mass emigration: 650,000 people left the country for the United States in the 1840s and one million in the 1850s. Thus also in these two decades, Ireland was the single most numerically important country of origin for migration to the United States.[15] In total, a full 19 percent of the Irish population is estimated to have left Europe in the 1850s (smaller fractions of which went to Canada, Australia and New Zealand).[16]

Irish emigration remained high also in the following decades. At 10–16 percent, Ireland had the highest population shares leaving Europe in each decade until 1900 when it was surpassed by Italy. By then, an accumulated 4.5 million in total had left the country, mostly for the United States.[17] The country's remaining population consisted of approximately as many, meaning it was only slightly more than half as large as it had been in 1841.

Apart from Ireland, the most important countries of origin for migration to the United States before 1890 were Great Britain and Germany.[18] The highest emigration rates were recorded for Sweden and Norway, where—as in

---

[14] Source: US Department of Homeland Security (2016).
[15] Source: US Department of Homeland Security (2016).
[16] Hatton and Williamson (1998).
[17] Hatton and Williamson (1998).
[18] US Department of Homeland Security (2016).

Ireland—populations were becoming too large for food production to reliably feed.[19] Hence European emigrants through this period came predominantly from the northern and western parts of Europe, which were the richest and the most industrialized, and whose populations could therefore to a larger extent afford to pay for the voyage.

After several decades, high accumulated shares of the populations of several Northern and Western European countries had emigrated and emigration began to fall. This happened around 1890, and total emigration from Europe was lower in the 1890s than it had been in the 1880s. But Europe's highest emigration by far was to be recorded between the turn of the century and the start of the First World War in 1914. As emigration was decreasing in the North and West, industrialization and rising incomes were beginning to reach larger populations in the South and East.[20] Several Eastern European countries were also liberalizing their previously strict emigration laws.[21]

The most important country of emigration in this period was Italy, from where around one-sixth of the population left Europe in these 15 years, and almost as many moved to other European countries.[22] (Almost half of all Italian transatlantic emigrants later returned to Italy. With faster and cheaper communications, by the turn of the century, transatlantic migration was no longer almost always for life.) Italian emigrants also differed from earlier—and other contemporary—emigrant groups in that almost half of those who left Europe did so for destinations other than the United States. The start of large-scale Italian emigration coincided with good economic opportunities in Argentina and Brazil. The scarcely populated Argentina had achieved more political stability than before and populating the large country was one of its government's top priorities. Likewise, the scarcely populated Brazil (the population in 1880 was only around one-fifteenth of its current size in each of these two countries) had eventually abolished slavery while at the same time going through a coffee export boom.

Resistance and decline. For many years immigration was almost completely unregulated in the United States. When people turn against immigration and strive to reduce it, it is normally due to either perceived economic competition from immigrants, or a dislike for ethnic or cultural mixing. And each of these two factors had comparably little reason to stir much sentiment in the United States during most of the nineteenth century. The cities had

---

19 Hatton and Williamson (1998).
20 Hatton and Williamson (1998).
21 Gould (1979).
22 Hatton and Williamson (1998).

labor shortages and could employ many millions of new immigrant workers for several decades while at the same time natives also saw their incomes rise steadily. And the western territories had vast areas of "unused" land. The only people who lost anything from immigrants or others putting these under the plow were Indian populations who almost completely lacked means to make themselves heard.

As for ethnic or cultural tensions, until 1890, the vast majority of immigrants originated in the same parts of Europe as most of the native-born population did. Thus most natives felt a relatively high degree of ethnic and cultural similarity to most immigrants. An obvious exception to this general pattern though, which serves well to illustrate the point, was the contemporary immigration from China. Chinese immigration was far smaller than European, but was met with all the more intense resistance.

Chinese migration to the United States took off with the Californian gold rush in 1848, and Chinese immigrants were meted a harsh welcome from day one. In its earliest low-technology days, gold mining was basically a zero-sum all-against-all competition between miners. If one group of miners could be kept away, there was simply more gold for the rest. Chinese immigrants comprised a fairly high share of all miners in many areas, and their foreignness provided a basis upon which other workers could attempt to exclude them. These attempts were quite successful. After some time, laws barring Chinese immigrants from mining or from owning mining claims were passed in several mining areas. Yet Chinese immigration continued, mostly because of industrial development and not least the construction of the first transcontinental railroad that created high demand for labor in Western United States.[23]

Representatives of domestic labor objected strongly to the Chinese immigration, claiming that it pressed down wages. Like today, the resistance was often framed as sympathy for the immigrants, who were said to be abused by their employers, and even to have been forced to migrate against their will.[24] Already in 1858, the State of California reacted by passing a law that barred all immigration of Chinese. The law was later overturned by the State Supreme Court, but also the first two national laws that restricted US immigration in any way, which were passed in 1875 and 1882, specifically targeted the Chinese.

The first of these two laws prohibited all immigration of three categories of people: Asians who immigrated for coerced labor, Asian women who intended to engage in prostitution and convicted criminals regardless of origin. In practice though, it was Chinese women in general who came to be affected by

---

[23] Kanazawa (2005).
[24] Kanazawa (2005).

the law. The way the law was implemented, almost all Chinese women were suspected of intending to engage in prostitution (this was not entirely without reason: a high share of all female Chinese immigrants in the previous years had really done just that), and were thus not allowed to immigrate. Chinese immigration in the following years thus came to consist almost entirely of men. Probably unsurprisingly, this in turn contributed to boosting the very vice that the law was said to aim to prevent, that is, prostitution. However, most likely, the main reason for wanting to exclude Chinese women was to prevent Chinese immigrants from having families and remaining in the country permanently.[25]

The second national US law restricting immigration was a more specific response to fears of wage competition. Passed in 1882 under the no-fuss name "the Chinese Exclusion Act," it prohibited all immigration of "workers" from China. Only those who could verify that they were, for example, businessmen or students were subsequently allowed to migrate from China to the United States and Chinese immigration thus fell strongly.[26]

This focus on workers in particular rather than Chinese people in general highlights the importance of economic arguments in the formulation of resistance toward immigration from China. Yet at the same time it is impossible to claim that Chinese immigration in particular would have been an exceptional problem in this regard. Merely around 2 percent of US immigration 1840–80 was from China.[27] If wage competition from immigrants was a problem, Chinese immigrants in particular would thus reasonably have been a very small part of the problem. (The share of immigrants being Chinese was substantially higher in the State of California, but not as high as the shares of other nationalities were in other states.) Hence in spite of its economic expressions, it is quite simply impossible to explain the particularly fierce resistance toward immigration from China other than as an expression of aversion toward people of other cultures, or skin colors.

(Chinese immigrants fared similarly also in Australia and Canada. The Australian State of Victoria saw a gold rush starting in 1851. The gold created an inflow of people from Europe, the United States and China. Victoria responded with a law in 1855 that limited immigration from China only. Canada imposed a fee on immigration from China in 1885, and immigration from China but not from any other country was almost entirely forbidden in 1923–46.)

---

[25] Abrams (2005).
[26] US Department of Homeland Security (2016).
[27] US Department of Homeland Security (2016).

Economic and cultural aspects and motivations seem to have been intertwined also in how the more general resistance toward immigration developed in the United States from about 1880 onward. A series of laws were passed in 1882–1917, which were aimed at raising the "quality" of the country's immigrants. Lists were formulated of categories of people who were not welcome, and when such people were denied entry it was the (economic) responsibility of the skipper who brought them there to take them back to their home country. Sorting out those of low potential economic productivity was a main focus—from the exclusion of any person "unable to take care of him or herself without becoming a public charge" in 1882 to that of those who could not read in 1917.

This also included a focus on mental disabilities that gives an almost paranoid impression. Together, the different laws enacted in this period list the unwanted categories: "lunatics," "idiots," "feeble-minded persons," "imbeciles," "insane persons" and those who were "mentally defective" or of "constitutional psychopathic inferiority."

Other categories who were not welcome, for mixed moral and political reasons, were alcoholics, epileptics, prostitutes, those with contagious diseases, polygamists, anarchists, political radicals and criminal convicts. The United States did however want to remain a haven for political refugees from other countries and hence excluded such from the category of criminal convicts.

The wish to use legislation to increase the economic productivity of the average immigrant may, of course, appear solidly grounded in economic concerns. And the productivity of the average immigrant indeed appears to have gone down in this period, that is, there was a real downward trend to combat. Literacy among immigrants was lower in the early twentieth century compared to the late nineteenth century and immigrants' average gap to native income levels was wider. But in particular, it was the economic performance of the Eastern and Southern European immigrants that was lower. And the cultural or racist dimension in how this was framed in public debate can hardly be denied, as it was commonly framed as being due to these Southern and Eastern Europeans belonging to less gifted "races" than Northern and Western Europeans.[28]

Although the list of categories of people who were not allowed to immigrate to the United States from 1917 onward was long, there were still a lot of people it did not cover. So in spite of this legislation, after the First World War ended in the following year, migration from Europe quickly

---

[28] Hatton and Williamson (1998).

rebounded to high levels. The next legislative counter-move was immigration quotas. A law passed in 1921 limited the annual inflow of people from each European country to the equivalent of 3 percent of the accumulated number of immigrants from the same country who lived in the United States in 1910. The sum of these quotas was 356,000 immigrants per year, corresponding to only half the number of immigrants who were admitted the year in which the law was passed. In 1924, the quotas were reduced to 2 percent of the numbers of immigrants who lived in the United States in 1890. The reference year was thus moved back a further 20 years, until just before migration from Eastern and Southern Europe took off, to further reduce immigration from that region. Furthermore immigration from Asia, which was already strongly limited by earlier legislation, was barred completely. Finally, in 1927, the total immigration quota was set to 150,000 people per year, to be distributed in proportion to the immigrant populations in 1920. Immigration from the rest of the American continent remained unrestricted. This legislation remained almost unchanged until the 1960s.[29]

For people from Northern and Western Europe, these quotas were in practice meaningless, as the number of people who wanted to migrate from there was no longer high enough to fill them. Immigration from Southern and Eastern Europe, on the contrary, fell strongly after the quotas were imposed. Yet what finally brought an end to the almost century-long period of high migration from Europe to the United States, as well as to migration to Canada, Argentina and Brazil, was not legislation but the economic downturn of the early 1930s. After one hundred years and around thirty million migrants, migration was no longer economically gainful and therefore stayed at levels far below the quota limits, from all parts of Europe.[30]

Also in Western Europe immigration was mostly unregulated before the First World War. Migration in Europe was then also mostly a matter of people leaving the whole continent. The war brought increased nationalism and animosity between European countries, and migration as well as trade became more restricted. The economic downturn of the early 1930s fueled further protectionism and restrictions.[31] These further restrictions most likely had little effect on actual migration though. There was not much economic reason

---

[29] Hatton and Williamson (2005).
[30] Gould (1979).
[31] Goldin, Cameron and Balarajan (2011).

to migrate when unemployment was soaring everywhere—in Europe as well as in America.[32]

1930 until today: First lower migration, then rising

This section describes how migration to Western countries has developed from the bottom levels of the 1930s until today. As almost all migration in this period has been limited and shaped by laws, this is to a large extent a story about how these laws have developed and interplayed with people's willingness to migrate. Therefore the presentation is also separated between the two main reasons for migration to the West, which have been governed by entirely different sets of laws. The first part deals with refugee migration and the second with economically motivated migration.

Refugee migration. For centuries it has been common for people who are persecuted in one country, for political, religious or other reasons, to flee to a different country. Borders have in large part been open. Yet when immigration became more regulated all over the Western world from the early 1920s, refugee migration became a more complicated international political issue. After more than one million people fled Russia in the years after the 1917 revolution, the League of Nations created the High Commissioner for Refugees to coordinate between countries and make sure that these refugees were received somewhere. An institution of that kind had not been needed before, and at first it was intended to exist only temporarily to deal with a temporary situation. But new conflicts kept generating new refugees, and the institution came to remain and later to be incorporated into the United Nations under the name UNHCR (United Nations High Commissioner for Refugees).[33]

The Russian refugee flow and others in the 1920s (e.g., Armenians from Turkey) could be handled relatively easily through coordinated voluntary resettlement in different countries. Yet in the 1930s when persecuted Jews began leaving Germany, the situation was different. Several countries decided that the number of people who chose to flee to their particular country was too high, and began returning them to Germany. No solution was found to prevent this from continuing. All refugee assistance was based on voluntariness from the part of receiving countries, and when the limits of that were reached nothing more could be done—or at least nothing more was.[34]

---

[32] Gould (1979).
[33] Barnett (2002).
[34] Barnett (2002).

The Second World War was probably the only period in world history when total international refugee migration was higher than total migration for economic reasons. When the war ended, between 10 and 30 million living people—there is great variation between estimates—had escaped their home countries.[35] However, most of these could rather quickly either return home or be received in a different country. In 1950, slightly more than one million refugees remained across Europe having nowhere to start a new life.[36]

As a joint guarantee that these remaining refugees would not be sent back to home countries where they would still be at risk of persecution, countries signed the United Nations' Refugee Convention in 1951. It stated that people who, as a result of events occurring before 1951 in Europe, were at risk of persecution in the home country for reasons of race, religion, nationality or membership of a particular social group or political opinion were not to be forcibly sent back to that country. Hence in this original form, the convention was limited to dealing with those whose refugee status was due to a certain episode. Yet with an additional protocol that was signed in 1967, its obligation upon signatories to not return a person to the home country was expanded to cover all persons at risk of persecution for the same above-mentioned reasons, without any limitations regarding time and place.

The 1967 protocol is the major watershed in the history of international refugee law. Before 1967, all refugee admittance was voluntary, except for that of the limited number to which the original refugee convention applied. International or domestic law did not force countries to receive refugees, although most of the time they did so anyway, with the German Jews of the 1930s being the main exception. But in 1967 it became an obligation upon all signatory countries to admit all refugees who were on their soil, regardless of how they arrived there. (Formally the convention and its protocol do not strictly oblige countries to *receive* refugees who are on their territory, only to not send them back to the home country. Yet in practice these two things tend to be the same. As long as no third country voluntarily receives the refugees, the country that has them on its territory is left with no other legal option than to receive them.)

Technically, what may more concretely have been the most important aspect of this new legal framework was that it gave all asylum seekers the right to have their cases tried. Actually returning a refugee to the home country after properly investigating the matter and concluding that the person's life is indeed in danger, is probably politically impossible in most instances, whether

---

[35] Compare, for example, Goldin, Cameron and Balarajan (2011), and Barnett (2002).
[36] Barnett (2002).

it is prohibited by law or not. It may therefore be more politically feasible to not try cases at all. For example, in the 1960s and the 1970s many people fled Haiti for the United States. The United States in many cases simply did not try their refugee status. It summarily declared that these were all economic migrants and sent them back. (This practice was formally legal in the United States throughout the 1970s. Although the country had ratified the protocol to the refugee convention already in 1968, it took a further 12 years—until 1980—before it was incorporated into its domestic law.)[37]

It took some time though for the far-reaching consequences of the change that had been made in 1967 to become evident. Compared with around the Second World War or with the latest decades, international refugee movements were relatively small in the 1960s and the 1970s. Refugee movements were thus not a contentious political issue, as is illustrated not least by how swiftly the conceptually far-reaching 1967 protocol was accepted in the United Nations' General Assembly even without much debate. That contrasted sharply with the more painstaking process of creating the original refugee convention in 1951. At that time countries were far more concerned not to promise too much, which explains why the original convention came to refer only to refugees from a limited region and time period.[38]

Yet in the early 1980s, the situation began taking a different turn. By then it had become easier and cheaper to travel long distances, and also more refugees did so. In many cases they found it more attractive to be given asylum in a rich Western country compared with in any of the poorer countries neighboring those from which they fled. And they could in practice often choose for themselves in which country to be received, by traveling to that country, because the 1967 protocol in practice placed the obligation to receive them upon any signatory country on whose territory they presented themselves. The receiving Western countries became increasingly unhappy with this situation. They do not appear to have foreseen, and were not much willing to accept, that the 1967 protocol obliged them to receive so many who had traveled thousands of kilometers to reach their countries, when more proximate options in many cases existed.[39]

If the 1967 protocol is the major watershed in the history of international refugee *law*, the major watershed in international refugee *policy* is how Western countries chose to react to the resulting situation in the early 1980s. Then, unhappy with the consequences of the protocol, they still chose to leave the

---

[37] Gibney (2004).

[38] See several among the contributions to Zimmermann, Dörschner and Machts (eds.) (2011).

[39] UNHCR (2000); Gibney (2004).

protocol intact (at least in public, abandoning the protocol does not appear to have been seriously discussed in any Western country). What they did instead was to start trying to avoid its consequences. This marked the beginning of the current era of refugee policy, where refugees are given an unlimited promise of support, yet in practice vast efforts are undertaken to keep this support out of their reach. Hence from the early 1980s, Western countries began applying different measures to prevent refugees from reaching their territories, because if refugees never reached a particular country and could apply for asylum there the 1967 protocol placed no obligation upon this country.

Today, Western countries apply a variety of such measures to keep refugees away. They have visa requirements for citizens of all countries from which any larger numbers of refugees may conceivably try to flee. Visas are denied to all who are seen as potential asylum seekers. Someone who is, for example, from Afghanistan and wants to travel to a Western country for tourism or business purposes is thus denied a visa if they cannot show credibly that they are not potential asylum seekers, which of course most cannot do. Visa requirements have been further complemented with carrier responsibilities, which place high fines upon carriers (e.g., airlines) if they bring a person without a visa to a country. Without carrier responsibility visa requirements would be pointless, as any person could then travel to a country without a visa and apply for asylum at the border or the airport. The United States, Australia and the EU have also used military or police boats to force boats carrying asylum seekers to return before reaching their shores. The EU has built walls around the Spanish enclaves Ceuta and Melilla that border Morocco. It has also made agreements with several North African and West Asian countries in which these, typically in return for money, have agreed to undertake operations on land and water to prevent people from departing for Europe.[40]

Europe is closer than other Western regions to those regions that have generated the largest numbers of refugees from the 1980s until today, and more refugees have tried to reach Europe. The measures that Europe has put in place to keep them out has forced them into dangerous clandestine methods such as traveling in small boats across the Mediterranean Sea in bad weather, and more generally into the hands of human smugglers. This has caused the death of tens of thousands and the suffering of hundreds of thousands.[41]

For decades, all of this was unknown to most Europeans. Today, the fact that many people who try to reach Europe drown in the Mediterranean Sea is

---

[40] UNHCR (2000); Gibney (2004); Andersson (2014).

[41] The NGO network *UNITED for Intercultural Action* has documented over 40,000 deaths among refugees attempting to travel to Europe since 1993 (http://www.unitedagainstracism.org).

well known. But the actual mechanisms behind it are still not as well known as they ought to be. Many still believe that migrants choose to travel in dangerous boats because it is cheap and they have little money. But it is in fact far from cheap. It often costs more than ten times more than a flight ticket. Instead, asylum seekers choose the dangerous boats because there is no legal and safe way by which they can reach Europe and exercise the universal right to asylum that Europe has formally stated that they have.[42]

European countries have also in several cases made agreements with North African or West Asian countries where the latter have promised to take "back" asylum seekers who have passed through their territories en route to Europe. Within the EU, all countries have also formally agreed to do the same between them. That is, they have agreed that an application for asylum shall be processed in the EU country in which the asylum seeker first set foot. This agreement was made in the Dublin Convention, which was signed in 1990.[43] Countries mostly followed its provisions until 2015, when it came to be generally seen as unreasonable, because it placed such a large share of the total burden of receiving refugees on Greece and Italy.

In practice though, most asylum seekers have always found ways around the Dublin Convention and other agreements to return them to countries they have passed through. This only requires that they do not reveal through which countries they have traveled. And the countries they travel through, including Greece and Italy, have also always had strong incentives to passively assist them in this by letting them pass through "unseen."

From the 1920s until today the basic problem in international refugee politics has been the same: All countries agree on the basic moral principle that those who are persecuted in their home country should be given an opportunity to live in another country. Yet there is no similarly obvious moral principle that dictates how a given number of refugees should be distributed across other countries. Typically, the populations of other countries are most content if refugees are received somewhere, but not in their country. And at no point in time has the international community been able to agree on a general principle for how to share refugees.

Under the existing framework, which is mainly determined by the 1967 protocol, the result of this is that all responsibility falls on the country to which refugees themselves choose—and succeed—to travel. The larger the number of refugees in the world, and the longer they can travel, the more politically explosive this becomes, because it means that refugees' potential

---

[42] UNHCR (2000); Gibney (2004); Andersson (2014).
[43] UNHCR (2000).

concentration in only a few "popular" destination countries increases. This in turn makes potential destination countries' efforts to keep them from arriving increase too.

All of this could be clearly seen in 2015 when there were more refugees in the world than ever before, or at least since the end of the Second World War, and many of them had the means to travel long distances. So many reached Europe that its border enforcement more or less fell apart and more than one million came in and applied for asylum. They distributed themselves very unevenly across the continent. Sweden, which is situated furthest from the source and home to only 2 percent of the population of the EU, received a full 20 percent of all applications for asylum in the three most intense months of September–November. Germany, with 16 percent of the Union's population, received 33 percent of all applications in the same period.[44]

The European reaction to this has been powerful, in several ways dominating and reshaping politics across the continent and earning the episode the well-deserved name "the refugee crisis." This strong reaction would appear quite remarkable though, if we tried to understand it solely on the basis of the number of refugee immigrants that were involved. It is simply impossible to refer to the refugee crisis as a period of "high" immigration. In all of 2008–16 together, total refugee immigration in the EU corresponded to no more than 0.37 percent of its population. The annual peak in 2016 (mostly due to applications submitted in 2015) corresponded to 0.14 percent.[45] These are small numbers—by any standard. The first corresponds to only one immigrant per 270 inhabitants in nine years, and the second to one per 700 in the peak year. For comparison, in the economic boom that preceded the financial crisis in 2008, some European countries had total immigration rates (i.e., consisting mostly of non-refugees) of several percent per year.[46]

In other words, to understand the European people's powerful reaction to this particular episode we must look beyond these aggregate numbers alone to find what sets it apart from other episodes. One aspect that clearly sets it apart from most other migration, but interestingly—as we shall see—not from a few other episodes that have also sparked strong backlashes, is that this immigration was strongly perceived of as *out of control*. While immigration itself was not high, the episode put Europe's lack of control over its volume starkly on display, as around two million asylum seekers entered the continent in 2015–16 despite fervent and visible efforts to stop them.

---

[44] Source: Eurostat.

[45] Source: Eurostat.

[46] Source: Eurostat.

When people think that immigration is out of control they have reason to evaluate the situation not just by the numbers who are actually entering. Because when control is lacking, there is no guarantee that future numbers will not be multiple times higher than the current. Then it is possible to explain a strong reaction to a small inflow not as a reaction to that small inflow itself, but rather to the situation creating an image of possibly very large inflows in the future.

This interpretation would still arguably be stretching the logic a little too far, if the European population was primarily evaluating events *at the European level*. Even if total European refugee immigration in 2015–16 would increase something like tenfold sometime in the future, it would still not be spectacularly high on a per capita basis compared with many other immigration flows in history. But arguably that would not be an accurate description of the European population. What is most important—politically, economically and socially—to most Europeans is what happens *in their specific country*. And at that level things are remarkably different. As the Swedish and German numbers above illustrate, refugee immigration that is small in relation to the total European population may still imply high refugee immigration in particular countries, if refugees' distribution across countries is uneven enough. In this particular recent episode, Sweden and Germany were at the extreme end of this unevenness and received many refugees per capita. But the episode nonetheless increases uncertainty about the future in all countries, not only in these particular two. It shows the extent of possible unevenness, and it is understood that it may be other countries that receive the highest concentrations next time. Countries' relative attractiveness to refugees change, sometimes fast, and for reasons that are seldom obvious. For example, the share of EU asylum seekers who chose to submit their applications in Germany had until recently before mostly been far lower than what it was in 2015–16.

Other Western countries have been more distant from the most important refugee-generating conflicts, and have thus been able to control their borders with somewhat less effort than Europe. (Australia is partly an exception and has received much international criticism in the last 10–15 years, both for military operations that have forced boats with asylum seekers to return to Indonesia, and because refugees who have arrived in Australia have been moved to detention centers in Papua New Guinea and Nauru. The criticism against the latter has targeted not so much the translocation as such, as the humanitarian conditions in these detention centers and Australia's unwillingness to admit any responsibility for these.)

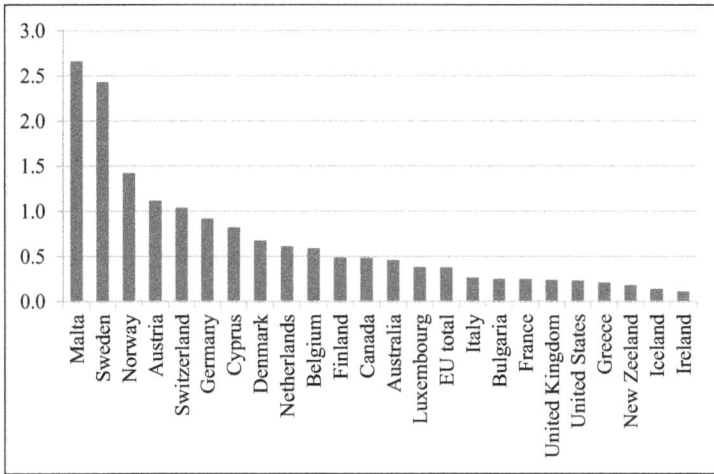

Figure 2.2 Total refugee immigration in 2008–16 (percent of population) in the United States, Canada, Australia, New Zealand, EU total and each individual EU country in which the share was above 0.04 percent.

Sources: Eurostat, US Department of Homeland Security, Immigration and Refugee Board of Canada, Australia Department of Home Affairs, and New Zealand Ministry of Business, Innovation, and Employment. Numbers for Australia and New Zealand refer to the fiscal years 2008/9–2016/17.

Hence, in contrast to what is the case in Europe, large shares of refugee immigration in these countries are made up of refugees who they voluntarily resettle from other countries, most often in the neighborhoods of a conflict. Such voluntarily resettled refugees made up only a few percent of the total refugee immigration of 2008–16 in the EU, yet almost half in Canada, two-thirds in the United States and Australia, and around 90 percent in New Zealand.[47] For reference, the size of the total refugee immigration per capita in different Western countries in 2008–16 is shown in Figure 2.2.

Australian refugee policy differs somewhat from that of other countries, in having for some time had a more clearly stated ambition to maintain a stable level of *total* refugee immigration. There has thus, at least part of the time, existed a more direct link in Australia between the "spontaneous" inflow of

---

[47] Sources: Eurostat, US Department of Homeland Security, Immigration and Refugee Board of Canada, Australia Department of Home Affairs, and New Zeeland Ministry of Business, Innovation, and Employment.

asylum seekers by their own means and the numbers that the country has voluntarily resettled from other countries. When the former number has risen the latter has gone down. One might say that this has enabled a different, and probably to some extent more honest, public discussion on refugee policy matters in Australia, compared most of all with Europe, but also to some extent with North America. Seeking asylum on site in Australia, although permitted, has been described as "jumping the queue" at the expense of other refugees who may have needed the support more acutely. Border enforcement has been described as what it really is—that is, aimed at limiting the inflow of asylum seekers. Europe, on the other hand, has for 30 years publicly described its border protection falsely as solely targeting illegal economically motivated immigration and organized crime.[48]

As a final point, the vast majority of the world's refugees do not reach the West. They are in countries that neighbor their home countries, sometimes in refugee camps. In June 2018, the UNHCR estimated that there were 19.9 million refugees in the world. This number refers to all those who are outside of their home country but have not been granted the formal right to stay in another country. (Palestinians and internally displaced—that is, those who have fled within the home country—are not included.) Among these, the highest numbers were in Turkey (3.5 million), Uganda (1.4 million), Pakistan (1.4 million), Lebanon (1 million) and Iran (1 million). By comparison, the total refugee immigration in 2008–16 was around 1.9 million in the EU and 700,000 in the United States.[49]

(This is a comparison between the total refugee stocks in neighboring countries and nine-year inflows in the EU and the United States. The UNHCR publishes refugee stocks also for the EU and United States. Yet—as is often not acknowledged—these do not give a relevant picture of their refugee populations. This is because these countries grant refugees formal residence permits, which makes the refugees disappear from UNHCR statistics. Hence these often-quoted statistics give the impression that the rich Western countries' share of global refugee hosting is even smaller than what is actually the case.)

Economic migration: Europe. The 1950s and the 1960s saw loosened immigration restrictions and increased labor immigration in much of the West. High economic growth created labor shortages in several countries. Labor immigration therefore not only became permitted but was also actively stimulated in several cases. For example, several European countries set up

---

[48] Gibney (2004).

[49] Sources: Eurostat, US Department of Homeland Security.

labor recruitment agencies in other countries that had labor surpluses, to make it easier for their companies at home to import labor from there. Several countries in Western Europe, for the first time, became countries to which many people moved, and their populations became multi-ethnic in ways that they had not been before. This refers mostly to West Germany (with high labor immigration mostly from Turkey, Italy, Yugoslavia and Greece), France (mostly from Algeria, Italy and Spain), the United Kingdom (mostly Ireland, India, Jamaica and Pakistan), Switzerland (mostly Italy and Spain), Belgium (mostly Italy, Spain, Morocco and Turkey), Sweden (mostly Finland and Yugoslavia) and Austria (mostly Yugoslavia and Turkey).[50]

These migrant workers received mostly permanent residence permits in some countries, and mostly temporary in others. West Germany in particular primarily issued temporary permits, intending workers to return home later when the country would not need them anymore. However, eventually, this return came to happen only to a very limited extent. West Germany had to accept that it had become the home of large Turkish and Southern European populations.[51]

There is an inherent conflict in temporary immigration programs. Declaring that immigration will be temporary often boosts the popular support for these programs when they are launched. It communicates that the country's ethnic composition will not be much affected in the long run, and also that when the business cycle turns downward and competition for jobs increases some of that competition will leave the country. Yet when that day arrives and workers and their families have already built lives in their new home country, it is often difficult to muster much popular support for sending back by force those who do not leave voluntarily. This tends to hold regardless of whether the temporary residence permits were issued for reasons of work or refuge.[52]

It is also not obvious from a purely economic standpoint whether temporary labor immigration would be better than permanent for the receiving country. On the one hand, it is convenient for the country of immigration to be able to "export" its unemployment in a downturn. Yet on the other, the productivity of the average immigrant increases substantially as they stay longer in the country and improve their linguistic skills and knowledge about the country's culture and institutions (see Chapter 4). Sending an immigrant home, only to receive another a few years later in the next upturn, thus implies that the initial "schooling" cost must be borne twice instead of only once.

---

[50] Source: OECD International Migration Database.
[51] Castles, De Haas and Miller (2013).
[52] Castles, De Haas and Miller (2013).

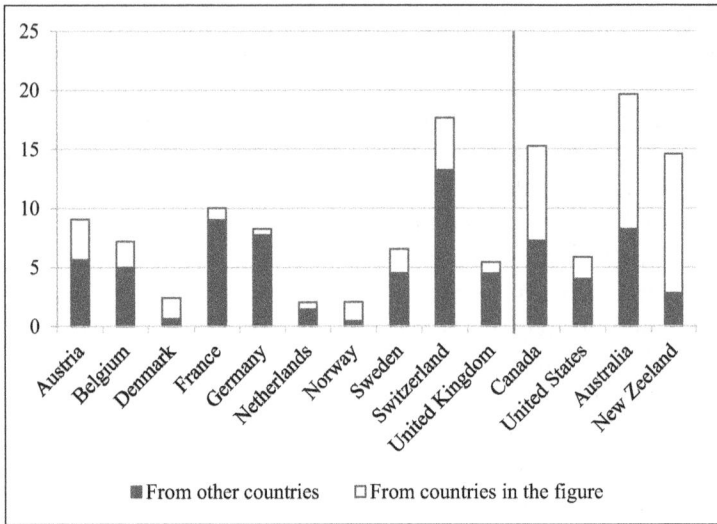

Figure 2.3 Foreign-born population shares (percent) 1970 in Western Europe and four non-European countries.

Source: OECD International Migration Database. Due to data limitations, "Germany" refers to current Germany, that is, West and East Germany combined.

In 1970, when the period of high economic growth and high labor immigration approached its end, 5–18 percent of the populations were foreign-born in the most important immigration countries in Western Europe. Foreign-born population shares in these countries, and for comparison in Canada, the United States, Australia and New Zealand, are shown in Figure 2.3. These shares are further split between those who were born in another of the countries that are shown in the figure (white) and those who were born in any other country in the world (black).

As the figure shows, only 40 years after their inhabitants' large-scale emigration to the United States ceased, in 1970 several countries in Western Europe hosted more immigrants per capita than the United States did. This is partly because the immigration share in the United States in this year was more or less at its historical all-time low, after having declined for about 40 years and just before it would start rebounding again. But most of all it illustrates the rapid transformation of parts of Western Europe in this period.

The labor shortages that had caused high labor immigration vanished in the 1970s as economic growth in Western Europe declined. Active labor recruitment abroad ceased and labor immigration has since in general been tightly restricted. Yet between countries in the European Economic Community

(EEC), subsequently the European Union (EU), workers have had considerably more freedom to move.

Free labor mobility in the EEC/EU. In the 1950s and the 1960s, as labor immigration brought obvious and important benefits to the growing economies of Western Europe and had broad popular support, the EEC was founded by Belgium, France, Italy, Luxembourg, the Netherlands and West Germany. The aim was to promote peace and economic growth through economic integration, specifically by enabling goods, labor, services and capital to move more freely across borders.

Today, the free labor mobility in the EU means that any EU citizen who is offered a job in a different member country is allowed to move there without restriction. It is thus not a free mobility of citizens but only of workers, that is, those with a job offer (and their accompanying family members). Other citizens are only allowed to stay for a maximum of three months in another member country.

At the EEC's inception in 1957, the five richer member countries feared that free labor mobility would flood them with workers from the sixth country—Italy—where wages were considerably lower. Yet when free labor mobility finally came into force, which was not until 1968, a considerable part of this wage gap had been closed and migration out of Italy stayed at modest levels.[53]

The fear of being flooded by workers has since been reignited each time the EEC/EU has expanded to include populous new member countries with substantially lower wage levels. This happened in 1981, 1986, 2004 and 2007 (the latest addition of Croatia with only four million inhabitants in 2013 did not cause much stir though). Therefore, on each of these occasions, the earlier members gave themselves the right to restrict access to their labor markets for citizens of the new member countries for in each case up to 7 years.

The biggest fears of low-wage competition were aroused when the major eastward expansion of the EU, in two steps in 2004 and 2007, was approaching. The 10 countries that were to be included in 2004 had a combined population corresponding to almost one-fourth of that of the earlier 15 member countries, a purchasing-power parity-adjusted average income that was only half as high and unemployment that was almost twice as high.[54] Hence, there was reason to expect migration from new to old member countries to become

---

[53] Fauri (2014).
[54] Source: Eurostat.

high. And in Romania and Bulgaria, who would join only three years later, average incomes were even lower.

Migration also turned out to be higher this time than it had been following the earlier EEC/EU expansions. Net outflows to the old EU members in 2004–9 corresponded to around 7 percent of the population in Romania, 4 percent in Lithuania and 2–3 percent each in Poland, Latvia and Bulgaria.[55] Yet as a fraction of the four times as large population in the old member countries combined, this still summed to a relatively limited inflow, with seemingly limited economic effects at the aggregate level. Inflows were also generally quite concentrated in the sectors of the receiving countries' economies where there was demand for additional workers, and the most economically important effect of the inflows appears to have been that they helped to reduce labor shortages in these sectors—most importantly the construction sector.[56] Such effects are the very idea of benefits of free labor mobility. Reducing sectoral shortages may also be important for aggregate economic growth as it may ease bottlenecks in production chains.

However in one country, that is, the United Kingdom, immigration from the new member countries caused a particularly strong negative reaction from a large share of the population. There is no agreement on exactly why the reaction was so strong in this particular country, but some explanations can easily be ruled out. The immigrant inflow per capita was not higher in the United Kingdom than in all other countries. It was higher than in several others, yet most likely not higher than in Ireland, Italy and Spain.[57] The United Kingdom was not in a more negative macroeconomic situation compared with other countries. It was hit quite hard by the economic downturn that started with the financial meltdown in late 2008 and this is likely to have added fuel to the fire. But a more negative reaction than in other EU countries was clearly there already in the preceding years when the country had strong economic growth. Immigrants' possibilities to compete for jobs by accepting lower wages is probably larger in the United Kingdom than in several other EU countries, yet not obviously so compared in particular with the three that were just mentioned as most likely having had higher Eastern European immigration per capita.

Quite likely, to fully understand the negative British response to this immigration, one needs to take into account not only "the facts on the ground" but also how these facts were interpreted in the prevailing political climate. It may be important that opposition to this new immigration became part of a bigger

---

[55] Kahanec (2013).
[56] Kahanec and Zimmermann (eds.) (2010).
[57] Kahanec and Zimmermann (eds.) (2010).

British discontent with the EU, which would later (probably much due to the extra fuel that was brought to the fire by Eastern European immigration) culminate in the vote in 2016 to leave the Union. Another explanation is that the new immigration came to create a public image of the country's immigration levels being almost completely unpredictable and out of control. This episode may therefore, as may the European refugee crisis, be an example of a strong popular backlash against immigration that was caused not by actual immigration levels as much as by a perceived lack of control, in turn causing fears of higher future immigration.[58]

Supporting this interpretation, the actual net inflow of new EU citizens to the United Kingdom in the years following the EU expansion was not remarkably high. Between the first-quarters of 2004 and 2009, the number of people living in the United Kingdom who were born in any of the countries that became EU members in 2004 increased by around 560,000 people or the equivalent of 0.9 percent of the country's total population. This amounted to less than half of the total increase in the number of foreign-born in the country in the same period.[59] Yet it was popular to interpret this and similar numbers against the background of a report that was commissioned by the government and published in 2003 and which predicted a net inflow of merely 5,000–13,000 per year.[60] This comparison was often repeated in British media as an illustration of the government's inability to predict and control its immigration. The harm was further increased when the government tried to prove that it was indeed in control, by promising in 2010 to reduce net immigration below 100,000 individuals per year, and then in subsequent years failing to come even close to this number.[61]

Ironically though, the entire comparison with 5,000–13,000 per year was based on (perhaps intentional) simply incorrect reporting of the results of the 2003 report. This prediction from the report was based on the crucial assumption that Germany would not use the option to temporarily limit immigration from the new member countries. Hence, the report reasoned, people from these countries would primarily migrate to Germany as they had done historically. Yet if Germany actually imposed limits—as eventually it did—the

---

[58] The book *Exodus*, written by the British economics professor Paul Collier and published in 2013, appears representative of this current of thought. The book's main theme is a warning against liberal immigration policies. Yet Collier states clearly that he does not think immigration has been too high in the United Kingdom so far. His concern is that liberal policies today may cause too high immigration in the future.

[59] Dustmann, Frattini and Halls (2010).

[60] Dustmann et al. (2003).

[61] Source: Office for National Statistics.

report predicted that migration to the United Kingdom would likely be several times higher.[62]

Economic migration: North America. The immigration policies that were put in place in the United States in the early 1920s used national quotas to favor migrants from Northern and Western Europe, and almost completely excluded those from much of Asia. (And in practice also Africa, as previous migration—on which the quotas were based—had been so low from there.) These quotas remained in place with only minor modifications until the 1960s. Their overtly discriminating intent was a major reason for their eventual abolishment. Yet also in the 1960s many Americans were still not excited about allowing immigration from Asia and Africa (and Latin America) to increase much. The new legislation that was passed in 1965, and came into force in 1968, may be seen as an attempt to reach almost as discriminating results yet with formally less discriminating legislation.[63]

The 1965 Immigration and Naturalization Act replaced the many national quotas with two large quotas: Immigration from the American continent, which had previously been unregulated yet in practice low, was allowed to reach a maximum of 120,000 individuals per year. Immigration from the rest of the world was capped at 170,000 individuals per year. Later, in 1978, the two quotas were merged into a global quota of 290,000 individuals per year, and in 1990 this quota was raised substantially to 675,000. (The immigration of immediate family members, and of refugees, follow separate rules and are not affected by these quotas.)

These new more aggregated quotas did not formally discriminate against migrants from Asia or Africa, who were in the same quota as those from Europe. However, it appears that this quota was intended and expected to be filled mostly by Europeans, because according to the rules those who had relatives who were American citizens or had permanent residence permits would be given priority within the quota. As there were many more Europeans than Asians or Africans in the United States in the 1960s, the annual quotas were also expected to be filled mostly by Europeans.[64]

It looks like a strategy that could have worked. Of all immigrants from Europe, Asia and Africa taken together, who lived in the United States in 1960, a full 93 percent were from Europe.[65] Yet what this plan—if it was

---

[62] Dustmann et al. (2003).

[63] Hatton (2015).

[64] Hatton (2015).

[65] Source: Own calculations using data from the US census in 1960, from Ruggles et al. (2015).

a plan—overlooked was the still declining interest among Europeans in migrating to the United States, which resulted in the annual quotas being filled mostly by Asians from the start.

However, the fairly high resulting immigration from Asia did not cause much public resistance. Most of the Asian immigrants who arrived were highly educated, entered highly productive jobs and were interpreted as contributing positively to the economy. In spite of the generally low education levels in their home countries, where the average length of education was in many cases only a few years, as many as two-thirds of all 25–40-year-olds from Asia who migrated to the United States in the 1970s, and four-fifths of all from Africa, had university education.[66]

However, in course of time, what instead came to create far more public resistance in the United States was the increasing immigration from Mexico. Similar to the trend from Asia, legal immigration from Mexico increased gradually from around 400,000 in the 1960s to nearly three million in the 1990s. Mexican legal immigration subsequently dropped below two million in the 2000s while that from Asia rose above three million. Yet in the Mexican case, illegal immigration in the last decades is estimated to have been roughly as high as legal. The total number of Mexican immigrants residing in the United States in 2017 was estimated to be 11 million. Half of these were estimated to lack permission to be in the country, and these were in turn estimated to make up half the total number of illegal immigrants in the country.[67] Furthermore, Mexican immigrants are on average less educated than almost all other immigrant groups in the United States. Only an estimated fifth of all (legal or illegal) 25–60-year-old Mexican immigrants in the United States in 2017 had attended university, that is, far below the corresponding three-fourths of all immigrants from Asia and the almost as high share of all from Africa.[68]

Mexican immigration has thus sparked much resistance for probably two main reasons. Due to their lower education levels, Mexican immigrants are expected to bring fewer benefits to the American economy, and to compete more strongly with the less-educated domestic workforce for jobs. And the illegal part of Mexican immigration is obviously another example of immigration that appears to be out of control. It has continued steadily for decades

---

[66] Source: Own calculations using data from the US census in 1980, from Ruggles et al. (2015). Some of these immigrants may have acquired the university degrees that they report having in 1980 after arrival to the United States.

[67] Krogstad, Passel and Cohn (2019).

[68] Source: Own calculations using data from the American Community Survey in 2017, from Ruggles et al. (2015).

in spite of the considerable resources that have been spent on border enforcement, by fences, patrolling vehicles, etc.[69]

It thus seems to fit a pattern. As noted in Chapter 1, and as will be shown in some detail in Chapter 6, when surveyed, populations of Western countries almost always lean more toward the opinion that immigration is too high in their country. But in most settings, this dissatisfaction remains mostly silent, and does not become a loud political voice demanding change. Yet I also noted that recent years have seen three major departures from this pattern, where recent refugee immigration in Europe, Eastern European immigration in the United Kingdom and illegal Mexican immigration in the United States have caused loud negative public reactions that have dominated and reshaped politics in the receiving countries to remarkable extents.

These three cases of migration are different in several ways. One is refugee migration, one is legal economically motivated migration and one is illegal economically motivated migration. They have not all been particularly large. Yet they seem to share this characteristic that sets them apart from most other migration flows, which is that all three have created public perceptions of migration being out of control. This does not prove that the perception of lost control is the central explanation for why precisely these three have created such far-reaching public and political reactions, but the pattern easily catches the eye.

Since some time back, illegal immigration from Mexico to the United States appears to have decreased, and the total number of illegal Mexican immigrants residing in the United States is estimated to have been two million less in 2017 compared with in the peak year 2007 (i.e., the year before the financial crisis and subsequent drop in labor demand). The number of illegal immigrants from the rest of the world residing in the United States is estimated to have been quite constant over the same period.[70] As previously mentioned, also legal migration from Mexico was considerably higher in the 1990s than what it has been since. After decades of high emigration, Mexico appears to have reached a saturation phase where emigration falls, just as Northern and Western European countries did in the late nineteenth century.

Like the United States' first phase of high immigration in 1840–1930, the second, since 1970, was initially characterized by decreasing economic performance of the average immigrant. Figure 2.4 shows 18–64-year-old immigrants' average incomes per week, in relation to the corresponding

---

[69] Hanson, Liu and McIntosh (2017).

[70] Krogstad, Passel and Cohn (2019).

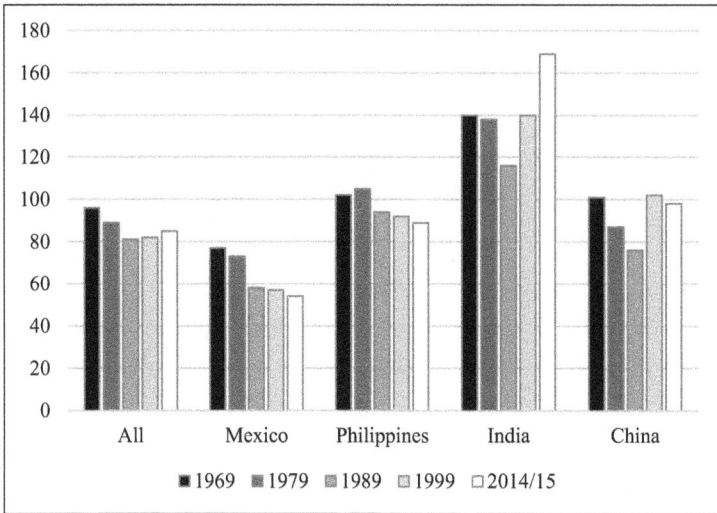

Figure 2.4 Average weekly wages among 18–64-year-old immigrants who have been in the United States for 6–10 years. Wages are expressed in percentages of average weekly wages of 18–64-year-old native-born.

Source: Own calculations using data from the respective US census or American Community Survey, from Ruggles et al. (2015).

averages for natives, at five different points in time since 1970. To increase comparability, all immigrants who are included in the analysis have been in the United States for 6–10 years.[71] The figure shows that from 1970 to 1990, the average income calculated over all immigrants fell substantially from 96 to 81 percent of the native average. It also fell by 8–25 percentage points in each of the four major immigrant groups that are shown separately in the figure, that is, those from Mexico, the Philippines, India and China.[72]

This average productivity decline was halted around 1990. Since then, the average income of immigrants compared with natives has increased moderately. For those from Mexico and the Philippines there have been moderate continued decreases, while for those from India and China there have been considerable increases.

This pattern can be rather easily explained by the change in immigration laws, in 1990, with the explicit purpose of increasing highly skilled immigration. A central change was a substantial increase in the annual number

---

[71] Averages were calculated over all individuals who reported being in the labor force and not self-employed.

[72] For similar results, see Borjas (1985), and Borjas (1995).

of H1-B visas, which are given to highly qualified workers predominantly in the science and technology sectors. These visas have since been issued primarily to workers from India, and secondly to workers from China, that is, corresponding well to the pattern in Figure 2.4.

However, although their numbers have increased, H1-B visas still make up a rather small share of the United States' total legal immigration. Altogether, the degree of selectivity in the country's immigration policy is still quite limited today. The large majority of residence permits are issued based on family connections and not on skills. Although the original intent (from 1965) with this may have been to create a selection mechanism favoring economically and culturally preferred countries, the result has been different. But attitudes also change as the world changes, and although there have been discontents, the country has mostly chosen to accept its new immigration for half a century, making only minor legislative changes. At the same time, although immigration policy has not been very selective there has been strong self-selection of migrants. Large shares of the country's immigrants have been highly educated and have done well economically in the country (see Chapters 3 and 4).

The path chosen by Canada and Australia in immigration policy differs from that of the United States. Their immigration has been higher per capita but also more strongly selected by policy. Canada's immigration history until the 1960s largely mirrors that of the United States, with mostly unregulated immigration from all countries except China until around the First World War, followed by strongly limited and mostly European immigration until the 1960s. In Canada, this framework was replaced in 1962 by one where residence permits were awarded mostly on the basis of measurable skills. Since 1967, this has been done by means of a points system, where applicants are given points for linguistic skills, formal education, etc., and the number of points determines who is allowed to immigrate (the points system does not apply to immediate family members or refugees).

Economic migration: Australia. The early immigration history of Australia is like a sharper version of that of North America. Similar to the United States and Canada, the country developed from British colonies. However, because it is situated considerably further from Britain, the monetary cost of the journey to Australia and the risk of not surviving it before the advent of steamboats were both considerably greater—and Europeans' settlement thus proceeded much more slowly. Until 1830, the different Australian colonies were mainly populated through the transportation of around 60,000 British convicts.[73] This filled multiple purposes: the colonies were populated, the population at home was deterred from committing crimes and less resources had to be spent on running prisons. Until the United States' declaration of independence in 1776, convicts had been transported to the American colonies for the same reasons. After a 12-year break, the foundation of the first Australian colony in 1788 enabled the transportations to resume.

Like in the case of North America, voluntary migration to Australia—mainly by people from Britain and Ireland—began to increase by the middle of the nineteenth century. Yet it remained at considerably lower levels, and many migrants even received financial government support for their moves. By around 1920, the population of the vast country was still only around five million. Even large areas that were suitable for agriculture or raising cattle were virtually desolate. For this, Australia received much international criticism. Taking the land from the aboriginal people had been motivated with resort to the "natural law" that those who make productive use of the land are entitled to it. Nevertheless, the land was not made productive. At the same time, China was overpopulated and many would have been willing to move from there to Australia to make use of the land. But this was not something that the white Australian population wanted to happen, for motives that can hardly be labeled anything but racist (economic motives can be ruled out, as the white population did not make use of the land, and did not even inhabit many of the areas concerned).[74]

The Australian solution was to fill the country with white, preferably British, immigrants. However, as the number of willing British migrants was limited, in spite of the financial support for the move that they received from the Australian government, immigration from Southern Europe—mostly Italy—was allowed as the second-best (or second worst) alternative. Southern European immigration was thus allowed as a tool for preventing Asian immigration.[75]

The need for more immigration came to be perceived as even more pressing after the Second World War. The need for populating the land to strengthen the state's legitimacy remained at least in part. The economy, and hence labor demand, was growing strongly. Furthermore, Australia had concluded from the war that its population was too small to secure its military defense. Yet the unwillingness to have immigration from Asia remained strong. Japan had

---

[73] Chiswick and Hatton (2003).
[74] McGregor (2016).
[75] McGregor (2016).

been the main adversary in the war, and China was ruled by communists. It was doubted whether immigrants from these countries would be loyal to their new home country in the case of a new war.[76] (The United States showed a similar attitude during its war with Japan when a large part of its population of Japanese ancestry was forcibly interned in camps. Not so in Hawaii though, where a full one-third of the population was of Japanese ancestry and interning them all would have ruined the economy.)

It was still preferred that immigration would originate in the United Kingdom, and although more people kept moving to Australia from there than from any other country they were still seen as too few. Financially supported migration was thus expanded to target migrants from other European countries—again Italy became the single most important. Australia also resettled many Eastern European refugees, although only those who were fit for work.[77] Many, in and outside of the country, thus criticized the Australian government for being more interested in labor recruitment than in the plight of refugees.[78] Yet, regardless of the aims, refugee immigration per capita in the postwar decades was considerably higher in Australia than anywhere else in the West.[79] A population's acceptance for refugee immigration has probably always been higher if refugees' self-sufficiency has been higher. Hence, although it may be instinctively tempting to deny it, there is often a real tradeoff between receiving more but less vulnerable, or fewer but more vulnerable refugees.

The Australian population grew fast, from around 8 million in 1950 to 13 million in 1970, in large part due to immigration. The population share of European ancestry remained almost as high as before, although the share of specifically British ancestry declined somewhat. Compared with European immigration in the same period, Australian immigration was higher per capita but still less controversial. This was most likely due to a combination of the common perception that it was even more necessary in Australia—not only for economic reasons—and that it was kept at least somewhat more ethnically homogenous.

Following only a few years behind the United States and Canada, Australia gradually abandoned immigration policies that discriminated by country of origin in the late 1960s and early 1970s. Like Canada, Australia instead began selecting immigrants on the basis of measurable skills. Also like in Canada,

---

[76] Gibney (2004).

[77] Gibney (2004).

[78] Price (1981).

[79] Gibney (2004).

today (since 1979) this is done in Australia by means of a points system where the number of points determines who may immigrate (apart from in the cases of close family members or refugees). Most migration to Australia today is from Asia.

Migration and migrants in the West today

The Western world is currently in a second period of high migration, the size of which is not second to the first in 1840–1930. We can make a relevant comparison by looking at the numbers of immigrants in the United States, which has been by far the most important country of immigration in both periods. In 1930 there were 15 million immigrants in the United States comprising 12 percent of the country's total population. In 2017 there were 50 million immigrants comprising 14 percent of the population.[80]

The number of migrants from the rest of the world in the West (the EU, Iceland, Norway, Switzerland, Canada, the United States, Australia and New Zealand), has increased by on average about two million per year during the last decades, from 40 million in 1990 to 92 million in 2017.[81] Being rather constant in absolute numbers, this net migration has decreased moderately as a share of the (moderately increasing) population in the West, and decreased markedly as a share of the (markedly increasing) population in the rest of the world (see further in Chapter 8).

Figure 2.5 shows the shares of immigrants in the populations in Western countries in 2017. Comparing it with Figure 2.3 reveals some of what has changed since 1970. A first major difference is that more countries were found worth including in Figure 2.5, as between these two years several countries have transitioned from mostly being countries of emigration to also being important countries of immigration. A second is that also among the "old" immigration countries, the immigrant share is higher in 2017 than in 1970 in each single country. As in 1970, the highest share in 2017 is found in Switzerland, followed by New Zealand and Canada. The immigrant share in the United States, which was at a bottom level in 1970, has more than doubled in 2017. In almost all countries, the large majority of migrant populations in 2017 are from countries outside the West (black bars).

---

[80] Source: Own calculations using data from the US census in 1930, and the American Community Survey in 2017, from Ruggles et al. (2015).
[81] Source: United Nations Global Migration Database.

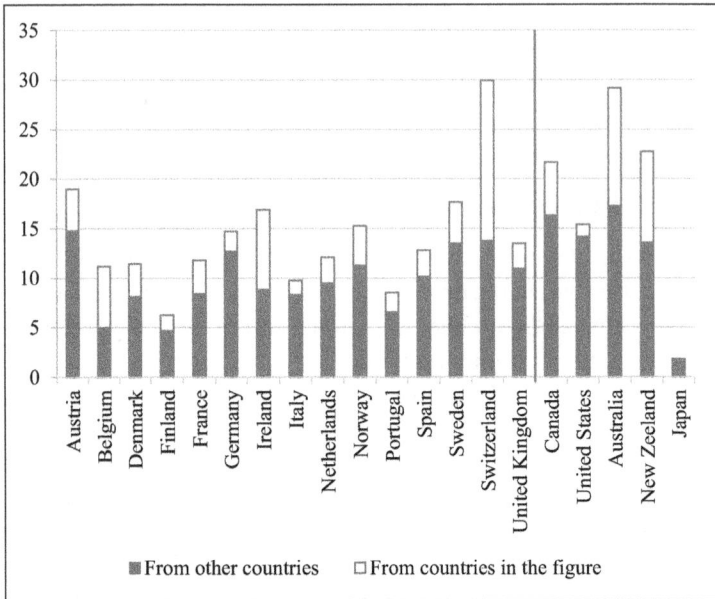

Figure 2.5 Foreign-born population shares (percent) 2017 in Western Europe and five non-European countries.

Source: United Nations Global Migration Database.

Japan is also included in the figure for illustration of the contrast to another high-income country, which differs strongly from Western countries in having allowed very little immigration, both during the country's period of strong economic growth in 1950–90 and today when low fertility means that the share of elderly in the country's population is expected to grow strongly in the near future.

Annual immigration in most Western countries corresponds to well below 1 percent of the country's population. Figure 2.6 shows annual immigration per capita in 2011–15 in Western European countries. Immigration from EU and non-EU countries are measured separately and that from non-EU countries is further divided between refugees and others. Average annual immigration per capita is on average around 0.5 percent. Around half of it is from another EU country. On average, only a small part is refugee immigration, but with much variation between countries.

Overall, there is less variation between the countries in the figure in non-European than in European immigration. This can easily be explained by the latter being determined to a large extent by variation in labor demand

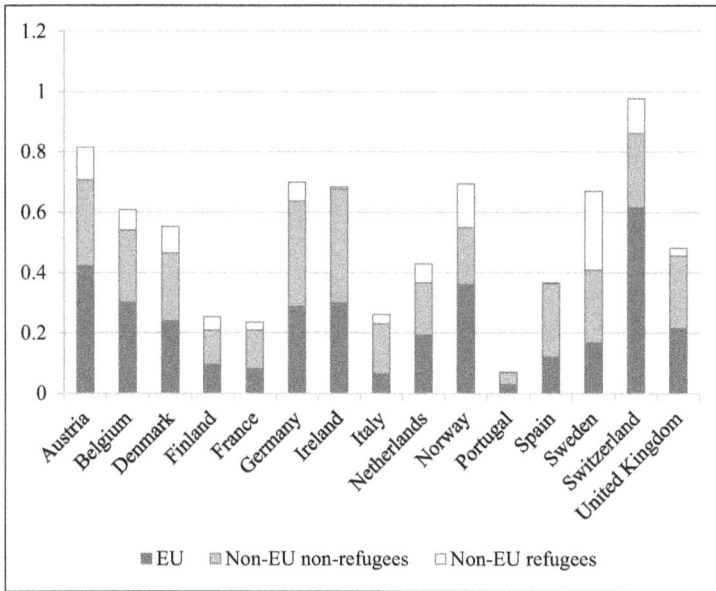

Figure 2.6 Average annual immigration in Western Europe in 2011–15 (percent of population).

Source: Eurostat. Family members of refugees are not separately identified. Hence these are included among non-refugees.

between European countries. Switzerland and Norway stand out with high labor demand and high wages during this period, thereby attracting many immigrants from the rest of Europe. Economic growth and labor demand were particularly weak in Portugal, which also experienced very low immigration (and quite high emigration) in this period.

Figure 2.6 also shows the decline of France as a country of immigration compared with other Western European countries. A look at Figures 2.3 and 2.5 also shows that France had the second highest share of immigrants in the population in 1970 but was far from that position in 2017. This may easily be explained by the country's relatively weak economic performance over the last several decades.

Final words: The importance of migration

Migration to the West may appear to be very high and important or a quite marginal phenomenon depending on from which direction one looks. And much of its theoretical and political complexity is because of that. Small annual inflows have, after more than half a century, accumulated to more than one-tenth of the population being immigrants in most Western countries, and almost one-third in two of them. In addition, many native-born have "foreign background" in the sense that their parents were immigrants. Yet from a more global perspective, even these accumulated numbers are quite small. As many as 97 percent of all humans on Earth live in the country in which they were born, and only slightly more than 1 percent have migrated from the rest of the world to the West.

Yet again, although only a small fraction of all people in low- and middle-income countries ever get the opportunity to migrate to the West, far higher numbers would also want to do it if they could. Gallup has asked people all over the world whether they would "like to move permanently to another country" if they "had the opportunity," and the alternative was to continue living in the present country. In the 2015–17 round of surveys, 33 percent in sub-Saharan Africa, 27 percent in Latin America and the Caribbean and 24 percent in the Middle East and North Africa said they would prefer to move—most of them to a Western country.[82]

It is probably wise to not take these numbers too literally, not least because the formulation "had the opportunity" is open to different interpretations. It is not clear exactly how much "opportunity" would be needed for these people to actually migrate. Or indeed what sort of opportunity is lacking for the 14 percent in the United States and Canada who say they would like to emigrate if they had the opportunity, but still have not done so. However if nothing more, these high numbers—and how stable they have been since these polls started in 2007—seem to give a clear sign that migration seems to be of great importance in the minds of very many in poorer countries.

And this again leads to the question touched upon repeatedly in this chapter, of whether we think migration is an important phenomenon because of the migration that we have actually seen so far or because of that which we imagine (or fear) may come to happen in the future. Perhaps the politically most important question about migration is to what extent it is possible to control it. Will it be possible for Western countries to keep out the hundreds of millions who say today that they would like to migrate, and perhaps a few hundred million more who might say the same in a decade or two, if they all decide to really make the move but the West does not want them? This question will be the focus of Chapter 8.

---

[82] These surveys are published at www.gallup.com.

Chapter 3

WHO MIGRATE?

International migrants comprise only a small fraction of all humans on Earth. Considering the small shares that migrate, it is easy to understand that these may potentially be very different from those who do not. The fewer the migrants are, the more different they are likely to be. (It is a mathematical fact that a small group may *potentially* differ more—in any sense—from the remaining population the smaller it is. The average height in a "group" consisting only of the world's tallest person is a simple illustration of this fact.)

This chapter is devoted to describing the migrants and their decision to migrate: the factors that are most decisive for the decision, and hence who is more likely to make a positive decision and become a migrant. The chapter title's plural form underscores one of the main themes of the chapter as well as of the book: migration is not one singular and easily summarized phenomenon where one type of person migrates for one reason. It is a vast array of things, where different circumstances in different places create different migrants.

How well-informed are migration decisions?

Migrants are thus likely to be different in some or many ways from non-migrants. And this may be in different ways for different migrant flows, and also for different migrants in the same flow. Historian John Gould wrote about the Europeans who moved to North America before the advent of transatlantic steam traffic in the 1860s, that the "appalling conditions [on the ships] deterred all but the most resolute, the most desperate, and the most ignorant of emigrants."[1]

The word "ignorant" was probably a quite fitting description of a large share of these early migrants, who had few ways of obtaining more detailed and reliable information about America than the rumors that it was much easier to make a living there. Considering the radical change—for life—that

---

[1] Gould (1979).

these migrants decided to make based on such scarce information, a greater willingness to accept risk is probably also a characteristic that set many migrants apart from non-migrants in this period, as well as in much of both earlier and later history.

Later on, as migrants—and hence letters to relatives in their home countries—became more numerous, knowledge about America also increased considerably among potential later European migrants. Yet that knowledge was still often limited to local conditions in the places where previous migrants from, for example, the same village lived. Hence, later migrants to a large extent went to the very same places.[2]

Today, in the Internet age, potential migrants' knowledge about conditions in far-away countries is most often (yet perhaps not always) much better than it was in the nineteenth century. We may, therefore, expect the decision of whether to migrate or not to most often be one where a quite well-informed individual or family measures the likely benefit of migration against the likely costs and decides whether the net effect would be an improvement or not. From this it follows in turn that we should generally expect that those who decide to migrate are largely those who have the most to gain from it.

It may be worth dwelling a moment on this expectation. In a world of perfect information, where every person knew exactly what their gains and losses from migration to another country would be, the logical outcome is that the expectation would be perfectly true: each individual who decided to migrate would have more to gain from it than each individual who did not. In reality, of course, nobody has perfect information even about their future opportunities in the home country—and typically even less so about their potential opportunities in a foreign country. Nevertheless, the more information potential migrants have about the likely benefits and costs of migration, the more we should expect it to be true that those who do migrate are primarily those who have the most to gain from it. We should thus, for example, often expect this to be more true in migration flows that have been going on for a long time than in those that have recently started. In the early phases, chance probably often plays a significant role in determining exactly who happens to receive the information—which may be correct or not—about promising opportunities somewhere far away.

Likewise, migration to escape violent conflict or persecution, which does not always allow sufficient time for careful gathering of information, may often leave more room for being determined by chance, or by very small pieces of information. Migration scholar George Borjas gives a vivid example in his book *We Wanted Workers*, where he recounts his own childhood arrival in the

---

[2] Wegge (1998).

United States as a refugee from Cuba in 1962. Most Cubans who arrived in this large inflow settled in Miami. That was where most other Cubans had settled before them and few had much information about other alternatives. An immigration officer tried to convince Borjas' mother that California was a good alternative. The mother listened to the advice, until someone further back in the queue shouted: "Don't go to California. There are earthquakes there." Based on this small piece of information the decision was made to settle in Miami.[3]

A wider example of something probably similar is the large refugee flow into Europe in the autumn of 2015. The stream of refugees across the sea from Turkey to Greece had increased steadily through 2014 and the first half of 2015. According to EU rules (the Dublin Convention, see Chapter 2), all asylum seekers who arrived in Greece would have to remain and submit their asylum applications there. In the eyes of most refugees, this was considerably less attractive than if they would have been allowed to continue their journey to Western Europe. But in the late summer of 2015, Greece suddenly and quite unexpectedly decided to stop adhering to these rules and instead let migrants pass through. The benefits of traveling to Europe thus suddenly increased for many refugees and many therefore made a fast decision to do this. They traveled to make use of the opportunity that had suddenly opened up before them and which they did not know how long it would last.

However as European governments were not prepared for the situation, and likewise reacted with little planning, it was not easy for refugees to determine exactly what their opportunities were. And in many cases opportunities also changed by the week, as different European governments changed their ways of responding to the refugee flow. One week Hungary kept refugees in the country by force. The next it assisted them to board trains to Austria. At different points in time different countries erected fences to stop the passage of refugees.

The result became a large mass of refugees, many of whom were uncertain about which country would be their final destination, moving—to a large extent on foot—through Europe and responding to new bits of information regarding which onward routes were feasible and which were not. In the end, as we saw in Chapter 2, a very disproportionately large share chose to seek asylum in Sweden: 20 percent of all asylum applications that were filed in the EU in September–November 2015 were filed in Sweden, which is home to only 2 percent of the Union's population. This was a considerable increase compared with the first eight months in the same year, when in each month between 5 and 8 percent of all applications had been filed in Sweden.[4]

---

[3] Borjas (2016).
[4] Source: Eurostat.

There was no legislative change in Sweden that could explain the strong increase in this share during these chaotic autumn months. What seems to be the only possible explanation for it is instead the difference between Sweden (and to a large extent Germany) and other EU countries in what signals they sent to refugees. The Swedish (and German) government, and many of the country's citizens, chose to depart from the main strategy that was adopted by the rest of Europe, which was to signal as clearly as possible that refugees were not wanted. They chose instead, by words, voluntary welcome committees, etc., to communicate that refugees were welcome. The difference may not appear huge. But with little other information available to refugees, who needed to make important decisions in little time and who were sometimes abused even to the point of being physically assaulted in other parts of Europe, it may have been decisive to many.

However, this example was mentioned to illustrate that large migration flows based on fairly poor information are indeed possible even in the age of telecommunications. Yet they are exceptions and not the rule. In particular, for economically motivated migration—which makes up the majority of migration to the West today—most potential migrants have good access to accurate information about conditions in receiving countries and may make well-founded decisions on whether and where to migrate.

Who have the most to gain from migrating?

Therefore, if we want to describe who are more likely to participate in the more large-scale economically motivated migration to the West, we may reformulate the question as who have the most to gain from doing so. Most of this chapter deals with providing answers to this. These are provided in the form of a list of factors that tend to increase the gains from migration, and hence the likelihood that someone will migrate. Not all factors apply to all migrants, but each factor can explain numerically important patterns.

Those who are allowed to. A first, obvious part of the answer to who have the most to gain from migration is *those who can migrate legally*. Any person who wants to move to a different country, but is not allowed to do so according to the laws of that country, has to make the decision whether to migrate or not by weighing the benefits and costs of trying to get in and live illegally in the country. This of course implies considerably lower benefits and higher costs than if the same person could have made the same migration legally. Hence, I first note the obvious conclusion that any given person is more likely to migrate if they are legally permitted to do so.

Those for whom the distance is shorter. The costs of migrating are lower, and migration thus generally becomes higher, over shorter distances. This is not only because of the one-time cost of a flight ticket. For many it is also because of the costs in time and money for regular visits to friends and relatives in the home country. It may also be because shorter distances often imply better knowledge about income opportunities in the receiving country,[5] something that tends to be true to some extent also in the Internet age.

Hence as a general pattern, there is on average more migration between two countries the closer they are geographically.[6] Migration to the United States is provided as an illustration in Figure 3.1. (Remember, figures like this are primarily for more effective illustration of results that have also been identified more generally.) For each country in the figure, the horizontal axis shows the distance from its capital to whichever of New York, Miami and Los Angeles is closest. The vertical axis shows the share of all living people born in the country who lived in the United States in 2010 (people living neither in the home country nor in the United States cannot be measured here and are thus excluded from these calculations). The figure clearly shows that migration is mostly higher from countries that are closer.

The highest emigration rates of all are from very small countries, as some of the highlighted markers in the figure illustrate.[7] Mexico has also been highlighted in the figure for having the highest emigration rate to the United States among larger countries. It may be interesting to compare the Mexican emigration rate of almost 10 percent with the considerably lower rate in the United States' second large neighbor Canada, which is also highlighted. This difference is most likely mainly a reflection of the higher expected income increases when migrating from Mexico where incomes are on average lower.

The "middle-rich." The primary economic benefit from migration equals the difference between the incomes that the migrant can earn in the destination

---

[5] Sjaastad (1962); Schwartz (1973).

[6] Grogger and Hanson (2011).

[7] For similar results in a broader analysis, see Beine, Docquier and Rapoport (2008). One may imagine different reasons why the size of a country has an impact on its emigration rate. It is more difficult for a smaller country to become self-sufficient in many goods that the population wants to consume. Therefore, smaller countries have stronger incentives to develop international economic relations (trade), and these relations may in turn also boost migration. One can also imagine a more direct effect, where people have more limited opportunities, in a wide sense, within smaller countries, which would create stronger incentives to move abroad.

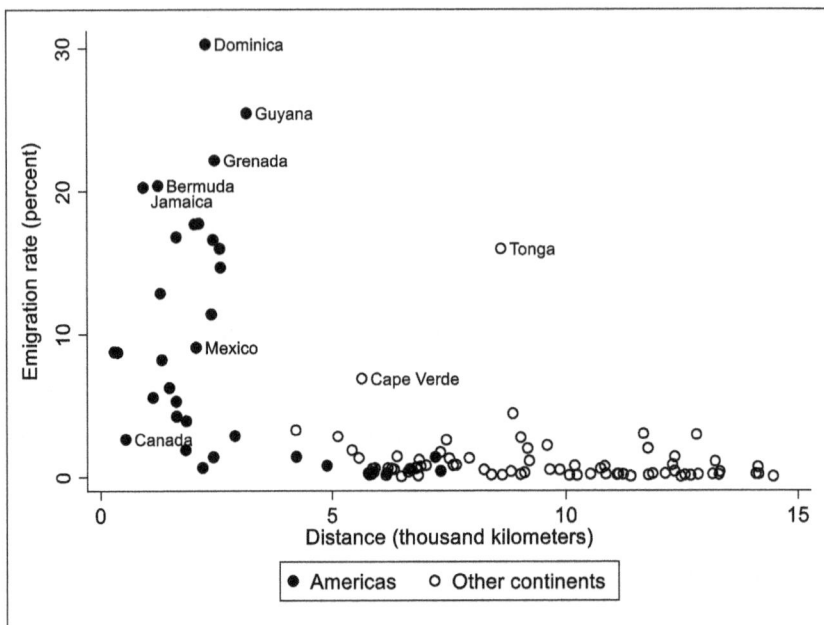

Figure 3.1 The correlation between a country's distance and emigration rate to the United States.

Sources: Number of migrants in the United States: Own calculations using data from the American Community Surveys in 2009–11 (the 2010 value is given by an average between these three), from Ruggles et al. (2015). Home country population: World Development Indicators, the World Bank.

country and in the home country. Therefore, we should expect more migration from countries where incomes are lower. Yet there is also a limiting factor. Many are too poor to afford the initial costs of migration, such as that of a flight ticket. This creates the one major exception from the insight that we should expect those who actually migrate to be those who have the most to gain from it (given the circumstances, including legislation). It does not help much if a person could gain US$100,000 over their lifetime by moving from Tanzania to the United States, if they are not able to pay the initial US$1,000 that is required for the flight. In most instances, it is very difficult to borrow for migration (outside of one's family) and promising to pay back once the gains have been realized. (One notable exception is when employers in the destination country pay for the journey and deduct the cost from future wage payments. We saw in Chapter 2 that this was fairly common in the Americas in the eighteenth and nineteenth centuries. Today it is rare in the West, to which many can afford to migrate by their own means anyway. It is more common in Gulf states though, which attract many migrants who are very poor.)

In sum we should therefore expect migration to be highest from countries where income levels are low, yet not so low that too many cannot afford migrating. The summary in Chapter 2 of migration from Europe to America in the nineteenth century provided one illustration of this. Large-scale migration did not happen until income levels in countries of origin became high enough to enable larger numbers of people to afford the journey. But as the income rise continued even further, it eventually caused migration to fall again (i.e., in Northern and Western Europe toward the end of the century). When incomes were already higher, further increases affected migration more importantly by lowering the gains than by relieving financial constraints.

Also today, emigration rates are on average higher from middle-income countries than from both low- and high-income countries. An example is illustrated in Figure 3.2, where the horizontal axis shows a country's GDP per capita in 2010 and the vertical axis shows the share of all living people born in the country, who in the same year lived in one of 20 countries[8] which together make up a very large part of the rich Western world.[9] Of all countries with an emigration rate above 20 percent, all except one have a GDP per capita in an interval of approximately US$3,000–20,000.[10] The exception is Ireland, which had spectacular GDP growth before 2010 and whose high accumulated emigration mostly happened earlier when the country was less rich.

---

[8] Also migrants between these 20 countries are thus included. The 20 countries are, by continent: Austria, Denmark, Finland, France, Germany, Greece, Ireland, Luxembourg, the Netherlands, Norway, Portugal, Spain, Sweden, Switzerland, the United Kingdom, Australia, New Zealand, Canada, the United States, and Chile (which is not typically included in "the West," but in the OECD and hence in the study from which the numbers originate). The two rich Western countries that are most notably not included are Belgium and Italy.

[9] For a broader analysis, see Clark, Hatton and Williamson (2007).

[10] Also in this case, we see that most countries with really high emigration rates have in common that they are small. Yet the pattern of countries within the given GDP per capita interval having on average higher emigration rates, remains also if we look separately at the smallest or the largest countries in the world, as well as in regression analysis that controls, for example, for second-degree polynomials in log land area and log population. An alternative candidate explanation for the pattern seen in the Figure 3.2 could be that, as poorer countries typically have less-educated populations, these can less often migrate legally to Western countries where immigration laws prioritize the more educated. However, the pattern shown in Figure 3.2 looks similar if we measure emigration rates specifically for those with low- or middle-education levels instead of total rates.

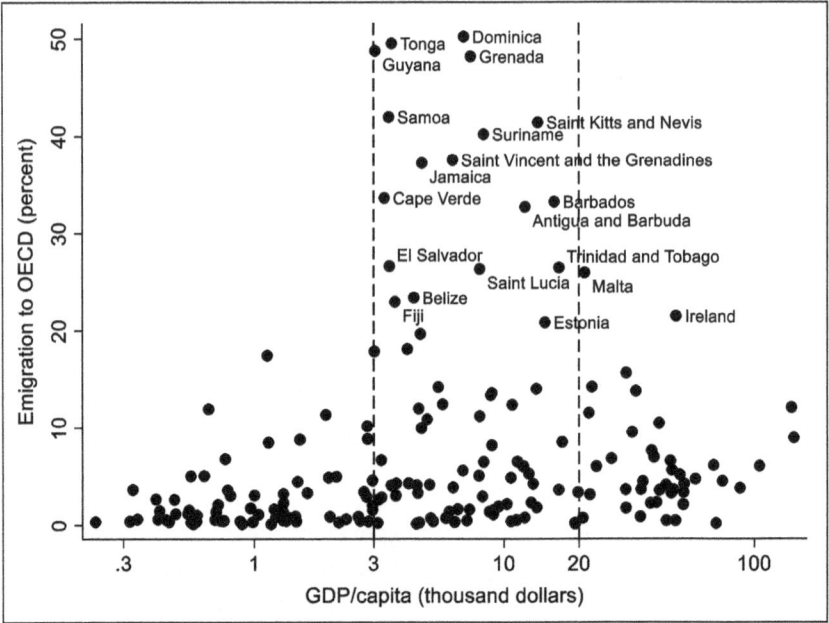

Figure 3.2 The correlation between GDP per capita and the accumulated emigration rate to 20 OECD countries in 2010. The horizontal axis is logarithmic, that is, higher values have been more compressed, for increased readability.

Sources: Emigration rates: Brücker, Capuano and Marfouk (2013). GDP per capita: World Development Indicators, the World Bank.

The young. We have seen that migration should be higher if expected income increases are higher and if costs are lower. Both these factors work in favor of higher migration among younger compared with older adults. (Psychological differences that make the young more prone to risk-taking may also play a role.) All else being equal, the longer the working life ahead of a person is, the larger is the potential income increase from migration measured over the person's entire lifetime. The costs of migration are also typically lower for the youngest adults, who have not yet invested so much in their adult life in the home country. Already at 35–40 years of age, most people have shaped much of their lives—their homes, families, education, careers and social contexts— and hence have more to lose from leaving all of that, compared with most people who are 20–25 years old and who have not yet invested in and created as much at home.

There is probably not a single case in history of a large migration flow where the age group 20–40 years, and 20–30 years even more, was not strongly

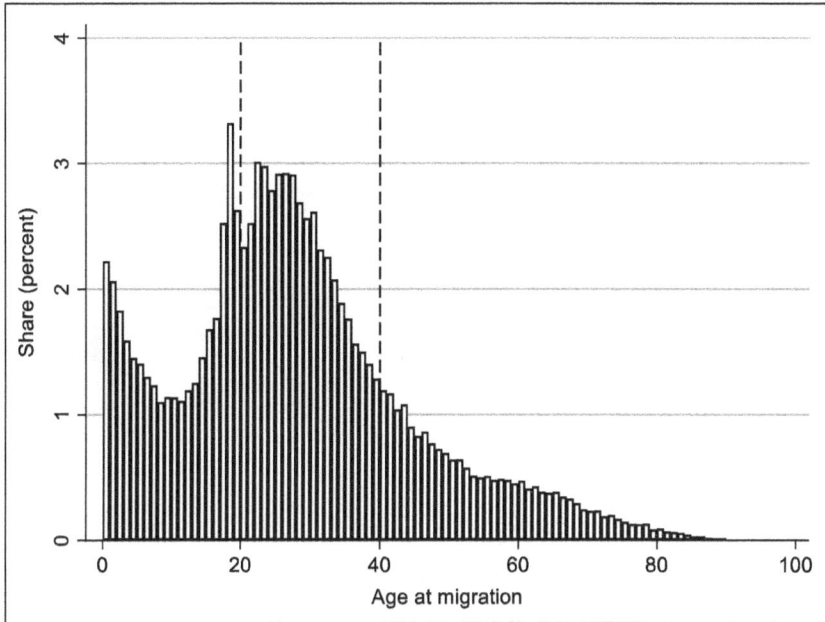

Figure 3.3 Distribution (percent) of age at migration among immigrants from Latin America, the Caribbean, Asia and Africa, who were in the United States in 2015–17, and had immigrated 0–5 years before.

Source: Own calculations using data from the American Community Surveys in 2015–17, from Ruggles et al. (2015).

overrepresented. Merely 8 percent of those who moved from Europe to the United States in 1868–1910 were above 40 years old.[11] Figure 3.3 shows the distribution of age at migration among all migrants from Latin America, the Caribbean, Asia and Africa, who lived in the United States in any of the years 2015–17 and had immigrated 0–5 years before. The migrants are strongly concentrated to approximately the ages 17–30 years. The distribution also has a second peak that represents very young children. It is a natural consequence of migration being highest among the youngest adults, that it is also high among young children.

Migration being more gainful for the youngest adults also in turn implies that a country's emigration rate should be higher the higher the share of young adults in the population is. In other words, it should be possible to

---

[11] Hatton and Williamson (1998).

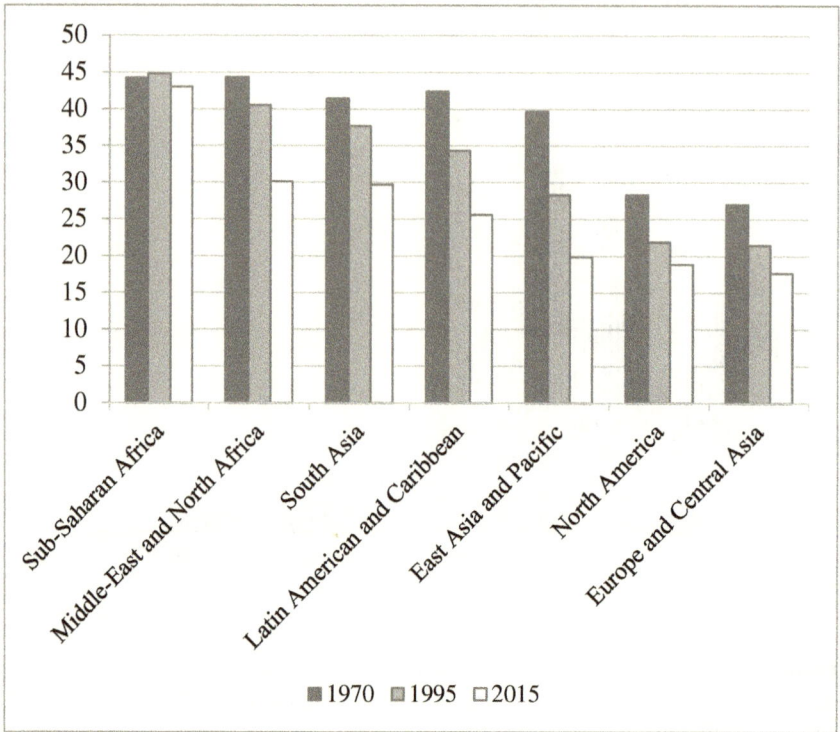

Figure 3.4 Population shares aged 0–14 years (percent per region), 1970, 1995 and 2015.

Source: World Development Indicators, the World Bank.

some extent to predict future migration from a country by studying the size of birth cohorts, that is, how many children are born in relation to the size of the population. When the share of children in the population increases or decreases, the future share of young adults, and hence the future emigration rate, should on average do the same.[12]

In most of the world, the share of children in the population has decreased considerably over the last half century. Figure 3.4 shows population shares in the ages 0–14 years, per continent, in each of the years 1970, 1995 and 2015. In 1970, most of Latin America and Asia were in the middle of the *demographic transition*, where the share of children typically becomes high. (Historically, when mortality was high, especially among small children, people on average had many children to compensate. Today, mortality is far lower in most of

---

[12] Hanson and McIntosh (2012); Hanson and McIntosh (2016).

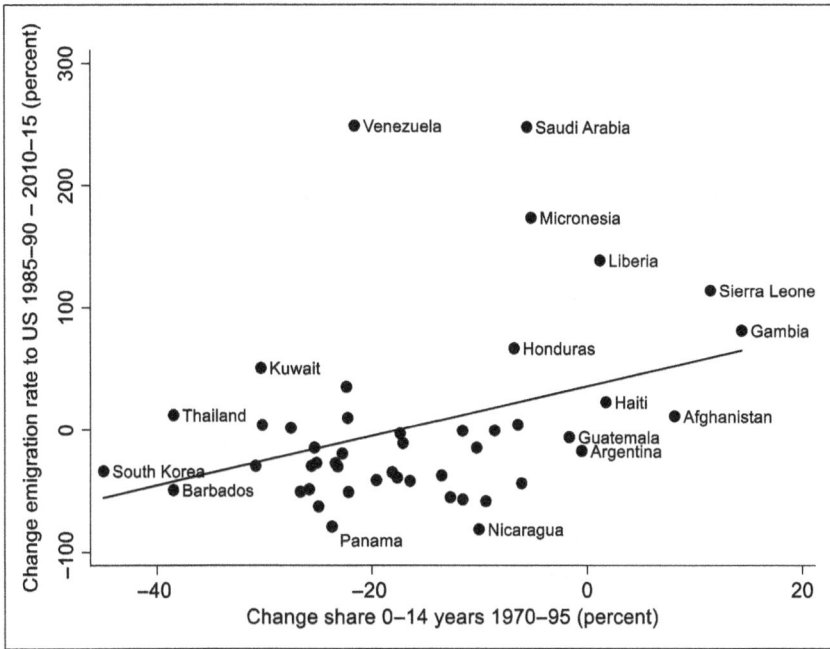

Figure 3.5 The correlation between the changes over time in the share of children in the population and the emigration rate to the United States.

Sources: Migration: Own calculations using data from the American Community Surveys in 2015–16, from Ruggles et al. (2015). Population and share of children in home country: World Development Indicators, the World Bank.

the world, which has also led to fewer births. Yet in most places, it took time for fertility to react to the falling mortality, creating a transition period—the demographic transition—where many children were born, few of them died, and hence the share of children in the population became high.) Forty-five years later, this transition is mostly complete in these regions and the shares of children in their total populations have fallen from 40–45 to 20–30 percent. The only large world region where the share of children is still really high is Sub-Saharan Africa.

The correlation between changes in the share of children in a country's population and emigration from the same country some years later is illustrated in Figure 3.5.[13] Its horizontal axis measures the percentage change in 1970–95 in the share of children (0–14 years) in a country's population.

---

[13] For a broader analysis, see Hanson and McIntosh (2012). The figure includes countries from which emigration to the United States in the earlier period was at least

(For example, if the share of children was 30 percent in 1970 and 24 percent in 1995, the value on the horizontal axis would be $-6/30 = -20$ percent.) Its vertical axis similarly measures the percentage change in the country's emigration rate to the United States between the two 5-year periods 1985–90 and 2010–15. Emigration is thus measured 15–20 years later than the respective child cohort size, for it to be measured when these child cohorts are approximately in the age interval where the propensity to emigrate is highest.

Figure 3.5 shows that both the share of children and the total emigration rate have fallen over time in the majority of countries. At their median values, the share of children is 18 percent lower in the latter compared with the earlier period and the emigration rate is 17 percent lower. We also saw in Chapter 2 that migration to the West from the rest of the world has been quite constant in absolute numbers since about 1990 and hence falling as a share of the—simultaneously increasing—population of the rest of the world.

The figure also shows the expected positive correlation between the two changes. The slope of the fitted regression line indicates that, on average, if the population share aged 0–14 years increases by 10 percent, emigration 15–20 years later will be around 20 percent higher. (However, it is not entirely easy to sort out to which extent this estimate is affected by changes in fertility coinciding with changes in average incomes. Especially so because—as we recently saw—changes in average incomes may either increase or decrease emigration.)

According to some analysts, this delayed effect of decreased fertility is a major explanation behind the apparent fall in illegal migration to the United States since 2007 (which was mentioned in Chapter 2). From this interpretation follows the forecast that this migration is likely to remain at lower levels also in the future.[14] This will be considered in more detail in Chapter 8.

The highly educated. Immigration laws in all Western countries to some—often a very high—extent favor migrants with higher probability of becoming economically productive and self-sufficient. A job offer makes it easier to obtain permission to immigrate in most countries. The Canadian and Australian points systems are designed to try to select the more productive candidates also among

---

0.05 percent of the population. Western countries, as well as Japan and Singapore have been excluded. Likewise excluded, because their migration to the United States was strongly dominated by refugee migration in at least one of the two periods studied, are Bhutan, Cambodia, Cuba, Eritrea, Iran, Iraq, Laos, Myanmar, Somalia and Vietnam.

[14] Hanson and McIntosh (2016); Hanson, Liu and McIntosh (2017).

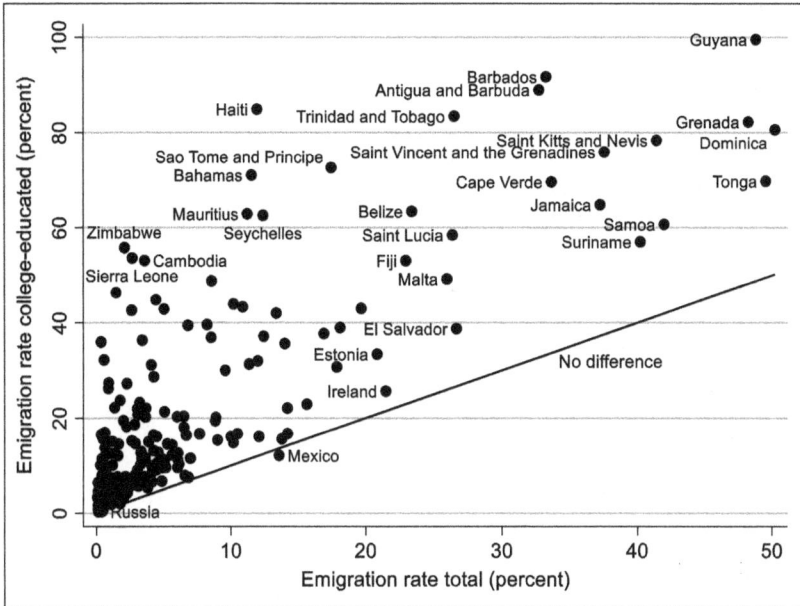

Figure 3.6 Share of all living people born in a country, who lived in one of 20 OECD countries in 2010.

Source: Brücker, Capuano and Marfouk (2013).

those who have not yet been evaluated by an employer in the country. They are described in more detail in Chapters 2 and 8, but an obvious consequence of them is that migration is substantially easier for the highly educated.

It is also easy to understand that expected economic gains from migration to a high-income country, where a large share of all jobs require advanced skills, are often higher among the highly educated. We should expect this to lead to positive self-selection where the highly educated more often choose migration regardless of whether immigration laws favor them or not.[15]

An image of the global correlation between education and migration is given in Figure 3.6. Its horizontal axis shows the share of all living people who

---

[15] It is also theoretically possible that economic gains from migration could sometimes be higher for the less educated, leading to negative self-selection. Yet theoretical models that lead to this result tend to require quite specific assumptions. For a theoretic framework that generally predicts more migration among the highly educated, see Sjaastad (1962), and Chiswick (1978). For one that predicts the opposite in certain cases, see Borjas (1987). For a discussion of the specific requirements that are crucial for the latter's conclusions, see Grogger and Hanson (2011).

were born in a country, who in 2010 lived in one of the earlier mentioned (same as in Figure 3.2) 20 rich Western countries. The vertical axis shows the corresponding share measured only among those with college education. The solid diagonal line represents the case where these two emigration rates are equally high. A marker above the line thus represents a country where emigration has been higher among those with college education than among those without and a marker below the line represents the opposite.

As the figure shows, the migration rate to these rich countries has been higher among the college-educated from as good as all countries. The only exceptions are Mexico and Russia and only with very small margins. And for many countries the difference is huge. Six countries even have emigration rates of the college-educated that are above 80 percent.

As we have just mentioned, the overrepresentation of the highly educated in migration to the West is likely due to a combination of selective immigration policies and migrants' self-selection. Plausibly, we may get closer to observing the importance of self-selection alone by looking at a corresponding pattern in a case where immigration laws were not strongly selective.

As we saw in Chapter 2, the US laws in 1968–90 may provide such a case. Therefore, the horizontal axis in Figure 3.7 shows the share of college-educated among all 20–34-year-olds in a non-Western country in 1990 and the vertical axis shows the share of college-educated among similarly aged migrants in the United States in the same year who immigrated 0–5 years before.[16] The solid diagonal line represents the case where the two shares are the same.

The conclusion drawn from Figure 3.7 is similar to that from Figure 3.6. Again, a marker above the solid line represents a case where those with college education have a higher emigration rate than those without. And this is the case for each single country of origin in the figure, that is, this time including Mexico although with a very small margin. Self-selection thus appears to have been quite enough to create a far higher migration rate among the college-educated also when immigration laws were fairly neutral with respect to education.

Another example of migration from countries with lower income levels to countries with higher income levels, where the selectivity of immigration

---

[16] Only countries with at least 30 migrants in the data are included. Western countries, and Japan and Singapore, were excluded from this analysis. The limitation to recently arrived migrants ensures that migrants have not had much time to add education in the United States, as the data source does not provide information on to what extent migrants have received part of their education after migrating, which would distort the measure of "college-educated migration." A similar limitation could not be done in Figure 3.6, hence that figure may exaggerate college-educated migration to a higher extent.

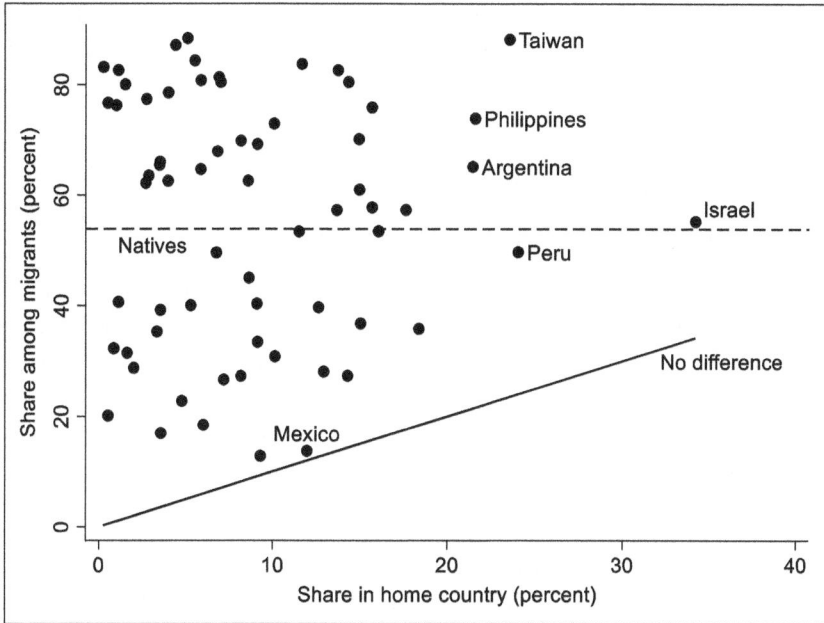

Figure 3.7 Share with college education among 20- to 34-year-olds in home country 1990, and among similarly aged migrants who moved to the United States in 1985–90.

Sources: Migrants in the United States: Own calculations using data from the US census in 1990, from Ruggles et al. (2015). Education levels in home countries: Barro and Lee (2013).

policies has been only marginal, is that of migration from new to old EU member states following the EU enlargement in 2004. Among those who moved to the United Kingdom between the first quarters of 2004 and 2009, 32 percent of all men and 40 percent of all women were college-educated.[17] Among those who moved to Sweden in 2004–5, at least 24 percent of all men and 48 percent of all women aged 20–45 had at least two years of college education. (Most likely, the shares were considerably higher. Information on education is lacking in the Swedish data for 36 percent of all men and 23 percent of all women in the group, and these missing values were included when the shares with college education were calculated.)[18] These shares are all considerably higher than the corresponding shares in the total or similarly aged populations in the home countries.[19]

---

[17] Dustmann, Frattini and Halls (2010).

[18] Ruist (2017a).

[19] Barro and Lee (2013).

Yet another indication of the importance of self-selection is that the highly educated are on average more overrepresented in migrant groups that have moved longer distances.[20] The theoretical explanation for this result is that when the costs of migration are higher—such as because of a longer distance—migration only becomes a net gain for those with the very highest expected income increases. And these are particularly often highly educated.[21]

However, the strong overrepresentation of the highly educated among migrants to the West does not automatically imply that migration always makes average education levels rise in the receiving countries. This is because these receiving countries typically have considerably higher education levels than the migrants' home countries. The dashed horizontal line in Figure 3.7 illustrates this. It shows the share with a college education, 53.9 percent, among natives in the same age interval as the migrants. Migration from the 37 countries whose markers are above the line in the figure has thus contributed to raising average education in this age interval in the United States, while migration from the 28 countries that are below the line has contributed to lowering it. Although the former countries are more numerous, the total number of migrants from the latter is higher. Thus the share of college-educated among all these migrants together, 37.8 percent, is lower than that among the natives. This non-Western immigration as a whole has thus lowered the average education level in this age group in the receiving country.

Those who follow in others' footsteps. Earlier in this chapter, I said that it ought to be reasonable to view a large part of current migration as the result of well-informed decisions where people weigh benefits against costs and conclude whether migration would be likely to bring them a net gain or not. Yet information is seldom entirely perfect. Not even the person who already has a job offer in the destination country when moving knows precisely what future opportunities will be beyond that immediate offer. And certain groups—refugees were mentioned—also sometimes seem to make their moves based on considerably less or poorer information than others.

Social ties to previous migrants who are already in the prospective destination may often make it easier to obtain good information about income opportunities, and thus to make a better founded and more often positive decision to migrate. Such ties may also reduce one of the major costs of migration for many, which is the threat of loneliness when arriving in an unknown place,

---

[20] Ruist (2017b). For similar results for migration within the United States, see Schwartz (1973).
[21] Sjaastad (1962); Schwartz (1973).

without friends and maybe with limited understanding of the local culture and social life. Even loose ties may provide a benefit, such as knowing that there is a friend of a friend at the destination, whom one has perhaps never even met, but who has promised to offer some help in getting to know the place and the people. Even the mere presence of other migrants from the home country, region or ethnicity may provide an assurance that one will not be completely alone in a place full of strange people with strange customs—also if one has no previous personal tie to any of these earlier migrants.[22]

It is thus easy to understand that the probability that a person will migrate increases if the person has some sort of connection to previous migrants at the destination. This is probably true to some extent for almost all migrants. Yet it is likely to be more pronounced in cases where also limited information is a major factor in determining who migrates and who does not. In other words, we should expect that migration always makes further migration easier, but much more so in some cases than others.

An empirical pattern that seems to confirm this expectation is that as good as all migrant groups cluster geographically to some extent, but some vastly more than others. Later migrants are always more likely to go to places where previous migrants from the same origin already live. In certain settings, where the lack of information or threat of social loneliness factors outlined above are plausibly more pronounced, these patterns may be very stark. I provide some illustrations below.

In the transatlantic migration of the nineteenth century, the importance of earlier migrants was particularly strong, as their letters were the all-dominant source of knowledge about conditions in potential destinations. The information that was provided in such letters was usually about very local conditions, that is, not so much about conditions in "the United States" as in the local area where the migrant who wrote the letter lived. This created a powerful force toward strong concentration of migrants.[23]

A stark illustration may be provided by a comparison of the settlement patterns in the United States of the nineteenth century migrants from Ireland and Norway. As was seen in Chapter 2, the Irish were the foremost pioneers of the transatlantic migration. Irish migration was high already in the 1840s, and peaked already in the 1850s. At that time, settlement of the American inland had not yet progressed far. Hence, these early Irish migrants predominantly settled along the East Coast. Large-scale Norwegian migration on the other

---

[22] Hatton and Williamson (1998).
[23] Wegge (1998).

Table 3.1 Shares (percent) of immigrants from Ireland and Norway living on the American "East Coast" and in the "Upper Midwest"

	1880 All immigrants	1900 Immigrated 1881–1900	2011–15 Immigrated 2000–2010
Ireland East Coast	64.7	77.3	45.7
Ireland Midwest	6.4	2.4	1.8
Norway East Coast	2.2	8.6	19.3
Norway Midwest	80.8	68.9	8.9

Source: Own calculations using data from the censuses in 1880 and 1900 and the American Community Surveys in 2011–15, from Ruggles et al. (2015).

hand did not take off until the 1870s. By then, economic opportunities further west had improved a lot, and most Norwegian migrants settled inland.

At a snapshot in 1880, which is shown in the first column of Table 3.1, we thus see that 65 percent of all Irish immigrants in the United States, yet only 2 percent of all Norwegian immigrants, lived along the "East Coast," which is here defined as ten States from Maine in the north to Pennsylvania and Delaware in the south. At the same time, 81 percent of those from Norway, but only 6 percent of those from Ireland, lived in the "Upper Midwest," which is here defined as Iowa, Wisconsin, Minnesota, North Dakota and South Dakota.

The root cause of this large difference in settlement patterns is that Irish migration started earlier than Norwegian, that is, when opportunities were relatively more favorable along the coast. This strongly influences what we see in this snapshot, as the Irish that we observe in 1880 on average arrived earlier than the Norwegians that we observe in the same year. Here we cannot compare migrants who arrived from different countries in exactly the same period, as the 1880 census did not collect information on immigrants' year of immigration.

Yet as we proceed, we shall discover that once a difference like this one has been established it may become very persistent also long after the root cause has disappeared. We see this in the second column in the table, which shows the corresponding settlement patterns in 1900 for migrants who immigrated in 1881–1900 (the 1900 census did collect information on year of immigration). Hence we are looking at Irish and Norwegian migrants who arrived during the same 20-year period, and with similar distributions over years within this period. Both groups arrived in the same United States with the same distribution of economic opportunities across different geographic areas.

Yet in spite of this, we see that their settlement patterns differ almost as much as those in the first column did. Relative to the 1880 populations, these later arrivals were somewhat more likely to settle along the coast in both groups. In this period, settlement of the Midwest had passed its peak, and labor demand was high from the industries along the coast. But still, most of the difference between the two groups in the first column remains also in the second; with 69 percent of Norwegian but only 2 percent of Irish immigrants in the Upper Midwest, and 77 percent of Irish but only 9 percent of Norwegian along the East Coast.

The only reasonable explanation for this is the direct effect of the earlier migrants on the settlement choices of the later. As many more Irish than Norwegians lived along the coast, information about new economic opportunities there reached Ireland more easily than Norway. And likewise, information about opportunities in the Upper Midwest reached Norway more easily than Ireland.

As a quite spectacular finale, the last column of the table shows how much remains of the early difference in settlement patterns between Irish and Norwegian migrants, even among those who immigrated from the same countries quite recently, in 2000–2010. Here we see that the ability of the Upper Midwest to attract European migrants has fallen considerably over the 100 years in between. The share of Norwegian migrants settling there is down to only 8.9 percent. Yet that fraction is still five times as high as the corresponding fraction among the recent Irish migrants that are depicted in the same column. Likewise, while the share of Norwegians settling on the East Coast has more than doubled since the late nineteenth century, it is still less than half of the corresponding share among the Irish. We thus see clear signs of chain effects, where migrants have followed migrants who have followed migrants, creating visible effects of the earliest settlement patterns even 120 years after their economic root cause disappeared.

Current migration is more diverse than that of the nineteenth century, and to what extent migrants follow in the footsteps of other migrants today depends a lot on the type of migration. At the end of the scale where poor information about income opportunities, or the risk of social isolation, would matter the most, that is, creating the most important chain effects, we probably find illegal migrants and refugees.

Illegal migrants lack access to formal, legal channels, for example, for job search, and therefore often rely strongly on their personal networks. One study of mostly illegal migration between Southwestern Mexico and the United States showed patterns of geographic concentration that were perhaps not as stark as those in the Irish-Norwegian example above, but not so far away either. For example, only 1 percent of all migrants from the Mexican State of Colima, but 21 percent of those from Michoacan, lived in San Francisco, and 0 percent of those from Colima, but 27 percent of those from Jalisco lived in San Diego. Such differences can obviously not appear by chance, but show the importance of links between migrants.[24]

Similarly strong geographic concentration can often be observed among refugees. Different mechanisms may explain this. The added comfort and social connectedness that is provided by relatives, friends, co-nationals or co-ethnics may be extra important in the insecure situations faced by many refugees. Perhaps even more so, as for refugees this factor does not have to be weighed against economic opportunities to the same extent as for economically motivated migrants. Possibly, refugees may also more often than other migrants make their moves based on limited information, also beyond the unique example I gave earlier from the European situation in the autumn of 2015.

I illustrate this with an example from Europe in the years before 2015, that is, in 2012–14. Also in these three years, Sweden received somewhat more asylum applications per capita than all other EU countries (but with a considerably smaller margin). Asylum seekers thus to a large extent had a certain preference for submitting their applications in Sweden. Yet so with great variation between asylum seekers from different countries. Among the 10 most important countries of origin of asylum seekers in the EU in this period (Serbia and Kosovo are excluded because border changes make these difficult to compare backwards in time, as I will do in the next step), the shares who applied for asylum in Sweden ranged between 1.6 percent among those from Pakistan and 29.8 percent among those from Somalia.

There exists no data that allow us to see directly how this variation relates to variation in where previous immigrants from these 10 home countries lived before this inflow. Yet we may come quite close by comparing this pattern among asylum seekers in 2012–14 with the corresponding pattern among asylum seekers who submitted their applications approximately 10 years earlier, in 2003–4, that is, the earliest years for which there is comparable data of reasonable quality.[25]

---

[24] Munshi (2003).

[25] Data quality is still poorer than in 2012–14. Data are missing from some EU countries, and no distinction can be made between applications submitted during the period and applications that were submitted earlier but had not yet been settled by the start of 2003.

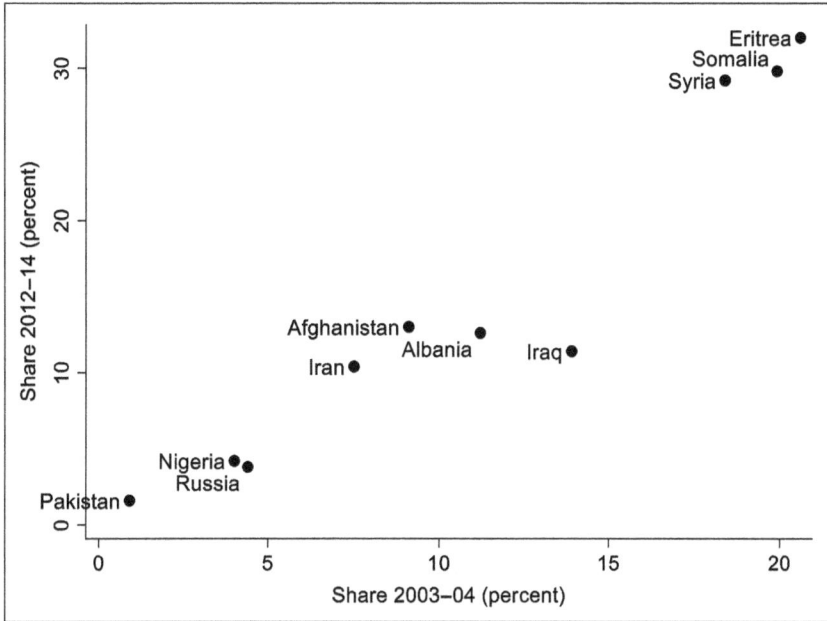

Figure 3.8 Share (percent) of all EU applications submitted in Sweden, per time period and country of origin.

Source: Eurostat. Shares in both periods are calculated based on EU borders in 2014.

This comparison is shown in Figure 3.8, with the share of asylum applications submitted in Sweden, by country of origin, in 2003–4 on the horizontal axis, and in 2012–14 on the vertical axis. The correlation is nearly perfect with all 10 markers almost on a straight line.[26] The most important, yet also modest, exception is asylum seekers from Iraq. However, even this exception can be explained in a way that further illustrates the point. A large fraction of all asylum seekers who arrived in the EU from Iraq in 2003–4 belonged to the Assyrian ethnic minority. Assyrians were strongly represented in Sweden since the 1970s, and therefore this particular group of Iraqi refugees choose Sweden as their country of destination to a particularly high extent.

---

[26] It is not obvious that this correlation only represents later refugees going after earlier. In theory, it could also be explained by persistent differences in how generously Sweden, compared with other EU countries, judges asylum applications from different countries. Yet it must be considered implausible that there would exist such variation in how different EU countries evaluate asylum applications from different countries, as to create the amount of variation that is depicted in the figure.

Further illustrating this, a large share of all Iraqi nationals who were granted asylum in Sweden in this period settled in Södertälje, a medium-sized city that had been a center for the Assyrian culture and in particular the Assyrian church, in Northern Europe since the 1970s, and where the share of Assyrians in the population before the Iraqi civil war started in 2003 was higher than in any other Western European city.[27]

Hence this deviation from the straight line in Figure 3.8 actually reinforces the story. In this particular case, country of origin does not sufficiently represent the community that has been most important for the people concerned. The Assyrian refugees were more interested in settling close to other Assyrians than to other non-Assyrian Iraqis. (Further underlining this point, the majority of Assyrian immigrants who lived in Södertälje before 2003 were born in Turkey and not in Iraq.)[28]

These were illustrations of some of the more extreme cases, where previous migrants appear to have had very strong influence on the settlement patterns of later migrants. In the typical case of legal, economically motivated migration today, this influence is considerably weaker than in these examples though. Yet it is as good as always possible, at least to some extent, to use the settlement patterns of earlier migrants to predict those of later migrants from the same country, and this is likely to at least in part reflect a direct effect of the earlier migration on the later.[29]

The final part of the Ireland–Norway example illustrated this, as it showed a visible impact of (far) earlier migrants also in one of the cases where we would probably have expected it the least. Today's migrants to the United States from Norway and Ireland are mostly well educated and working in relatively high-paying jobs, often in multinational corporations. They have ample opportunities to communicate with friends and relatives in the home countries and also to make relatively frequent visits. Poor information about income opportunities in the United States, and risks of social isolation, certainly apply less to most of these than to many other migrants. Still, at least to some extent, they have conformed to the pattern that was created more than one century earlier.

Having shown this, it is also important to issue a word of caution. The patterns that I have depicted here obviously illustrate that migration makes further migration easier. From this insight, it is sometimes concluded that

[27] Pripp (2001).
[28] Pripp (2001).
[29] Bartel (1989); Card (2001); Pedersen, Pytlikova and Smith (2008).

future migration may be ever-increasing, as migration creates more migration that creates even more migration and so on. Yet this conclusion is not at all as obvious as it might seem at first. Elaborating further on this point fits better into Chapter 8 though and is hence saved for there.

Who remain in the destination country?

Most migration to the West happens because income levels are higher there than in the rest of the world. Hence there is also good reason to expect most of this migration to be permanent, that is, that the migrants would stay for life. The longer they remain the greater is their benefit from the higher incomes. Also, after a few years, the receiving country may have come to feel more like home socially, not least for childhood arrivals and for families who have had children in the receiving country.

Yet there are also reasons to not remain for life. Some migrants from the outset decide that their migration is for a limited period, for working or studying for a few years and gathering money or useful experiences, and then living the rest of their lives in the country where they grew up and still would prefer to live. In other cases, migration may turn out to be temporary also if this was not the initial intention, if migrants are less successful in the receiving country than what they had hoped they would be. The decision to migrate is often made based on a partly uncertain expectation of high future incomes in the destination country. If this expectation is not realized to the extent that migrants had hoped for, they may decide to return home (or more seldom to give it a new try in a third country).[30]

On the other hand, there is also clear evidence that many migrants do not initially foresee how rooted they will become and that they eventually stay longer than what they intended to at first. One study of people who moved to (West) Germany in 1983–92, and who eventually turned out to stay for at least 20 years, reports that during their first one to four years in the country only around one-third said they aimed to remain for life. Yet when exactly the same people had stayed for 12–15 years this share had risen to around 60 percent.[31]

From this, one can almost guess another common observation, that is, that remigration is most likely to happen during a migrant's first few years in a new country. The longer one stays the more rooted one is likely to become and

---

[30] Borjas and Bratsberg (1996); Dustmann and Görlach (2016).
[31] Dustmann and Görlach (2016).

hence the less likely to ever move again.[32] (This may also be related to the age factor that was covered earlier in the chapter.)

The share of a migrant group that remains for a long time differs a lot between different groups. For example, in one study of labor migrants who moved from low- or middle-income countries to the Netherlands in 1999–2007, only one-third remained in the country nine years after their immigration.[33] But in my study of migrants who moved from the new EU member countries to Sweden in 2004–5, a full 83 percent remained in 2013, that is, eight to nine years later.[34]

Refugees on average remain longer than other migrants.[35] Alas, wars and persecution often last long and most refugees have much time to settle and get rooted in the new country before it becomes time to ask themselves the question about whether to return or not.

For those who migrated for economic reasons, economic success is of course crucial in determining who remains shorter and who remains longer. The just-mentioned study of labor migrants in the Netherlands, which is based on data of particularly high quality, reports that the probability of remigration was lowest among those who earned €1,000–3,000 per month, and higher among those who earned less or more than that.[36] My study of Eastern European migrants in Sweden also reports considerably higher remigration rates among those earning less than 100,000 kronor (around €10,000) per year.[37]

As it is difficult to survive on such low incomes, these results are very consistent with the explanation that much remigration happens because migrants turn out not to do as well as they had hoped to in the new country. The higher remigration rates among those with the very highest incomes in the Dutch study may to a larger extent reflect that these very successful people, for whom many opportunities are likely to exist, may to a larger extent have intended already from the start that migration was to be a temporary step in their careers. Related to this, several other studies show that people with college degrees more often than others intend their migration to be temporary.[38]

---

[32] Dustmann and Görlach (2016).
[33] Bijwaard and Wahba (2014).
[34] Ruist (2017a).
[35] Borjas and Bratsberg (1996); Edin, LaLonde and Åslund (2000).
[36] Bijwaard and Wahba (2014).
[37] Ruist (2017a).
[38] Dustmann and Görlach (2016).

Final words

Only a small fraction, 3 percent, of the population of the world are international migrants, and only around 1.5 percent of all those born outside of the West live in the West today. How these small shares differ from the rest of the Earth's population may be very different for different migrant groups, as these have migrated from different places, to different other places, and for different reasons. To take one very clear example, many things separate the successful software developers of Silicon Valley from the world's most vulnerable refugees.

Yet even though there is a lot of variation and uniqueness, some patterns are also evident. Migrants more often originate in middle-income than in low-income countries. They are more often young, and more often highly educated, compared with non-migrants from the same countries. This is more or less without exceptions. Migration between two countries also becomes more likely the shorter the distance is between them and the more migrants have already beaten the path. And the longer migrants have already stayed in a destination country the more likely they are to stay for life.

The high level of education of many migrants naturally has a positive effect on their chances to do well on the receiving country's labor market. At the same time, migrants often have other obstacles to overcome to succeed, such as limited knowledge about the language, culture and institutions of the receiving country. How migrants fare on the labor markets in receiving Western countries will be the subject of the next chapter.

One question that has not been considered in this chapter is which migrants move to which destinations. This is saved for the next chapter because the basic conclusions that we may draw about it are in fact drawn from migrants' performances on labor markets.

Chapter 4

MIGRANTS' INCOMES IN RECEIVING COUNTRIES

This chapter is about how migrants fare economically, that is, what their incomes look like, in the receiving countries. Its central message is that even when they are averaged over large groups, migrants' incomes look very different in different cases. Some groups have higher average incomes than natives already upon arrival, and their incomes keep rising further the longer they stay in the country. Others begin with incomes far below those of natives and not even their children—or their grandchildren—fully catch up. The chapter thus emphasizes that migration comprises manifold things, and underscores the importance of separating these when thinking about migration.

The main focus is to illustrate how large differences often are. When it is easy to explain why the differences that are shown look the particular way that they do then explanations are provided. Yet in several cases no effort is made to provide explanations. Much of the point is that the performance of each single migrant group is the unique outcome of a combination of many factors. Some—like education levels and selectivity of immigration laws— are measurable. Others—probably much related to ability, motivation and self-selection—are not. It is often difficult to explain why a particular group performs better or worse than another. And the aim of the chapter is not to highlight particular groups as much as the vast amount of variation itself.

Variation across sending and receiving countries

There are clear differences between receiving countries in who the "typical" immigrant is. Immigrants are, for example, more often highly educated labor immigrants in Anglo-Saxon countries, more often less-educated labor immigrants in the Netherlands and Germany and more often refugees in Sweden and Norway. Immigration in some countries is, or at least was, much shaped by historical colonial relations. In Italy and Spain the typical immigrant arrived quite recently, while, for example, in France it is more common to have been in the country for decades (or to be a native-born child of immigrants).

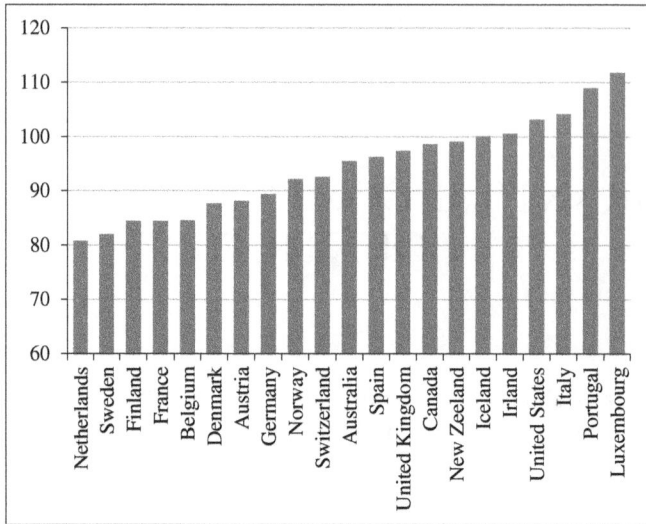

Figure 4.1 Employment rates among 15–64-year-old immigrants, as percentage shares of those of similarly aged natives, per country in 2016.

Source: OECD.

It is thus not surprising to find considerable variation in immigrants' labor market performance even when we take averages over the entire immigrant populations in different receiving countries. Figure 4.1 shows, per country of immigration in the richer part of the Western world, the employment rate in 2016 among 15–64-year-old immigrants by host country, expressed as a fraction of the employment rate of natives in the same age interval in the same country. It shows large differences. Immigrants are on average 20 percent less likely than natives to be employed in the Netherlands and Sweden, but 10 percent more likely than natives in Luxembourg and Portugal.

Certainly, part of the explanation for these differences may be that some countries have better policies than others for getting (similar) immigrants employed. However, it is quite obvious that at least a large share of them are due to variations in types of immigration. Different countries receive most of their immigrants from different sending countries, immigrants on average have more education in some countries than in others, etc.

Perhaps the most obvious point in this respect is the variation across countries in how heavily very recently arrived refugees weigh on the averages that are shown in the figure. Refugees typically encounter more difficulties than other immigrants to find employment, as will be illustrated in some detail later in the chapter. And this is particularly true for the most recently arrived

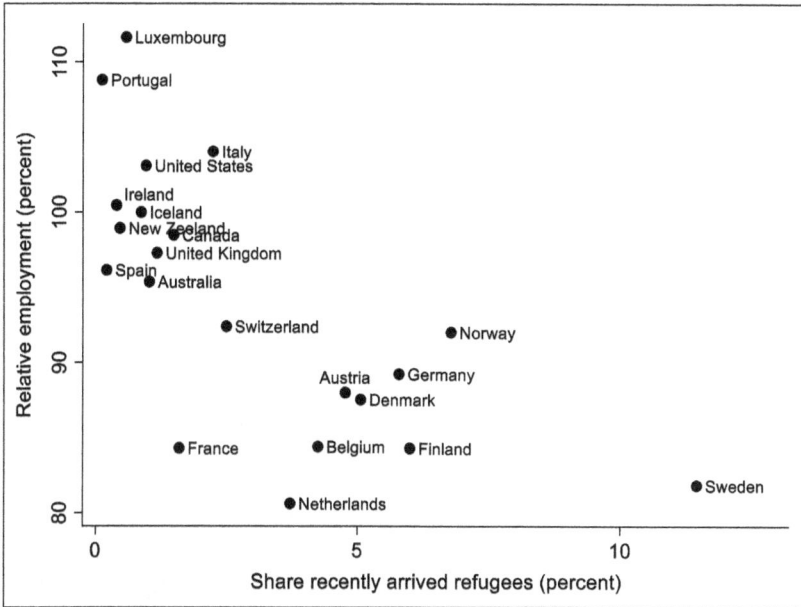

Figure 4.2 The correlation between immigrants' employment in 2016 relative to natives', and the percentage share of immigrants being recently arrived (2011–16) refugees.

Sources: Employment: OECD. Total immigrant population sizes (in 2017): United Nations Global Migration Database. Numbers of newly arrived refugees: Eurostat, US Department of Homeland Security, Immigration and Refugee Board of Canada, Australia Department of Home Affairs and New Zealand Ministry of Business, Innovation, and Employment.

refugees. Hence, an average as shown in Figure 4.1 will be lower the higher the share of recently arrived refugees is in a total immigrant population.

This is directly illustrated in Figure 4.2. The vertical axis shows the same measure of relative employment as Figure 4.1. The horizontal axis shows the share of recent (2011–16) refugee immigrants in the immigrant population over which this employment was measured.[1] The figure clearly shows that the employment gap between immigrants and natives is on average more negative when a higher share of the immigrant group is made up of recently arrived refugees.

---

[1] There is some measurement error. What is measured is in fact the size of the refugee inflow in 2011–16 divided by the size of the total immigrant population. Yet given the low remigration of refugees, this should be a minor source of error. It is also not possible to limit this measure to those aged 15–64 years.

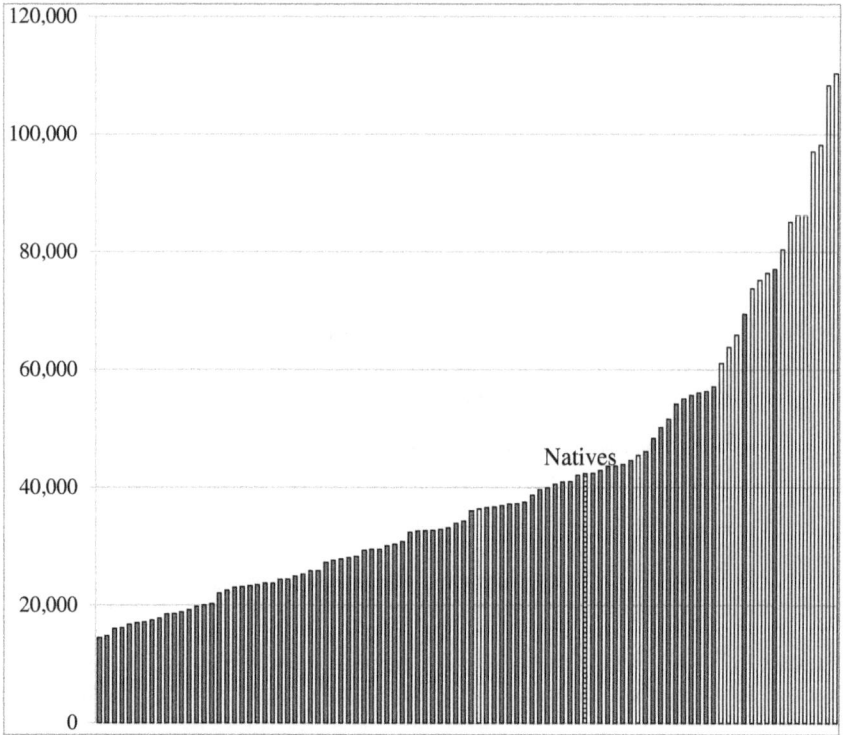

Figure 4.3 Average annual labor incomes 2012–15 (dollars) among 30–50-year-old immigrants in the United States, who have been in the country for 6–10 years, by 97 countries of origin.

Source: Own calculations using data from the American Community Surveys in 2013–16, from Ruggles et al. (2015). Countries with fewer than thirty observations have been excluded.

Further large differences in immigrants' incomes across both receiving and sending countries are illustrated in Figures 4.3 and 4.4. These show average annual labor incomes, by country of origin, for 30–50-year-old immigrants who have spent 6–10 years in the receiving country, in the United States in 2012–15 and Sweden in 2007, respectively. White bars represent richer countries of origin (Western Europe, Canada, the United States [in Sweden], Australia, New Zealand, Japan and Singapore). For comparison, the striped bar in each figure shows the average income of natives in the same age interval.

Both figures show huge variation in immigrants' average incomes by country of origin. In both of them the highest bar is around a whopping seven times as high as the lowest. We thus see clearly that different migrants

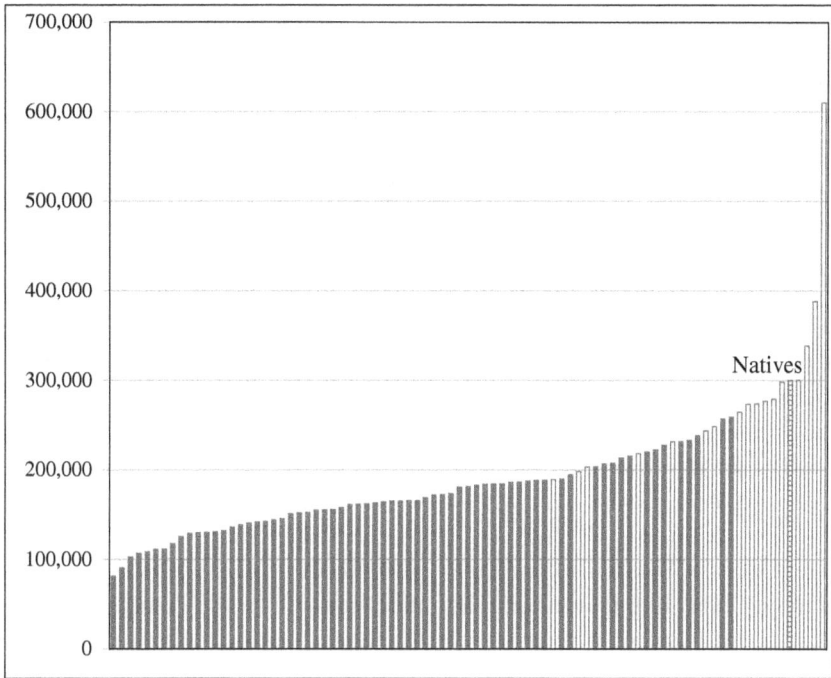

Figure 4.4 Average annual labor incomes 2007 (kronor) among 30–50-year-old immigrants in Sweden, who have been in the country for 6–10 years, by 84 countries of origin.

Source: Own calculations using Statistics Sweden's database Linda, 2007. Countries with fewer than thirty observations have been excluded.

perform very differently on the receiving countries' labor markets, also when taking averages over really large groups.

The main reason for showing these two graphs is to show the sheer amount of variation. Yet taken together they also provide a second insight. There is a big difference between them in where we find the bar that represents natives. In the Swedish case, only migrants from the four Western European countries Belgium, Iceland, the Netherlands and Switzerland have higher average incomes than similarly aged natives after 6–10 years in the country. But in the United States, the same is true for a full 33 out of the 97 countries of origin that are shown in the figure. Furthermore, 18 of these 33 have black bars, that is, they are not among the richest countries of origin. They even include countries with as low incomes per capita and as low-educated populations as India, Syria, Venezuela, Iran, Lebanon and Cape Verde.

This provides a clear sign of how strongly positively selected migrants in many cases are on productive characteristics. If Indian or Syrian immigrants in the United States had been random samples from the entire Indian and Syrian populations, then obviously their average incomes would have been far below those of natives. They would have been far less educated than natives and had really poor English skills in addition to less knowledge about everything related to how things are done in America. But these actual migrant groups are very far from any random samples. We saw in Figures 3.6 and 3.7 how strongly positively selected migrants could be in terms of education only, and the same is likely to be true also for other skills and characteristics that are more difficult to measure. Here, we now see that this positive selection is in many cases enough to more than outweigh the obstacles to strong labor market performance that come from not being born in the host country.

Yet while we see this clearly in the American case, it is not as evident in the Swedish. Again, it is difficult to rule out with full certainty that this could be a reflection of Sweden having far poorer policies than the United States for getting similar immigrants into the labor market. Yet the common explanation for this kind of large differences between receiving countries is that the migrants are not similar, but were self-selected through different processes, as different countries attract and allow different migrants.[2] Hence at this point we encounter the issue that was saved from the last chapter: who migrate where?

In the last chapter, I concluded that migration decisions seem to be most often well-informed and, therefore, we should expect that those who migrate are those who have the most to gain from it. Economic gain is a major part of this. Yet who would have the most to gain economically from migrating to a country differs quite a bit between the case where that country is the United States and that where it is Sweden, because these two countries are quite different. The United States has the highest wage inequality in the Western world and Sweden has one of the lowest.[3] Sweden has higher and more progressive taxes and a far more generous welfare system.

All of this should make the United States a particularly attractive destination for migrants who expect to be able to earn high wages. High wage inequality and low taxes imply that these may expect to earn considerably more (in particular after taxes) in the United States compared with in Sweden. These also probably bother relatively little about the limited social insurance

---

[2] Grogger and Hanson (2011); Belot and Hatton (2012).
[3] According to OECD statistics for 2010, the United States was the OECD country with the highest ratio between the 50th and 10th wage percentiles. The Swedish ratio was second from the bottom, with a very small margin to the lowest, in Belgium.

in the United States as they strongly expect to get by without such assistance. Sweden, on the other hand, should be a relatively more attractive destination for those who do not expect to perform spectacularly on the receiving country's labor market. As even the lowest wages in Sweden are fairly high, and social protection is strong, one can expect to do reasonably well in Sweden even if one only manages to secure a job near the bottom of the pay scale, or even no job at all. (Remember that we are discussing averages over large groups here. Obviously, there are many immigrants in each of these two countries who do not fit into this broad pattern.)

A country's labor market, taxes and welfare systems thus impact on who decides to move there, and in turn on how the resulting immigrant population performs on the country's labor market. The difference between migrants' average incomes in the United States and Sweden is likely to be an illustration of this result. A more general result that points in the same direction is that countries with higher average wage gaps between high- and low-educated workers on average attract more educated migrants.[4]

Yet another result that appears to indicate something similar is from a study of entry wages for newly arrived 25–29-year-old men with college degrees (from other countries) in Australia, Canada and the United States.[5] Figure 4.5 shows these average wages, expressed as fractions of average wages among similarly aged native-born men with college degrees in the same country. Information is shown separately for five groups that immigrated in different five-year periods between 1986 and 2010.[6]

All immigrants who are compared in this analysis are thus similar in age and in having college degrees. However, the figure shows a clear difference where the immigrants have considerably higher entry wages in the United States than in both Australia and Canada in all five periods. For the groups that immigrated later, this result may plausibly—in line with what was shown in Chapter 2—be partly explained by the expansion of the H1-B visa program in the United States during the 1990s. That made a higher share of the college-educated immigration in the United States consist of people in very highly productive jobs in science and technology.

Yet there are big differences in the figure also between those who immigrated in 1986–90, that is, before this policy change in the United States. In this period, immigrants' entry wages were on average about at par with those of

---

[4] Grogger and Hanson (2011); Belot and Hatton (2012).

[5] Clarke, Ferrer and Skuterud (2019).

[6] These entry wages are not pure averages. They are predicted wages from regression models where wages were estimated as a function of years since immigration and a number of additional variables.

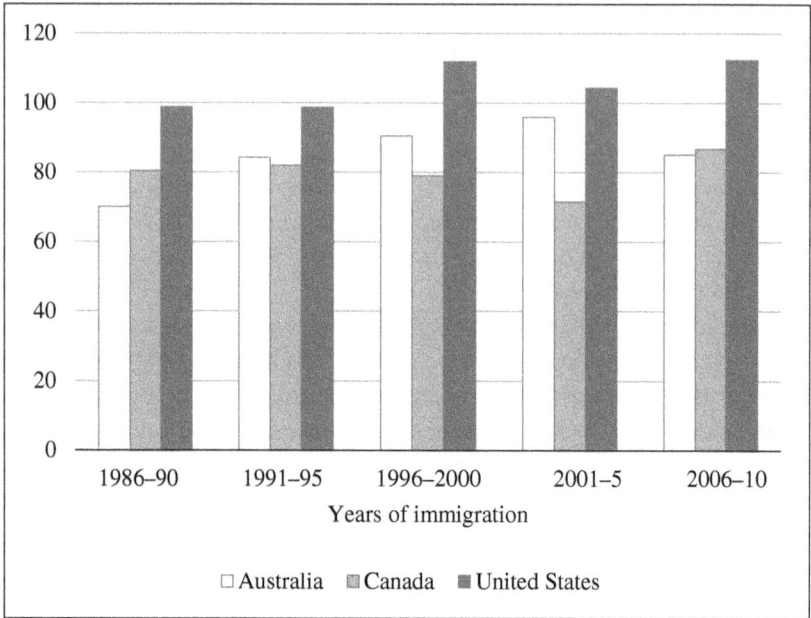

Figure 4.5 Estimated average entry wages of male 25–29-year-old newly arrived immigrants with college degrees in Australia, Canada and the United States, per immigration period. Wages are expressed as percentages of average wages among similarly old native male college graduates.

Source: Clarke, Ferrer and Skuterud (2019).

natives in the United States, whereas they were about 20 percent below them in Canada and 30 percent below in Australia. Most likely, this is also primarily a result of it having been more economically beneficial for the most highly productive to opt for moving to the United States.[7]

These differences between the three receiving countries thus appear to say something interesting about the limits of migration policy in shaping migration. The Canadian and Australian points systems have ensured that large shares of all their immigrants have college degrees. But it still appears that out of the total international pool of migrants with college degrees, the United States has got more of the very most productive ones. Further insights about what migration policy can and cannot do might also be drawn from how the

---

[7] The study also shows similar patterns separately for migrants from each of the three countries that have been major countries of origin for migration to all three destinations: China, India and the Philippines. Hence the differences do not appear to be explained to a large extent by which sending countries dominate in each receiving country.

relative heights of the three bars in the figure have evolved over time. I will return to this in more detail in Chapter 8.

We have seen thus far that the average income of an immigrant group can be almost anything, from far below to far above the native average in a country. "Immigrants" is thus a category that encompasses a large variety of people, who have moved for different reasons and who bring different skills to the receiving country. This tends to make "immigrants" a quite uninteresting category. What we learn from studying "the average immigrant" in a country is often of limited value. We should strive to more often break down this category into somewhat more narrowly defined, homogenous and thus more relevant groupings.

A second conclusion that follows from this is that one should always be careful with drawing conclusions from comparing different migrant groups with each other. Many factors make groups different, both within and across countries. Hence, if we observe a difference between the economic or social positions of two immigrant groups, it is seldom obvious whether this is primarily due to differences in what was in their baggage when they immigrated or to differences in how they were received. We should always be careful with labeling any outcome of any migrant group as a success or a failure, because we almost never know what is the appropriate yardstick with which to measure it.

Variation in income developments over time

It is also difficult to identify any consistent pattern in how migrants' incomes tend to develop with time spent in their host countries. Again there are large differences both between different receiving countries and between different immigrant groups in the same country. Some groups improve strongly over time whereas others do not improve much. A good illustration may be provided by comparing some of the largest migrant groups in the United States. Again, groups are defined by countries of origin, which often seem to capture quite well several important differences in why people migrate.

Figure 4.6 shows average incomes from work per year (2004–16), by country of origin, for men who were born in 1968–78 and immigrated to the United States in 2002–3.[8] The countries included are those that sent the largest migrant groups in those years, that is, Mexico, India, the Philippines and China, the largest from a Western country, that is, Canada, the largest from a Latin American country besides Mexico, that is, El Salvador, and the largest from an African country, that is, Nigeria. Incomes are expressed as percentage shares of the average income in

---

[8] Individual incomes were Winsorized at the 95th percentile.

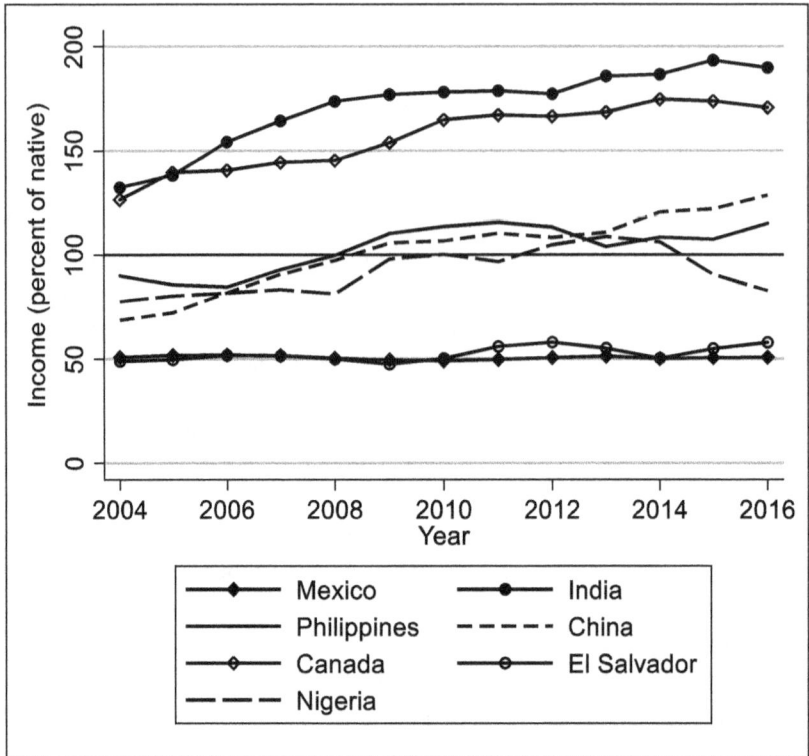

Figure 4.6 Average annual labor incomes (moving averages), by country of origin, for men born in 1968–78 who migrated to the United States in 2002–3. Incomes are expressed as percentage shares of the average income among similarly old native men in each year.

Source: Own calculations using data from the American Community Surveys in 2005–17, from Ruggles et al. (2015).

each year among native men who were born in the same period. Hence income increases are also measured in relation to these. An upward sloping curve in the figure represents that the average income in a migrant group has increased more than that of the natives, while a flat curve represents that it has increased just enough to keep the percentage gap to the natives unchanged.

We may group together the income development patterns of the seven migrant groups that are represented in the figure into three main categories. Immigrants from India and Canada had higher average incomes than natives already on arrival in the United States, and after that they kept rising. After slightly more than one decade in the country these immigrant men earned on average not so far from twice as much as similarly aged native men. Migrants from the Philippines, China and Nigeria initially earned less than natives.

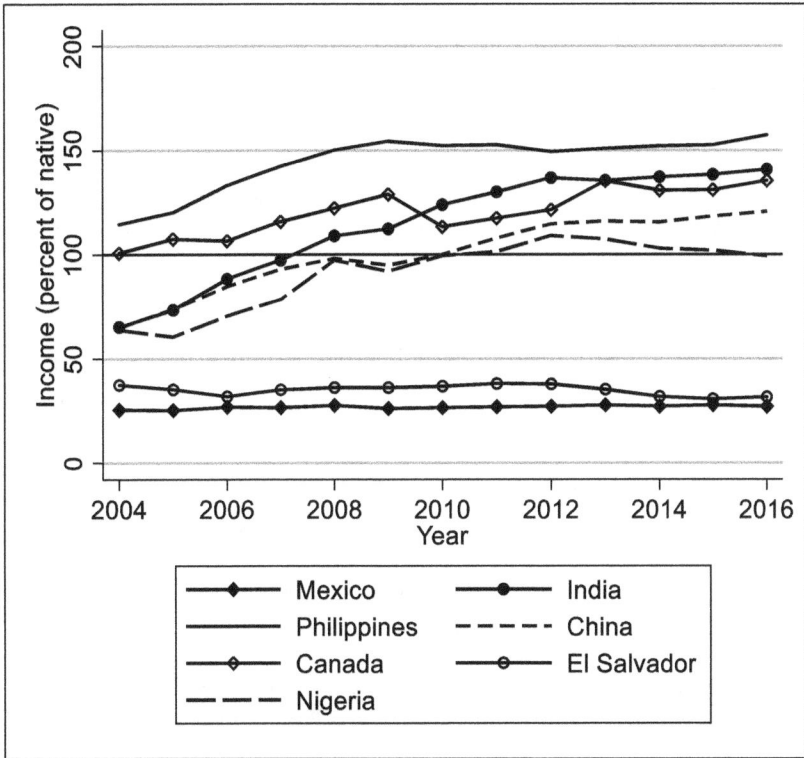

Figure 4.7 Average annual labor incomes (moving averages), by country of origin, for women born in 1968–78 who migrated to the United States in 2002–3. Incomes are expressed as percentage shares of the average income among similarly old native women in each year.

Source: Own calculations using data from the American Community Surveys in 2005–17, from Ruggles et al. (2015).

But their gaps were closed fairly quickly, and after less than a decade they on average earned more (this conclusion is quite uncertain in the Nigerian case, where the annual samples are smaller and estimates thus less precise). Male migrants from Mexico and El Salvador initially only earned about half of what the native group did, and they continued to do so for ten years thereafter: their curves are virtually flat.[9]

Figure 4.7 shows the corresponding information for female immigrants from the same countries, with their incomes expressed in relation to those

---

[9] A limitation to this analysis is that we cannot determine to what extent these patterns are influenced by remigration. When we see the average income in a group rising, we do not know to what extent this is because actual people's incomes increased, and to

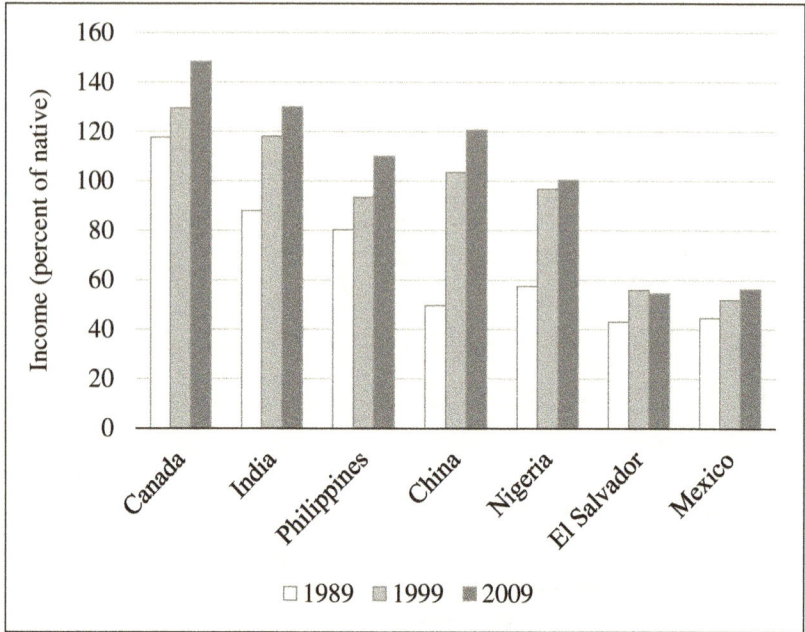

Figure 4.8 Average annual labor incomes, by country of origin, for men born in 1951–61 who migrated to the United States in 1985–86. Incomes are expressed as percentage shares of the average income among similarly old native men in each year.

Source: Own calculations using data from the US censuses in 1990 and 2000, and the American Community Surveys in 2009–11, from Ruggles et al. (2015).

of native women. The Philippine curve is higher for women than for men while the Indian is lower. Generally, female immigrants have somewhat lower incomes in relation to native women than male immigrants do in relation to native men. Mexican and Salvadorian female average incomes are particularly low: only around 30 percent of those of native women.

We see similar variation between groups also over a longer period for earlier immigrants. Figures 4.8 and 4.9 follow those who migrated to the United States in the same age interval and from the same countries in 1985–86. Their patterns are mostly similar to those represented in Figures 4.6 and

what extent it is because those with the lowest incomes left the country. If those with the lowest incomes leave a group, the average in the group will increase even if nobody's income actually does so. As the analysis is based on a new sample each year, that is, does not follow a consistent sample of people from year to year, nothing can be done about this in the analysis.

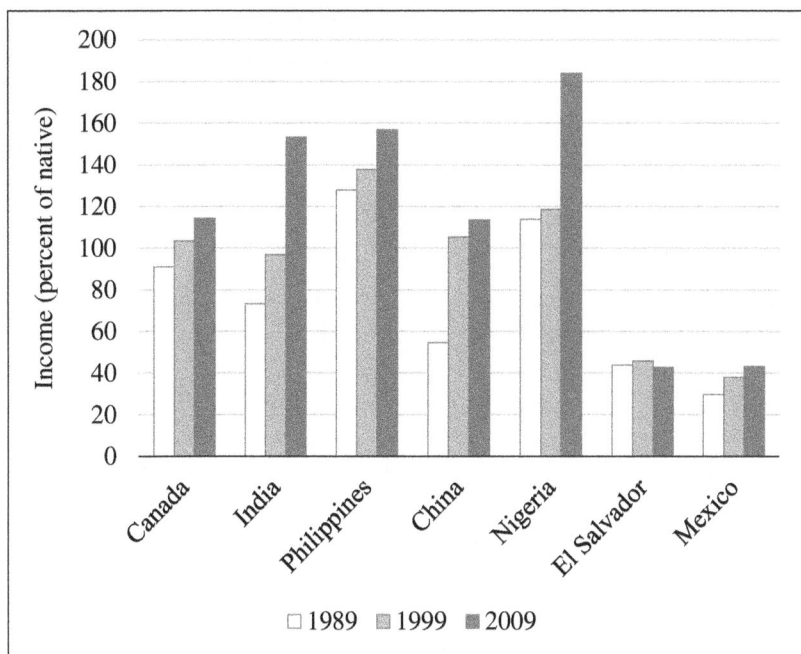

Figure 4.9 Average annual labor incomes, by country of origin, for women born in 1951–61 who migrated to the United States in 1985–86. Incomes are expressed as percentage shares of the average income among similarly old native women in each year.

Source: Own calculations using data from the US censuses in 1990 and 2000, and the American Community Surveys in 2009–11, from Ruggles et al. (2015).

4.7. Migrants from the five non-Latin American countries sometimes start at higher, yet most often at lower, average incomes compared with similarly aged natives of the same sex. Yet their incomes on average increase faster than those of natives, in most cases also between the later points in time, that is, between when the migrants have spent 13–14 years and 22–25 years in the country. After 22–25 years,[10] all of these 10 non-Latin American groups have equally high or higher average incomes compared with natives of the same sex. Some of them have experienced quite spectacular increases. In 20 years, the women from India, and both the men and the women from China, have more than doubled their average incomes in relation to similarly aged natives of the same sex.

---

[10] "2009" in these figures refers to averages over 2008–10.

However, for migrants from the two Latin American countries of origin income convergence to natives is limited also over this long time horizon. For three of these four groups, the income gap is at least somewhat smaller in 2009 compared with in 1989, yet not by any large margin.

Refugees

In contrast to other migrants, refugees did not move to another country because they saw opportunities for work. Hence unsurprisingly, they tend to be employed less often and on average earn less compared with most other migrants.

In the United States, we see in Figure 4.10 that recent refugee immigrants' average labor income is at par with those of similarly recent immigrants from Mexico and El Salvador. The figure shows average incomes in 2016 for refugees and for migrants from Mexico and El Salvador, who are all 20–40 years old and have spent 1–5 years in the country. These curves thus—somewhat

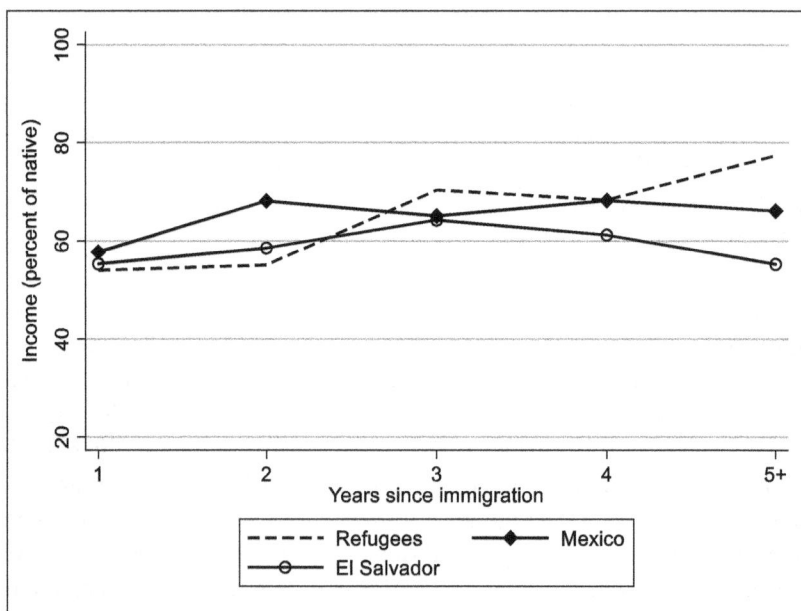

Figure 4.10 Average labor incomes in 2016, by years since immigration and origin for US immigrants born in 1976–96. Incomes are expressed as percentage shares of the average income in the same year among similarly aged natives.

Sources: Mexico and El Salvador: Own calculations using data from the American Community Survey in 2017, from Ruggles et al. (2015). Refugees: Own calculations using data from the Annual Survey of Refugees, 2016.

inappropriately and in contrast to Figures 4.6–4.9—tie together migrants who immigrated in different years, rather than follow migrants who immigrated in a given year. Most refugees are from Bhutan, Iraq, Myanmar and Somalia. Annual incomes are expressed as fractions of the average labor income among similarly aged natives.

Refugees' incomes are thus found to be near the bottom of the range of large immigrant groups' average incomes (cf. Figures 4.6 and 4.7). To a large extent this is due to large shares of all these groups—the women in particular—having no work at all. However for non-refugees, permission to immigrate to the United States without a job offer most often requires that someone else with sufficient financial resources—most often a relative—undertakes to support the immigrant for them not to be a burden on public finances. But for refugees this is not so. Hence, although average incomes are fairly similar between the three groups that are represented in Figure 4.10, in Figure 4.11 we see among the same groups that the share receiving public financial support is considerably higher among refugees than in the other two groups. The figure shows the share of each group that received food

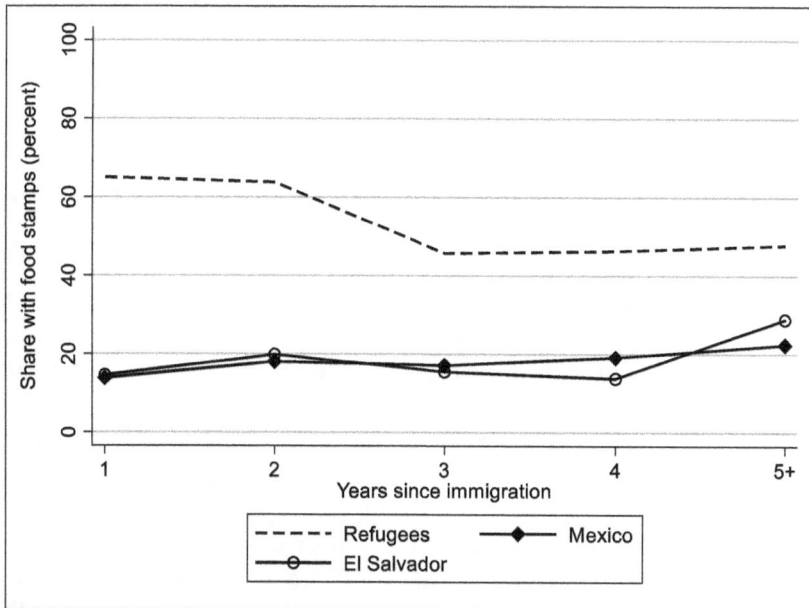

Figure 4.11 Percentage shares living in a household that received food stamps in 2016, by years since immigration and origin, for US immigrants born in 1976–96.

Sources: Mexico and El Salvador: Own calculations using data from the American Community Survey in 2017, from Ruggles et al. (2015). Refugees: Own calculations using data from the Annual Survey of Refugees, 2016.

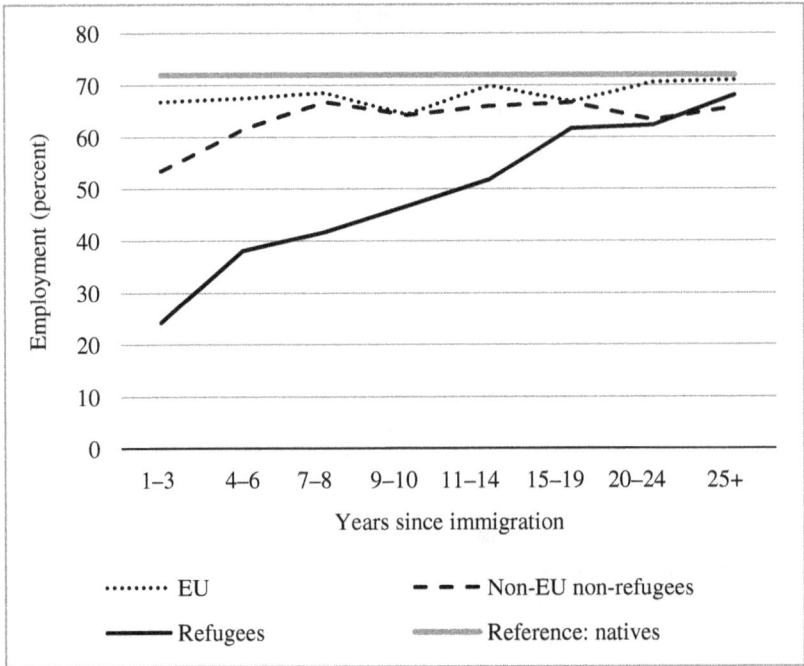

Figure 4.12 Employment rates (percent) by years since immigration, among immigrants in Europe.

Source: The figure is reproduced based on information from Fasani, Frattini and Minale (2018). I am grateful to Luigi Minale for his assistance with this.

stamps in 2016. For those who have been only 1–2 years in the country this share is a full 40 percentage points higher among refugees compared with in the other two groups. The differences are smaller among those who have been a few years longer in the country, but still around 20 percentage points also among those who have been so for five years or more.

Also in Europe, refugees fare on average considerably worse than other immigrants on labor markets. Figure 4.12 shows average employment rates for three categories of immigrants who are 25–64 years old, across 20 European countries, depending on the number of years since their immigration. All observations were made in 2008 or 2014. Again, the curves tie together immigrants who immigrated at different points in time.[11] For

---

[11] The numbers are not directly measured employment rates. They are obtained from employment gaps to natives that were in turn estimated by regression analysis to remove differences between the three groups with respect to age, sex, educations, country of residence and year of observation.

the two groups of non-refugees, from EU and non-EU countries, respectively, the employment rate is always fairly close to that of natives, which is 72 percent (the gray line in the figure). Yet, refugees' employment is considerably lower, also after a long time spent in the receiving country. It takes 15–19 years for refugees' employment to reach levels similar to those where the other groups were to be found more or less from the year after their immigration.

Refugees thus face considerable challenges on labor markets on both sides of the Atlantic. Yet also with large differences between refugee groups. This is illustrated here using data from Sweden. Figures 4.13 and 4.14 show, for men and women respectively, average income by years since immigration for refugees who immigrated to Sweden in 1992–96 at the age of 20–50 years (the vast majority were in the lower half of this age interval). Incomes are expressed as fractions of the median income of 20–50-year-old native men (also for female refugees) in each year. Data quality is particularly high in this case, and the curves are based on observing the very same refugees each year (remigration of refugees is very low and has negligible impact on the

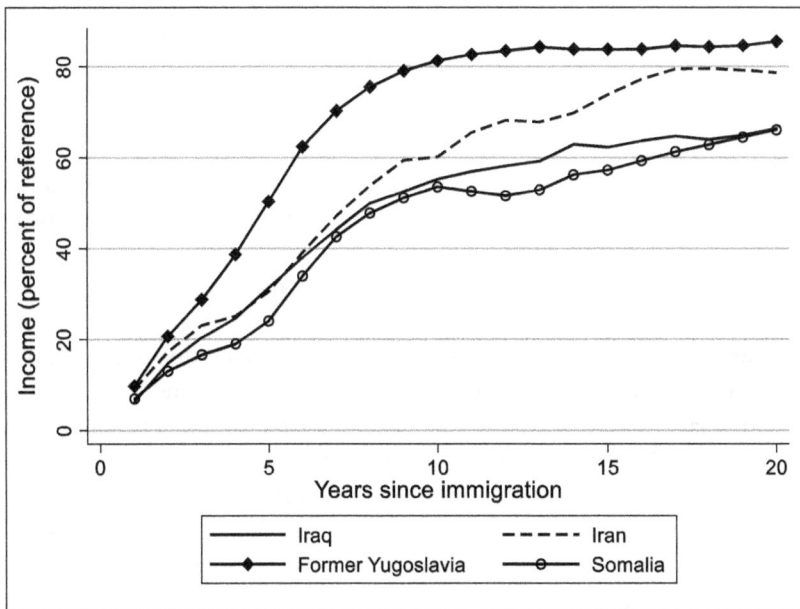

Figure 4.13 Average incomes, in percent of the median income among 20–50-year-old native men in each year, per years since immigration, for male refugees who immigrated to Sweden in 1992–96, at ages 20–50 years.

Source: Own calculations using Statistics Sweden's database Linda, 1993–2015.

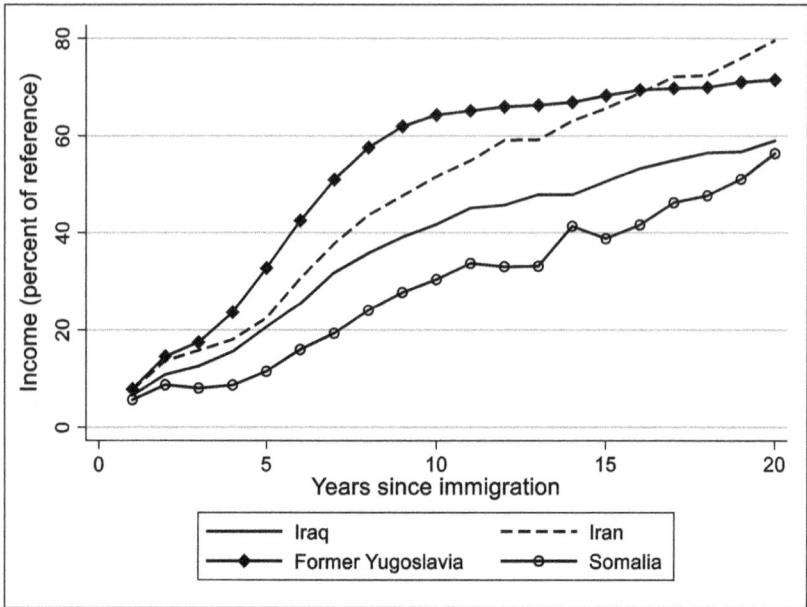

Figure 4.14 Average incomes, in percent of the median income among 20–50-year-old native men in each year, per years since immigration, for female refugees who immigrated to Sweden in 1992–96, at ages 20–50 years.

Source: Own calculations using Statistics Sweden's database Linda, 1993–2015.

patterns). Numbers are shown separately for the four countries of origin that sent the largest numbers of refugees to Sweden in this period, that is, former Yugoslavia (treated here as one country), Iraq, Somalia and Iran.

Just like Figure 4.12 showed very low employment rates among refugees in their first few years in the receiving European countries, Figures 4.13 and 4.14 show low average incomes, which in turn are much due to low employment, for many years among refugees in Sweden. Average incomes start near zero, then rise steadily for 20 years—or at least for almost that long—in all groups. But the differences are large between countries of origin. Much of the time the difference between the highest and the lowest curves—for each sex—corresponds to around 20–30 percent of the reference income, with only limited convergence even after as much as 20 years in the country. There exists no widely accepted explanation for these large differences.[12] Knowledge about

---

[12] Ruist (2018b).

how effective different policies are in improving the employment of refugees is also fairly scarce.[13]

In contrast to Figures 4.6–4.9, the refugee incomes as given in Figures 4.13 and 4.14 were expressed in relation to the same (male) reference income for both women and men. This is to also enable a direct comparison between the income levels in the two figures. We then see that average male incomes rise much faster than female in the first decade after immigration. However in the second decade, average male incomes change only little in relation to the reference income while average female incomes keep rising. After 20 years in the country, there is basically no difference between these average male and female incomes. The same conclusion holds in most refugee groups in Sweden historically.[14] This appears to represent a quite remarkable degree of adjustment to the Swedish norm of equal labor market participation for men and women, considering how far most of the major refugee-sending countries have been from sharing this norm.

Descendants of immigrants

We have seen several examples of how different income levels often are across different migrant groups, and so for a long time. Average incomes in different groups do not necessarily converge, neither toward each other nor toward native averages, even near the end of immigrants' working lives. And even this is not the end of it. In several cases, average incomes have not even converged during the working lives of immigrants' native-born children. Large differences have persisted even after several generations.

Again, I provide illustrations from the United States, which is quite unique in enabling analyses over multiple generations.[15] But these analyses are far from perfect. There is not much data that reveals who is the parent of whom, and even less who is the grandparent or great-grandparent of whom. We must resort to approximations, which creates more room for measurement error.

The horizontal axis of Figure 4.15 shows average labor incomes in 1979, by country of origin, for men who were born in 1920–31 and immigrated to the United States in 1950–59.[16] Hence they are observed when they are

---

[13] Frattini (2017).

[14] Ruist (2018a).

[15] For similar analyses, see Borjas (1993).

[16] The countries of origin in the figure are those for which the values on both axes could be calculated over at least thirty individuals. Individual incomes were Winsorized at the 95th percentile.

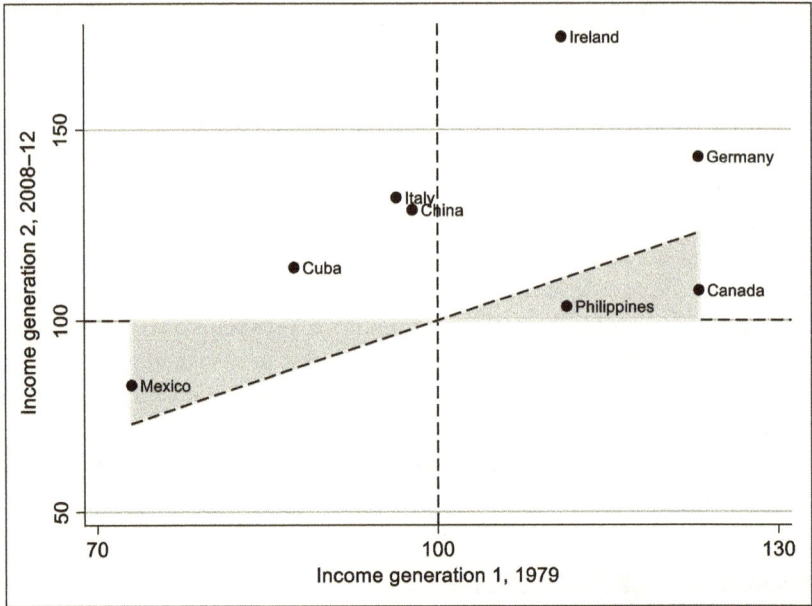

Figure 4.15 Average male labor incomes, as percentage shares of native averages, for immigrants in 1979, and native children of immigrants in 2008–12.

Source: Own calculations using data from the US census in 1980, and the Current Population Surveys in 2009–13, from Ruggles et al. (2015).

48–59 years old and have been 20–29 years in the country. We may thus assume that they are at this point near the end of their income development. Their incomes are expressed as percentages of the average annual income of similarly aged men. Hence a marker to the left of the vertical dashed line represents an immigrant group that, late in its working life, on average earns less than natives, while a marker to the right represent a group that earns more. We see that two groups on average earn considerably less, two marginally less and four considerably more than natives.

The vertical axis in the same figure shows average incomes in 2008–12 for native-born men who were born in 1952–63 and whose two parents were born in one of the countries that are represented in the figure. This is thus an attempt to identify the sons of the immigrant men whose earlier incomes were measured on the horizontal axis. There is no data to reveal how successful this attempt is, yet it ought to be a reasonable approximation when observing such large groups. These sons of immigrants are thus 45–60 years old, and they should also be close to the end of their income development when they are observed.

The average incomes among these men are measured as percentages of the average income of similarly aged native men with two native-born parents. A marker above the horizontal dashed line thus represents that a group of native-born sons of two immigrants on average earns more than similarly aged native sons of two natives. Hence the shaded areas in the figure represent that the incomes of sons of immigrants are on average closer to those of sons of natives than what the incomes of their immigrant fathers were to the incomes of native men. In other words, they represent convergence, that is, that the difference between two groups is smaller in the second generation compared with in the first.

What we see in the figure is thus that even when we follow migrants far beyond their own working lives, all the way to the end of their children's working lives, convergence to native incomes has happened in far from all groups. In the case that is shown in the figure, it has happened in only three out of eight cases. The remaining five markers are all above the shaded area. This means that between these two generations, these groups have either "overtaken" natives (the three groups to the left) or started above natives and then moved even further away (the remaining two).

Average incomes have also diverged rather than converged between the studied immigrant groups. In the first generation, the highest-earning group earned on average around 70 percent more than the lowest-earning. In the second generation, the corresponding number is around 110 percent.

Figure 4.16 shows the corresponding information for female immigrants and their daughters. Here, convergence toward average income levels of native women has happened only in four out of nine groups. The remaining five have moved away from natives in the positive direction. Hence in conclusion, many children of immigrants—men as well as women—perform very strongly on the labor market. The female immigrant groups that are shown in Figure 4.16 have converged in relation to each other though. This contrast to the male groups is perhaps not surprising given that the female groups were further apart in the first generation. In the first generation of female groups, the highest average income was around 200 percent higher than the lowest, while in the second generation it was around 120 percent higher.

Later generations. Income differences between immigrant groups can thus remain large—or even increase—in the second generation compared with the first, and several groups may on average earn considerably more than natives with native parents.

Considerable differences may also remain after an additional generation or two. Later generations can be identified in existing data from the United

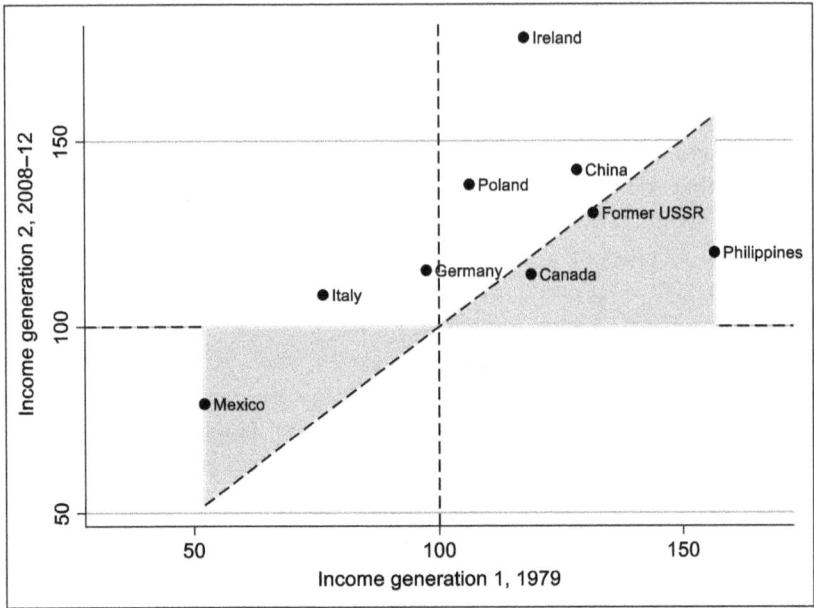

Figure 4.16 Average female labor incomes, as percentage shares of native averages, for immigrants in 1979, and native children of immigrants in 2008–12.

Source: Own calculations using data from the US census in 1980, and the Current Population Surveys in 2009–13, from Ruggles et al. (2015).

States yet not perfectly. American Community Surveys collect information on ancestry, that is, which country or countries outside of the US respondents say their ancestors came from. Yet these surveys do not simultaneously collect information on who is a second, third or higher generation immigrant. Therefore, the comparison in the following text will focus only on 22 countries of origin, from which migration to the United States was so much higher before compared with after 1930 that most current Americans who identify them as their main ancestry should be immigrants of at least the fourth generation. Average incomes in these 22 ancestry groups, among 25–60-year old men in 2004–13, are shown in Figure 4.17.[17] Differences are quite large, with the two highest bars being about 40 percent higher than the lowest.

These differences are also not random. They correlate strongly with the corresponding differences between the immigrant groups that plausibly to a

---

[17] For details on the selection of these 22 countries, see Ruist (2017b). Countries that split during the period are considered as one unit throughout. Individual incomes were Winsorized at the 95th percentile. Group differences in age and region have been leveled out through regression analysis. The values shown are regression predictions for a man who is 40 years old and lives in the East North Central Division.

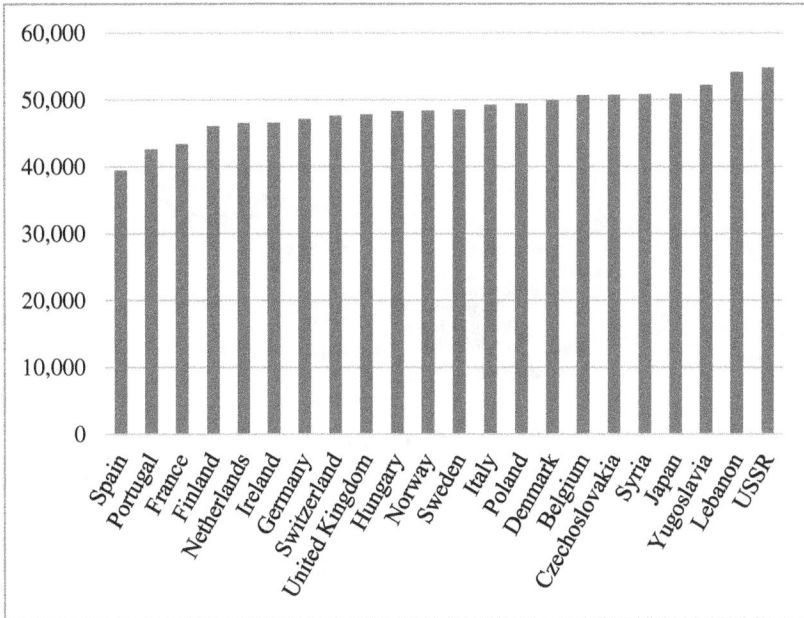

Figure 4.17 Average annual incomes in dollars for 25–60-year-old native men in the United States in 2004–13, by ancestry.

Source: Own calculations using data from the American Community Surveys in 2005–14, from Ruggles et al. (2015).

large extent were their ancestors. In other words, they appear to a considerable extent to represent the remains of differences between the ancestors. To illustrate this I use data from 1930. This early, information on annual incomes was not collected in American censuses. Therefore, I use a measure called *occupational prestige score*. It is an index for the social and economic status of a person's occupation. (The measure was created based on surveys where people were asked to rank the prestige of different occupations. It is strongly, yet not perfectly, correlated with income levels in different occupations. For example, jobs in the public sector, or artistic jobs, are often somewhat higher in the prestige ranking compared with in the income ranking.) The vertical axis of Figure 4.18 shows the average prestige score in 2005–14 of the groups for which average incomes were shown in Figure 4.17. The horizontal axis shows the average score in 1930 of 25–60-year-old immigrant men from the corresponding countries of origin.[18]

---

[18] Group differences in age and region—and year of immigration in the immigrant group—have been leveled out through regression analysis. The values shown are regression predictions for a man who is 40 years old and lives in the East North Central Division—who immigrated in 1915 in the immigrant group.

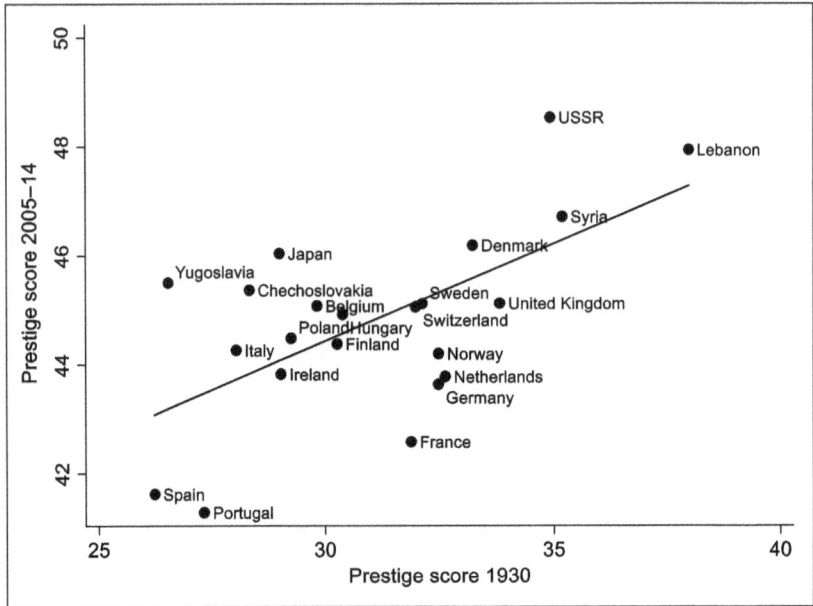

Figure 4.18 Average occupational prestige scores, by country of origin, for immigrant men in the United States in 1930, and approximately for their male descendants in 2005–14.

Source: Ruist (2017b).

I thus try approximately to see the prestige score correlation between native-born men today and their great-grandfathers in 1930. This identification of ancestors is of course far from perfect, which should introduce noise and make the observed correlation weaker. However, in spite of this the correlation is strong. The variation in average prestige scores in the immigrant generation explains as much as 36 percent (according to the R^2 measure) of the variation between current mostly fourth- to fifth-generation immigrants. In other words, a significant share of the variation across immigrant groups appears to have remained for several generations.[19]

In part, this should not be a surprise. It is common for income or prestige score differences between people to be to some extent visible even after multiple generations also if these people were all native-born. Parents' and children's incomes are positively correlated in all countries where this has been studied.[20] Yet differences between immigrant groups appear to be extra

---

[19] For similar analyses, see Borjas (1992), Borjas (1993) and Borjas (1994).
[20] Corak (2006).

persistent, at least in the United States.[21] Different possible explanations exist for this. The most popular is that differences between groups of different origins are cemented by ethnic segregation. Someone who is, for example, of Italian ancestry remains more Italian by growing up among other Italians.[22] Another possible explanation is discrimination.[23] Personally I have, with quite limited success so far, tried to propose the hypothesis that it may be an effect of the personal characteristics on which immigrants were self-selected being particularly persistent across multiple generations.[24]

Final words

How do migrants perform economically in their receiving countries? This chapter has shown that the answer can be almost anything. Some groups perform on average approximately like natives, whereas some perform far worse and some far better. Some have positive or negative income gaps to natives that are stable for two or three decades, while others' incomes increase considerably over time compared with similarly aged natives. Clearly visible differences between different migrant groups may remain for several generations.

Two migrant groups are never fully comparable. Each group is the result of a unique situation, and different groups may have very different potentials to succeed on the receiving country's labor market. Some of these differences are easily identified while others are not. We know, for example, almost nothing about why refugee groups from different countries of origin perform so differently on the labor market in Sweden.

An important conclusion from this, from the perspective of the receiving country, is that it strongly limits the possibilities to draw firm conclusions on whether an immigrant group's performance on the labor market should be seen as a success or a failure. We cannot simply use a different group, in the same country or a different country, as the yardstick against which to measure success. We basically never know how appropriate any comparison is.

Differences in economic success between different migrant groups also create potentially important differences in how their immigration impacts economically and socially on the receiving countries. These are the questions to which we now turn in the next two chapters.

---

[21] Borjas (1992); Ruist (2017b).

[22] Borjas (1992).

[23] Solon (2014).

[24] Ruist (2017b).

Chapter 5

ECONOMIC CONSEQUENCES IN RECEIVING COUNTRIES

Certain forms of migration are desired in many receiving countries for their presumed positive economic effects. This is probably most obvious in the case of talented and highly educated people who work in highly productive science and technology sectors. If a country succeeds in attracting more such people, it may also more easily attract more highly productive industry and generate more innovation. This in turn increases the country's average productivity, incomes and tax revenues, which benefits its entire population. Most likely, virtually no one in the country loses from this. These people have an excellent labor market. They do in most cases not compete for jobs as much as they help each other to create productive and innovative environments, where they gain from the presence of each other. This, most of all, is why high-tech industry clusters geographically, such as most famously in Silicon Valley.[1]

If there are losers from the migration of these people, they would be their countries of origin, who lost them, and other potential destination countries, who did not get them either. Western countries compete with each other to attract them. I will treat this in some more detail in Chapter 8. Here it suffices to say that this type of immigration is looked positively upon by almost everybody.

Another category of immigration that is viewed positively at least by most people is that which helps to more easily fill labor shortages. If an economy otherwise has good potential for further productivity development, yet is held back by shortage of workers in certain sectors (quite often this will be the construction sector, where labor demand is highly volatile), an inflow of workers from abroad may ease the bottleneck and allow productivity, incomes and tax revenues to increase more broadly in the economy. This is to almost everyone's gain, although the domestic workers who were previously in short supply may have been deprived of some spectacular short-term income increases.[2] (On the other hand, if many immigrant workers leave again in the next economic

---

[1] Kerr et al. (2017).
[2] Borjas (2001).

downturn, these domestic workers may eventually become winners too, as it makes an unemployment increase affect them less strongly.)

Enabling this type of migration is a main reason for the free mobility of workers in the EU (see Chapter 2). If workers can move freely across the Union, the risk of labor shortage in any particular place is reduced. Also, as the mirror image of this, the negative consequences of local economic downturns, that is, which do not affect the entire Union at the same time, are reduced. Unemployment in the affected areas will increase by less, if part of the labor force moves to better opportunities elsewhere. (However, such effects have so far turned out to be meagre in practice. The economic downturn in 2008 affected certain Southern European countries much harder than the rest of the Union. This caused migration from Greece, Spain and Portugal to other countries, but not enough to have considerable impact on the steeply rising unemployment in the countries they left.)[3]

These were examples of migration that is predominantly seen as increasing productivity throughout the economy, that is, where immigrants are thought to create rather than compete for jobs. Such migration thus tends to receive quite broad public support. However, it constitutes only a small minority of all Western immigration. Most immigration is looked more skeptically upon by populations in the receiving countries, who – in the realm of economic consequences – may fear that it makes domestic workers' wages fall, or their unemployment rise or that it puts public finances under strain. Yet at the same time, many also hope that immigration could be a way of strengthening public finances, not least as these are currently being put under increased strain by population aging all over the West. The rest of this chapter deals with how immigration impacts on these aspects of the receiving country's economy: the labor market and public finances.

Consequences for labor markets

The main question about how immigration may affect a labor market is to what extent wages may fall or unemployment rise among existing workers if the size of the labor force increases because of immigration. A first thing to be noted regarding this question is that we do not expect it to have one answer that is applicable to all migration. Instead, what we expect from basic economic theory is that the effect should depend partly on the characteristics of the immigrants, and probably most of all on how expected their immigration was.

This is a mostly empirically oriented book, which favors empirical results and illustrations over theoretical reasoning. However, the question of the

---

[3] Bertoli, Brücker and Fernández-Huertas Moraga (2016); Ruist (2018b).

consequences of immigration on labor markets is special in the sense that reliable empirical results are extremely difficult to produce—for reasons soon to be explained—while at the same time there is relative consensus among researchers behind some core theoretical insights. Therefore, this section begins with some simple and hopefully convincing theory, before we turn to the challenging empirics.

Theory. We do not generally expect increases in the size of a labor force to have negative consequences for wage levels or unemployment rates. In many countries, the labor force increases every year as the inflow of young people who graduate from school is relatively larger than the outflow of people into retirement. The main reason why we do not expect this to be negative for existing workers is that it is a predictable event that happens every year to approximately the same extent. Employers thus learn that the labor force gradually increases and hence if they gradually expand their side of the labor market, that is, by gradually creating more jobs, there will be workers to fill them approximately as easily next year as it was this year, and so on.

Hence we do not expect, and also do not observe empirically, any general negative correlations between population size and per capita income levels. The fact that the number of inhabitants per square kilometer is around 20 times as high in the Netherlands and Belgium as in Sweden and Finland does not make us expect average income levels to be lower in the former two countries, not even slightly so. (If anything, we probably expect a little of the opposite due to positive economies of scale. But that is a relatively minor point.) With similar production technologies available in all four countries, but 20 times as many workers per square kilometer in the former two, firms' profit-maximizing decisions have been to invest in 20 times as much physical capital and whatever else is required for production, per square kilometer in these two. In effect, creating 20 times as many jobs at similar levels of productivity, and thus also paying similar wages.

Normally, this insight about workforce growth in general should apply also to workforce growth that is due to immigration. This is because normally immigration is also quite stable and predictable. We notice immigration more when it is unexpected. That is when we hear about it on the news and when it may become a hot political issue. But most Western immigration, like youths reaching adulthood, contributes to a slow gradual increase in the labor force every year, without major surprises, and which employers can easily match with gradual expansion of their activities.

Major exceptions have occurred in history though. At times the size of immigration has changed strongly and unexpectedly. Quite likely you would not be reading this book otherwise (not to mention what a different book it would have been—if any book at all). Yet most—although not all—examples of this have been refugee migration. And although the inflow itself of refugees into a country may sometimes come as a big surprise, this does not in itself imply that refugees' entry into employment will do the same. As we saw in the previous chapter, even after 9–10 years only somewhat less than half of all refugees in Europe who were 25–64 years old were employed. Hence, in many cases, when most refugees finally manage to enter the labor market this hardly comes as a surprise for anybody. Rather, the presence of a large pool of unemployed refugees presents employers with a clear incentive to create jobs that are targeted to those refugees.

Hence we can only reasonably expect immigration to have any important negative effects on existing workers' wages or unemployment in cases of unexpected major changes, not only in the inflow of immigrants into an area, but also in their inflow into employment. And such events are rare. The immigration into the United Kingdom from Eastern Europe that began in 2004 was one of them. Thus there may be reason to believe that British workers' perception that these immigrants negatively affected their own opportunities on the labor market (see Chapter 2) were well founded. At least in the short run.

If a negative effect of unexpected immigration happens, it will persist for as long as it takes employers to react and adjust to the new situation. An unexpected inflow of immigrants means there are suddenly more workers in the economy than what employers were expecting when they made their production plans. Hence their profit-maximizing decisions will be to adjust these plans and invest more in physical capital, etc., to create the additional jobs that suddenly became easier to fill— eventually neutralizing any negative effects of the inflow on other workers. Hence also when immigration has a negative effect on wages or unemployment in the short run, the effect should be zero in the longer run after employers have had the time to react.

What has been said here is very basic theory. The large majority of scholars who are active in this field would agree that there is a convincing theoretical case for immigration having a negative effect on wages or unemployment only in cases of an unexpected inflow of immigrants.[4] Yet theory can only point out direction, not size. In other words, how large these rare negative effects may be, and how long-lasting, must be the realm of empirical studies to which I turn shortly.

If immigrant workers impact negatively on the opportunities of existing workers, we naturally also expect this impact to be more pronounced for

---

[4] National Academies of Sciences, Engineering and Medicine (2017) provides a good illustration. A large number of the most influential scholars in the field stand behind it—hence it only contains conclusions on which they could all agree.

those existing workers whose qualifications are more similar to those of the immigrants. Less-educated immigrants most likely compete with other less-educated workers, etc. Often, the other workers with the most similar qualifications will be previous immigrants. These may, for example, share weaker language skills with the newly arrived and may hence compete more for jobs with lower language requirements.[5]

On this matter, there appears to be at least fairly strong scholarly consensus that the theoretical reasoning that stable and predictable immigration should have a zero effect on other workers applies only to their average wages and total unemployment, and not to the wage and unemployment gaps between groups that are more similar and groups that are less similar to the immigrants. Here, I am one of those whose opinions deviate from the consensus. I find it difficult to see why the theoretical reasoning behind the conclusion of no effect should only apply to the average wage in an economy and not also to the averages in smaller groups of workers. Nothing in how this reasoning was presented here says that there should be any difference. Hence as I see it, if employers, for example, learn that each year the pool of workers without college degrees increases, yet the pool of workers with college degrees does not, they would expand production processes in such a way as to create more jobs for the former group but not for the latter. And if only the pool of workers without college degrees increases unexpectedly, they will react by creating more of those jobs later, thereby neutralizing the initial effect on the wage gap.

However, many others do not agree but rather believe in a theoretical framework where also stable and predictable immigration can impact on wage or unemployment gaps between different types of workers, and where these effects may also be permanent, that is, may not be neutralized over time the way any impact on average wages will.[6]

---

[5] National Academies of Sciences, Engineering and Medicine (2017).

[6] National Academies of Sciences, Engineering and Medicine (2017). For this question, there does not exist anything similar to the quite convincing illustration that it is possible for average wages to be similar in the Netherlands and Finland in spite of their vastly different population densities. There are no two "otherwise similar" Western countries with hugely differing shares of college-educated workers, on which we could build a similar story about wage gaps. I am happy to concede though that the reasoning that relative supply of workers should have no effect on their relative wages appears unrea-sonable if we take it far enough. For sure, an advanced economy could not function without a single college-educated worker, to make the argument very clear. (The Netherlands–Finland comparison on the other hand appears to show that, for average wages, the argument can be taken very far.) Yet I do not think this has to prevent the argument from holding within the limits of variation that may actually occur in reality. Western economies are very open to trade and investment, and production can swiftly

Empirical research. Theory could thus quite convincingly answer some questions about the impact of immigration on labor markets but others less so. For these we would therefore want to add empirical results. Yet producing reliable empirical research on the consequences of immigration on labor markets is very difficult. To make it possible, we first of all need historical variation in immigration. We need to be able to compare how labor markets have developed in different places depending on how much immigration there were in these places. However, this is not enough. We also need a large share of this variation in immigration to be *exogenous* (literally: "created outside"). This means that the variation in immigration must not itself be influenced by that on which we want to measure effects (or by some third factor that also affects that on which we want to measure effects, yet through other channels than immigration). In other words, the variation in immigration between places that we study must not in turn depend on differences in wages or unemployment between these places.

And such variation has been very rare in history. As we have seen repeatedly through this book, it is precisely the opportunities to earn higher incomes that causes most of Western countries' immigration. Therefore we expect migration to quite consistently be higher to places where wages are higher and unemployment lower. And it is no surprise that in many cases we can even observe clear patterns where places with higher immigration have had more positive, not more negative, wage developments compared with places with less immigration. There is not much reason to believe this to have been because higher immigration created more positive wages. More likely it is due to the reverse causal relation, that is, that stronger labor markets attracted more immigrants.[7]

For this reason, the best empirical research on the topic is primarily about finding historical episodes where immigration has varied between locations for reasons that were plausibly to a large extent not due to conditions on their labor markets. Most such episodes concern migration of refugees. Yet most of these in turn come with the problem that refugees' entry into employment has

---

relocate to where it is more profitable. If the share of the workforce that, for example, has college degrees increases gradually every year (as it has done for a long time in many countries), this could enable more production (also globally) that requires these skills, while shifting simpler production to other countries or to automation, without implying a decrease in the wages of college-educated workers. Or if, for example, through immigration, the share without college degrees increases, this could be accommodated without wage effects, through a slowdown in the processes of automation or relocation of simpler production to other (mostly non-Western) countries.

[7] Borjas (1999).

been too slow to make these episodes feasible to exploit in empirical studies. Entry into employment only happened at the same time as entry into the area for a minority of the refugees. And when it actually happened for the rest of them is of course strongly dependent on the development of the local labor market, that is, it is far from the exogenous kind of variation that we need.

Some interesting episodes have been identified though, where we have seen large variation in immigration across locations, for reasons plausibly not much due to labor markets, and where most immigrants have been employed within a short time. These episodes most likely provide the most reliable conditions for evaluations of labor market consequences of immigration. I will present those that I find most credible in some detail below.

Yet unfortunately, these episodes are only suitable for answering part of the questions that were asked in the theory section. They all have in common that they resulted from quite (or very) unexpected political changes. They are thus only suitable for studying the labor market effects of immigration *in the case where we expect these effects to be the most negative*, that is, when immigration comes as a surprise to economies that were not prepared. There exists no historical episode that enables us to make a credible empirical study of the labor market effects of immigration *such as it most often looks.*[8] This is the main reason why the theory section was included. When it comes to the normal case of immigration, that is, where it is stable and predictable, reliable empirical estimates of its consequences for the labor market do not exist. In this case, theory is the best that we have.

Furthermore, even the empirical studies that are probably the most reliable that we have also have their issues with credibility or interpretation. Therefore I do not simply summarize their results. Instead I review them in some detail, explaining their issues, to allow readers to make their own assessments.

Mariel. The oldest—and by far the most well-known, also in non-academic circles—example of an evaluation of labor market consequences of immigration in a case where one may plausibly argue that the variation in immigration between areas was mostly due to factors other than wages or unemployment, is from the Mariel crisis of 1980. When Cuba temporarily—and unexpectedly—removed its ban on emigration and allowed people to leave from the port of Mariel, an estimated 125,000 people left the country by boat during the five months that followed. Nearly all these boats arrived in Miami, where also half

---

[8] Many attempts have been made though to study the labor market effects of immigration also in other settings. For recent reviews, see Dustmann, Schönberg and Stuhler (2016), and National Academies of Sciences, Engineering and Medicine (2017).

of all previous Cuban immigrants in the United States lived. The fact that around 60 percent of the Mariel refugees settled in Miami is commonly seen as due to these factors and not much related to the labor market in the city at the time.[9]

The refugee inflow increased the size of the workforce in Miami by probably 7–8 percent in only a few months, and that of the workforce without something corresponding to a high school degree by a full 20 percent. Many of the refugees also quickly entered into employment.[10]

The size of the inflow, and its plausibly not much labor-market related concentration in Miami, contribute to the suitability of the episode for an evaluation of labor market effects. Yet two factors make it less suitable. One is that the episode does not provide variation between many places. The only statistical analysis it enables is a comparison between how labor markets subsequently developed in Miami, which received many refugees, and in all or some other cities, which did not. This basically comes down to a comparison between only two observations. The reliability of a statistical analysis becomes higher the more observations we can compare, because more observations reduce the risk that chance creeps in and affects the results. In the current case, the comparison between wage trends in Miami and other cities will give a biased account of the wage impact of immigration, if something else happened to occur in Miami at the same time, which importantly affected wages in either direction.

(There is a conflict here between reliability and popularity that is good to be aware of. The fact that the research on the effects of the Mariel migration only compares two observations increases its sensitivity and decreases its reliability. Yet it also makes it very easy to understand, both for people with and for people without training in research methods. This is probably the main reason why this research has become so well known and influential in both academic and non-academic circles.)

The second weakness concerns data collection. If wage impacts of immigration had been a question of more political or academic interest in 1980 (it was as good as nonexistent) there would certainly have been considerable efforts to collect data in Miami in the years thereafter in order to enable accurate measurement of wage trends following this very unusual event. However, this did not happen. The only data source that is available is, therefore, the annual nationwide Current Population Surveys, where few of the sampled individuals live in Miami. This creates a major risk that these annual samples are not fully representative of the Miami population.

---

[9] Card (1990); Borjas (2017).
[10] Borjas (2017).

These two weaknesses have been handled in different ways in the most influential studies on the topic, which reach very different results regarding how workers in Miami were affected by the immigrant inflow. The estimated effects range from nonexistent to an effect where wages for workers without high school degrees decreased by 1 percent or even more for each percent increase in the similarly low-educated workforce through immigration.[11]

Many of us find it difficult to establish which among these estimates is the most credible. The differences are mostly due to small differences in data treatment where one can hardly claim that either method is obviously better than the other. The main takeaway therefore becomes that the Mariel episode hints that wage effects *may* have been very strongly negative for the existing workers who were most similar to the immigrants, yet that this result is not certain.

Less concentrated inflows, and instrumental variables. The Mariel case was extreme with respect to the immigrants' high concentration to only one city in the receiving country. Hence the empirical evaluation was a simple (in one sense) comparison between this city and all or some others. Otherwise, immigrants tend to spread out somewhat more evenly across a receiving country, yet often still quite unevenly. Some regions and cities always tend to get more immigrants than others.

This in itself is good for the possibilities to evaluate labor market effects of immigration. To be able to perform an empirical evaluation we need variation in immigration across localities, and the more localities we may compare the more stable and reliable results we may obtain. The problem with the Mariel case was that although we had large variation, all that variation was due to only one place.

Hence what we want to find most of all is a case where we have much variation in immigration between many places and at the same time this variation is exogenous, that is, not caused by variation in labor market opportunities between these places. This criterion has probably not been fulfilled to 100 percent anywhere at any time. The labor market always matters, at least to some extent, in migrants' location choices. However, we do not necessarily need it to be fulfilled to 100 percent. It may be sufficient that some other factor, which we can identify and measure, has been responsible for at least a large share of the variation in immigration across cities. We can then use a technique that is called *instrumental variables* to isolate the part of all variation in immigration that can be explained by this other factor, and only measure how subsequent wage or unemployment trends correlate with that part.

---

[11] Card (1990); Borjas (2017); Peri and Yasenov (2019); Clemens and Hunt (2019).

This is quite complicated in all its detail and cannot be fully explained here. Yet it is fairly simple to provide a basic intuition that is sufficient to enable the reader to assess the credibility of the technique, which is very much case-specific and dependent upon how convincingly we can identify a credible other factor, that is, a credible *instrument*, in each specific case.

I explain this by a very simple example. Following what we saw in Chapter 3 (Figure 3.1), one instrument that could be used to explain variation in immigration across places is the distance to the migrants' home country. The fact that, through history, so many Cuban immigrants in the United States have chosen to settle in Miami of all cities is of course not by chance. It is rather mostly because Miami is so close to Cuba. Because it is so close it will probably more or less always get more Cuban immigration than, for example, San Francisco, even in times when the labor market is better in San Francisco. On average, the further to the north or west we look in the United States the fewer Cubans we see.

The distance to Cuba could therefore be used as an instrumental variable, which we can use to predict a fundamental pattern in Cuban settlements that will matter regardless of what local labor markets look like. Better labor markets will always get more immigrants, but we can still identify a broad pattern of how the concentration of Cubans on average declines with the distance to Cuba.

This is an overly simple example of an instrument, which is only meant to illustrate the technique. If we want to use it to evaluate the wage impact of an inflow of Cubans, we thus investigate how the variation in wage trends across cities correlates not with actual local inflows of Cubans—which partly depend on these very wage trends—but with the instrument, that is, with the distance to Cuba. We thus investigate if there is a pattern where wages on average increase or decrease with the distance to Cuba, and if we find such a correlation we ascribe it to be *entirely* due to the inflow of Cubans.

The over-simplicity of the instrument in this example illustrates the critical point of the instrumental variables technique: it only gives correct results if the instrument (here: distance) does not correlate with the outcome variable (here: wage trends) for any other reason than the one we claim (here: immigration). For every candidate to be an instrument one has to decide if this appears plausible or not. In the present example, it is difficult to be convinced because the instrument is as simple as the distance to a point. The business cycle is not the same across all of the United States. A multitude of factors could accidentally create a pattern where wage trends are on average either more positive or more negative as we move further to the northwest or southeast in the country, regardless of whether there has been any Cuban immigration or not. Hence it appears that we would go too far if we tried to explain any such pattern as exclusively a result of Cuban immigration. (And if we did, we would certainly conclude that Cuban immigration increased wages in some periods and decreased them in others.)

The remaining three studies that I shall cover in this section all evaluate labor market consequences of immigration in settings where plausibly factors other than labor markets were responsible for large shares of the variation in immigrant concentrations across places. They all try to capture these factors with measurable instruments. Hence a very central element in an evaluation of the credibility of any of them is an evaluation of the credibility of its instruments.

Again, I also repeat that these studies all cover cases where immigration was quite unexpected, and where we thus expect its labor market consequences to be more negative than in the normal case.

French "repatriates" from Algeria. Algeria was under French rule in 1830–1962. While other French colonies were mostly only administered by small numbers of French bureaucrats and soldiers, Algeria was a place where French people settled in larger numbers. (Formally Algeria was not a colony but a part of France proper, although its inhabitants could not become French citizens with equal voting rights unless they renounced Islam.) In March 1962, when the peace agreement that gave Algeria its independence was signed, around one million people of French ancestry lived on Algerian soil. Most of them "returned" (many of them were born in Algeria) to France within a year thereafter. After a few years, migration from Algeria had thus increased the size of the French labor force by 1.6 percent, yet with large regional variation. The increases were 5.6 and 4.4 percent, respectively, in the southern regions of Provence-Côte d'Azur and Languedoc-Roussillon but merely 0.4 percent in the northern region Nord.[12]

These "repatriates" were French in language and culture and on average slightly more educated than the rest of the French population. Most of them found employment quite easily, and there is good reason to believe that they competed for different types of jobs to approximately the same extent as the rest of the population.[13]

Two studies have estimated how this large and unexpected inflow had affected wages and unemployment in France six years later, in 1968. They could not measure the impact earlier than that, since they had to wait for the census of 1968 to see the geographical distribution of immigrants across the country. Hence there is a risk that parts of the effects on labor markets had

---

[12] Hunt (1992).
[13] Edo (2020).

time to be neutralized in the meantime. These two studies used different data sources, with different advantages and disadvantages, and their estimates of the effects differ somewhat. But both agree that the effects were fairly substantial. One study concluded that for each percentage increase in the size of the labor force in an area due to immigration, unemployment increased by 0.2 percentage points and wages decreased by about 0.5 percent.[14] The other concluded that the wage decrease was even more than twice as large as that.[15] Hence, as in the Mariel case, there is quite some discrepancy between estimates, although in this case both studies report some fairly large effects.

To obtain these results, the first study used two instrumental variables together to predict the distribution of immigrants across France: the local average temperature and the concentration of immigrants from Algeria in the earlier period 1954–62. Hence it investigates how local labor market trends in 1962–68 correlated with the local climate, and interpret the result as due to the settlement of immigrants. And it investigates how the same trends correlated with where immigrants from Algeria had settled in the previous period, and interpret the result as an effect of the settlement, not of the previous, but of the contemporary immigrants. The second study uses a different version of the second instrument only: the concentration of all immigrants from Algeria who lived in France at the beginning of 1962 (i.e., regardless of whether they arrived after 1954 or not).

Both these instruments have their pros and cons. The idea of using annual mean temperatures is that those who were used to the warm Algerian climate preferred to settle in warmer parts of France. The study also supports this by showing a strong correlation between mean temperature and the concentration of immigrants. However, almost the same objection can be raised against the mean temperature as an instrument as in the earlier simple example with the distance to a point. Apart from a couple of mountain areas, there is not much more detailed local variation in mean temperatures across France than in the distance to a point (to Algiers, for example). Hence also this instrumental variable carries a considerable risk of accidentally picking up regional business cycle variation that is due to other reasons than immigration. Depending on the direction of such variation, this could mean that the estimated labor market impact in the study is either more positive or more negative than the true impact.

The idea of using the settlement pattern of previous migrants as an instrumental variable is based on the thought that the settlement pattern of a group is due in part to the labor market and in part to other factors. The local labor

---

[14] Hunt (1992).
[15] Edo (2020).

market changes over time. It is better in some areas in one period and in other areas in the next period. We do not have perfect knowledge about exactly which the other factors are. Yet plausibly several of them (preferences for certain types of milieus) do—in contrast to labor markets—not change much over time. The later immigrants plausibly had largely the same preferences as the previous immigrants over factors that were not related to the labor market. But they faced a different labor market. Hence the settlement pattern of the previous group may contain information on many non-labor market-related things that affected where also the later group settled. But the only information it contains on settlement because of labor market factors is from a different period, that is, it (supposedly) does not contain information about the labor market of 1962–68. (Note that we cannot evaluate this assumption empirically, as such an evaluation cannot be separated from the measurement of effects of immigration, which is the whole point of the analysis.)

The main weakness of this strategy is that it only works if labor market developments in the two periods were completely unrelated (hence the word "supposedly" above). And in this case, when the two periods are adjacent, this may be quite strongly questioned. Even if the immigrants who arrived in the later period certainly only cared about what the labor market looked like in that period and not what it looked like before, there is a major risk that those two things looked quite similar. The local labor markets that were the strongest in 1954–62 may still have been the strongest in 1962–68. If this is so, it will make the estimated labor market effects in these studies less negative than the true effects, that is, we might expect that the true effects were larger than those that were reported in these studies.

Bulgarian Turks in Turkey.[16] A similar, yet probably better, example is from the forced migration of ethnic Turks from Bulgaria to Turkey in the summer of 1989. Today's Bulgaria has had a large population of ethnic Turks since the days when the area belonged to the Ottoman empire. After the foundation of the country Bulgaria in the early twentieth century, many of these Turks were forced, in several waves, out of the country. Almost all of them then moved to Turkey. In 1951, Turkey stopped accepting such refugees, which made the expulsions cease. The only exception for a long time was a large family reunification program that was agreed by the two countries in 1968.

But in May 1989, Bulgaria made a new committed attempt to rid itself of those parts of its remaining Turkish population who then refused to follow new hard assimilation laws, including by changing to Bulgarian names,

---

[16] This part is entirely based on Aydemir and Kirdar (2017).

ceasing to speak Turkish and denying the very existence of a Turkish people. Turkey gave in and received around 170,000 refugees during three months. This increased the country's total labor force by a quite meager 0.7 percent. But as the refugees mostly settled in limited parts of the country, inflows were really high in some of these parts. The labor force increased by more than 4 percent in 20 cities, whereof by more than 10 percent in two.

As in the French example, these refugees were of the same ethnicity and spoke the same language as the majority population of the receiving country, and most of them quickly found employment. And also the effect of this inflow on existing workers has been evaluated in a study that uses the settlement pattern of similar previous immigrants—in this case earlier immigrants of the Turkish ethnicity from Bulgaria—as an instrument for the settlement pattern of the immigrant group that is being studied.

The major advantage of this study in relation to the French is that these earlier Turkish immigrants arrived so long before those under study. Almost all of them arrived before 1951, or at the family reunification in 1968. Therefore, the risk that settlements of the earlier group were influenced by local labor market conditions that were still relevant when the later group arrived in 1989 should reasonably be very small.

The labor market impact of this inflow is studied by comparing changes in local unemployment across 342 cities between the Turkish censuses of 1985 and 1990. The 1990 census was conducted in October, that is, 12–14 months after the refugees' arrival. Hence in this case, local labor markets have had relatively little time to adjust to the unexpected immigrant inflow. The results indicate that for each percentage increase in the size of the labor force due to immigration, male unemployment increased by 0.26 percentage points (female labor force participation in Turkey in 1990 was low). The effects on wages could not be studied due to lack of wage data.

Daily commuters in Germany. The overview thus far paints a mixed picture of short-term labor market consequences of unexpected immigration. The estimated effects range from almost zero in some of the Mariel studies to very large in one of the Mariel studies and one of the French studies.[17] Yet although the studies reviewed here are among the most reliable that have been made, they all have their obvious potential weaknesses. The Mariel studies rely entirely on the assumption that nothing else of importance happened in Miami at the same time as the immigrant inflow. The studies of French and

---

[17] For results from other empirical studies, see reviews in Dustmann, Schönberg and Stuhler (2016), and National Academies of Sciences, Engineering and Medicine (2017).

Turkish immigration rely on the belief that their instrumental variable strategies have really worked.

The Turkish study could indeed present a fairly strong argumentation for its instrumental variable because it was based on events so far back in time, and I think it is clearly the most reliable among the studies that have been reviewed so far (hence it is unfortunate that it could not also study effects on wages). At the same time, any instrumentation of migrants' settlement patterns has an inherent weakness in that these settlements are choices of the human free will. Every person decides where to settle. We do not know who decides to act according to the predictions of the instrument and who does not, why they do it, and if their choices or motifs eventually in some way that is intractable to us, builds some additional links between the instrument and the labor market into the analysis, distorting it.

This is almost always an issue with instrumental variable estimation. It is normally referred to in terms of who the "compliers" with the instrument are, and whether it is likely or not that compliers and non-compliers have the same effects on the outcome variable. Generally, an instrument is weaker the more scope people have to choose whether to act according to its predictions or not. The strongest instruments in this sense are those that people cannot avoid complying with.

In this lies the major strength of the last study that I will review in this section.[18] It covers a case of "migration" where the "migrants" had very restricted options to decide where in the receiving country to add themselves to the labor force. This was because they were not allowed to settle, only to commute daily for work. By night they had to be out of the country again (alternatively they were allowed to stay overnight if they worked no more than two days per week).

This system was introduced in Germany in 1991. The country was experiencing shortage of workers, and as one of multiple strategies to attract foreign workers it was decided to issue working permits to workers from the neighboring countries Poland and Czechoslovakia (The Czech Republic after the separation in 1993). Communist rule and its ban on emigration had recently ended in these countries, and their unemployment rates were high. However, the earlier experiences of guest workers who did not want to return home in the next economic downturn had made a lasting impression on Germany (see Chapter 2). The solution for this not to be repeated was that this time the workers would not be allowed to settle at all, only to commute to work on a daily basis. This was also feasible in practice, because this time they would be from neighboring countries.

---

[18] This part is entirely based on Dustmann, Schönberg and Stuhler (2017).

This rule obviously limited where in Germany these daily commuters could work, and hence affect local labor markets: it could not be very far from the border with the home country. Therefore, the distance to this border becomes a very reliable instrument in a study of the labor market effects of this commuting. Workers' actual behavior *cannot* deviate far from the predictions of the instrument: the closer to the border the more workers there will be on average. And beyond a certain distance (about 80 kilometers) there will be almost no workers at all. (This instrument is also quite different from the earlier examples of a simple distance to a point. The affected area in Germany is a fairly long stretch of land that is 80 kilometers wide. The nearest point on the border is far from the same point along all of this stretch.)

This legislation caused fairly large inflows of workers in areas close to Poland and Czechoslovakia. However, most of these areas are not so suitable for evaluations of effects on labor markets. The entire Polish and about half of the Czechoslovakian border was with former East Germany, which was itself at the same time in the middle of a gigantic economic transformation. A large part of the remaining border, that is, that between Czechoslovakia and former West Germany, was also so close to former East Germany that the economy in this border area was probably also much affected by the East German transformation, such as through an inflow of workers from East Germany.

Therefore, the study limits its geographical coverage to the part of former West Germany (Eastern Bavaria) that was within 80 kilometers from Czechoslovakia and more than 80 kilometers from former East Germany. In this area, the share of Czechs among all employed workers rose from virtually zero in 1990 to around 3 percent in 1992–93. Fewer permits were issued after 1993, and the share gradually fell again. The variation in the concentration of daily commuters is predicted in the study with the distance to the border as an instrument. The study thus investigates whether wage and unemployment trends in these border areas correlate with the distance to the border, and interprets the result as the effect of the inflow of daily commuters.

This setting is also an example of an unexpected inflow of workers and one to which employers had little time to prepare in advance. The first work permits were issued only 4 months after the commuting scheme was made public by the German government (and only 14 months after the fall of the Berlin wall and the Czechoslovakian revolution).

The study estimates fairly small effects of the worker inflow on existing workers' wages but quite large effects on their employment. For each percent increase in the number of employed workers in an area due to the inflow of commuters in 1990–92, the employment rate of other workers was 0.6 percent lower in 1993.[19]

Due to the particularly trustworthy instrument that was used in this study, its estimates must in themselves reasonably be considered the most reliable that have been produced in any study in this research field. Indeed they are probably more reliable than what I think most of us expected we would ever see before this study was published in 2016. And it took a quite unique historical episode—which was previously not so well known even in most of Germany—to enable it.

But this does not imply that this research field can now close its books and conclude that the best possible empirical answer to the question of labor market effects of unexpected immigration has now been found. However reliable these estimates are in themselves, it is less evident what we may learn from them outside of the specific example. A daily commuter and an immigrant are not fully the same thing. Most importantly, immigrants consume most of their income in the receiving area but daily commuters most likely do not. Hence with immigration a country gets both workers and consumers but with commuters it mostly gets workers.

To what extent this creates a difference in how immigrants and commuters affect demand for other workers in the affected area—and hence employment and wages—depends most importantly on what is produced in the area. To the extent that the area produces goods that are traded internationally, there should be no difference, because then it does not matter where the consumers live. (This was the perspective taken in the earlier theory section.) Yet to the extent that the area produces goods for local consumption there will be a difference.

We can thus be as good as certain that the estimated negative effects of unexpected commuting (a seldom-used expression indeed) are to some extent larger than the negative effects of unexpected immigration. But we do not know to what extent.[20] At least this may provide a reason to perhaps believe

---

[19] This study itself mostly emphasizes that *employment* in 1993 was 0.9 percent lower. The effect on employment is larger than that on the employment *rate*, because the inflow of commuters also had a negative effect on the size of the resident native population (fewer other people moved into the areas into which many Czechs commuted).

[20] There is also no good data available on to what extent the affected area produces internationally traded goods in this particular case, which may have enabled us to get a sense of orders of magnitude.

less in the estimates of larger effects than in the German study, which were obtained in other studies with less-credible estimation strategies. But we should also not completely rule out that contextual differences between the different cases that were studied in different studies may have implied that labor market effects of immigration were in fact more negative in other cases than in the German case.

Final words, labor markets. Few historical episodes exist that provide reasonable opportunities to evaluate consequences of immigration on labor markets. Some of the best candidates have been reviewed here, and together they paint quite a disparate picture, including both quite modest and really large negative effects.

Yet all these episodes are also examples of quite unexpected immigration. Hence they are examples of rare events where we expect the effects to be unusually negative. They are not examples of immigration such as it normally looks in the West, that is, quite stable and predictable. For this normal case, good empirical evaluations do not exist. But there is a strong theoretical case for effects being as good as nonexistent, at least on average wages and total unemployment.

In those cases where immigration does have considerable labor market effects, because it was unexpected, we expect those effects to be neutralized over time as the economy eventually reacts. But there is no good empirical picture of how long that time would typically be.

Consequences for public finances

The average person who lives in a Western country gives a positive net contribution to that country's public finances in approximately the age interval of 20 65 years, that is, the interval within which most people work and pay income taxes. Those who are younger or older than this are on average net costs for public finances, as most of them do not work.

For this reason, immigration has an obvious potential to have a positive impact on a country's public finances. As we saw in Chapters 2 and 3, virtually all migration flows are concentrated in the age interval of 20–35 years. Hence in a typical immigrant, a country receives a person for whom the first 20—costly—years have already been paid. Another country covered the costs of education, hospital care, etc. in this period. The receiving country receives a person with many potentially productive years ahead before the advent of the costly old age.[21]

---

[21] Storesletten (2000).

If an immigrant group works, earns income and pays taxes to a higher extent than the rest of the population, the effect of its immigration on public finances of course becomes even more positive. But if it instead does so to a lower extent, the effect will be less positive, or may even be negative, in spite of the positive age factor. In the previous chapter we saw large differences between different migrant groups' outcomes on labor markets. Some performed on average far better, others far worse, than natives. In consequence, there are also large differences between these groups in their net contributions to public finances.

This section presents the results of some estimates of the effects of the immigration of certain groups on public finances. Yet before presenting these, we need a discussion of how they are calculated, and of the sources of error that are involved.

Method.[22] In a modern welfare state the public sector collects somewhere between around one-third and one-half of the monetary value of all goods and services that are produced in the country, that is, of GDP.[23] Most of its revenues are in the form of income, payroll and consumption taxes. They are used for two things: transfers, that is, direct payments to people in the form of income support, pensions, etc.; and public consumption, that is, the costs of schools, hospitals, roads and so on. The public sector is thus both a system for redistributing resources between people and one where the population collectively pays for common goods.

Different people contribute different amounts to the public sector. Some pay higher taxes, some receive more transfers, some use more hospital care, etc. Some people are net contributors and others net costs. The idea of estimating exactly who contributes and who does not, and by how much, is conceptually quite obvious to a certain point. The vast majority of public revenues are collected from individuals who work and consume, and are thus obviously linked to those individuals. Yet for minor revenue shares, such as taxes on corporate profits, it is less conceptually obvious which individuals paid the taxes: was it the firm's owners, its workers or who?

On the cost side, it is similarly evident who receives the costs that consist of transfers. Likewise, when the public sector pays, for example, for hospital or elderly care, it is quite simple to define who the receiver is. Yet large shares of public costs target much larger groups, or the entire population: for example, costs of infrastructure and defense.

---

[22] For more detailed reviews, see Rowthorn (2008), and Preston (2014).
[23] Source: OECD.

Actually estimating the net contributions to public finances from individuals or groups in practice adds additional difficulties above the conceptual ones. In some countries there are available data where researchers can see who paid different taxes. In others this must be estimated, for example, from income data. It is never possible to see who paid consumption taxes. However, we know approximately what the relations between income and consumption look like on average and can use that knowledge for approximation. On the cost side it is often possible to see who received transfers. Most often we cannot see exactly who visits hospitals, uses public child care, etc. But we often have quite good information on how utilization of these services correlates with age—and sometimes also immigrant status—and can use that for approximation.

In sum, we can observe some revenues and costs at the individual level and we have quite good knowledge about others at various group levels. Hence we cannot calculate *individual* contributions to public finances with much precision. But neither are we very interested in doing this. We are more interested in how revenues and costs are distributed over larger population groups, and at those levels we can often calculate them quite accurately.

The benefit of such calculations may be, for example, to predict how the public sector's financial strength will be affected by the increasing share of elderly in the population that is projected to happen in all Western countries in the coming decades. We can use our knowledge about how much higher public net costs are for older compared with younger people, and use this information to estimate the expected impact of an increasing share of the former group. Another benefit may be to estimate to what extent public finances become stronger or weaker if a country receives more or fewer of a certain type of immigrants. Whether, for example, the increasing costs that follow from population aging may be balanced by increased immigration, or if such would instead add yet another stone to the burden.

However, the latter calculation has additional sources of error. According to what has been described here, we may calculate the (positive or negative) net contribution of an immigrant group to the public finances. But this is not really what we want to know. What we want to know is the *effect* of receiving a similar group in the country. These two things are most likely not identical. For them to be identical, it is required that receiving an immigrant group does not have any effect on public revenues from, or costs directed to, other people in the country.

For example: If an immigrant gets employed and starts to pay taxes, this is a revenue for the country. If this job was created because the immigrant arrived, this revenue also constitutes the effect of the arrival of the immigrant on revenues. Yet if, on the contrary, this job would have existed anyway and would then have been done by someone who is now unemployed because the immigrant took the job instead, the effect of the immigrant's arrival on revenues is instead zero. Then the more important effect of the immigrant's arrival on public finances may instead be an increased cost for public finances, in the form of public income support to the worker who is now unemployed.

In this example, the effect of the immigrant's arrival on public finances is thus more negative than the net contribution from the immigrant. Other sources of error may instead imply that the effect is more positive than the net contribution. If the immigrant takes a low-paid job with low language requirements, perhaps opportunities increase for other workers with better language skills to advance to better-paid (thus created) jobs, making them pay higher taxes. Another example is economies of scale. Quite likely, not all public costs increase proportionally with a population increase. For example, even more sparsely populated areas have a certain density of roads. If the population increases in such areas perhaps the need for additional roads is almost zero. Likewise the costs of a country's military defense are probably not fully proportional to its population size but depend also on its area. Hence if the population increases by 1 percent, perhaps costs for infrastructure and defense may increase by less than that.

These are the most commonly mentioned examples of why net contributions from immigrants and effects of their immigration are not necessarily equivalent, and there are also others. It is very difficult though to try to take these into account when estimating the effects of immigration on public finances. The relations are complex and we basically never know very much about exactly what they look like. The most common strategy is therefore to not make any attempt at all to take them into account. This is for two main reasons. First, we generally believe that most of them are quite small. We saw earlier in this chapter that the effects of immigration on other people's employment opportunities are believed to be small or nonexistent in most cases. It is similar with other sources of error.

Secondly—and importantly—by not actively attempting to take these sources of error into account in the analysis, we avoid making active choices that affect the outcome of the calculation in a direction that is obvious in advance. The effects of immigration on public finances is a politically contentious issue. Hence there is a value in keeping the calculations as neutral as possible. This value would be questionable, of course, if we had a clear perception of whether it is the positive or the negative sources of error that are the most important ones, that is, of whether by this strategy we obtain too positive or too negative estimates of the effect of immigration. But at least my interpretation is that we do not have such a clear perception.

Policy-relevant questions. There exist quite a few studies, from many different Western countries, of the consequences of immigration for public finances. But surprisingly few of these have been made in such a way as to make their results relevant for evaluating or informing policy. The typical study calculates the net contribution to public finances of all immigrants, or the average immigrant, in a country. They tend to conclude that the total net contribution is fairly small. It is sometimes found to be positive and sometimes negative, but in almost all countries less than the equivalent of 1 percent of the country's GDP.[24]

The values thus calculated represent the sums of the net contributions of immigrants who arrived in the country last year, those who arrived 10 years ago and those who arrived 50 years ago—those who arrived as refugees, as labor migrants, and for family reasons, all taken together. For the purposes of evaluating the consequences of immigration policy in the country, they are thus an impenetrable sum of the consequences of different policies that have been in place over the decades, vis-à-vis different types of immigration that have occurred for different reasons and originated in different parts of the world. They show the sum of the net contributions of all immigrants who have been allowed in under a range of different policies. It becomes quite impossible to see which policies and which immigrant groups contribute to making the results more positive or more negative. To me, this makes the results of such studies quite uninteresting.[25]

However, there also exists a smaller number of studies that aim at providing results that are more directly informative on the consequences of different policies. The earliest of these were evaluations of the consequences for public finances of the free migration of workers from new to old EU member countries following the EU enlargement in 2004. The background to these studies was the widespread fear that this enlargement would lead to large migration of people with poor abilities to earn their own living, who would qualify for public income support and remain in receiving Western European countries as a burden on their public finances.

The first empirical evaluation of this was made in the United Kingdom, where the issue was more politically contentious than anywhere else (see Chapter 2). The evaluation showed no sign of the immigrant group in question placing a burden on public finances—quite the contrary. In the fiscal year 2008–09, the new EU migrants made up 0.91 percent of the population

---

[24] Rowthorn (2008).

[25] Readers who want to know more about this larger literature are advised to consult the accessible article by Rowthorn (2008). It is a few years old, but so is much of this literature.

in the country. They were marginally overrepresented on the revenue side of public finances, contributing 0.96 percent of all revenues. And they were more markedly underrepresented on the cost side, being the target of only an estimated 0.60 percent of all costs. Hence the average immigrant in this group paid in 37 percent more to public finances than they received.[26]

I later made a similar evaluation in Sweden. There was reason to expect less positive results there. Few non-Swedes speak Swedish. The Swedish labor market is more regulated and more difficult to enter compared with the British. And Sweden has higher taxes and in total more generous welfare benefits, which should make Sweden relatively less attractive than the United Kingdom for migrants who expect to earn well, yet relatively more attractive for those who expect a weaker position on the labor market (see Chapter 4 for this reasoning in more detail).

The evaluation also showed somewhat less positive results in Sweden compared with in the United Kingdom. In 2007, the average migrant from the new EU member states paid in approximately 2 percent more to Swedish public finances than they received. The net contribution was in other words very near zero.[27] A follow-up study of how these immigrants' income developments looked during their first 9–10 years in Sweden indicates that the net contribution will likely remain quite near zero also over these immigrants' entire time in Sweden, if they remain for life.[28]

These evaluations did away with the fears of large net costs for public finances due to the new EU migration. There were good reasons to claim that these fears were unwarranted already at the outset, and rather based on poor understanding of the regulations that were in place. (As described in Chapter 2, only those who have a job offer are allowed to migrate. Immigrants must first work and earn their own income in the country for a period before they become entitled to public income support.) But empirics are sometimes more convincing than logic.

How good can it get? However, although these studies may have answered a question that was quite unnecessary to ask from the start, there may be scope to obtain a more general and more interesting insight from their results. The primary interpretation of them so far has been as evidence of absence of bad outcomes. Yet what they might more interestingly provide today may in fact be evaluations of how good it can reasonably get (and thus—as we shall see—as evidence also of absence of great outcomes).

---

[26] Dustmann, Frattini and Halls (2010).
[27] Ruist (2014).
[28] Ruist (2017a).

As Western populations are aging many hope that it will be possible to counter some of the resulting burden on public finances with increased immigration. Several studies have explicitly attempted to investigate the scope for this. But these are all in the category of studies of the total immigrant population, or the average immigrant, in a country. Hence all they provide are evaluations of the consequences for public finances of allowing more immigration *that on average looks exactly like immigration into the country has done historically*. But this is not what we want to know. For example, in a country like Sweden, where a large share of historical immigration was of refugees, such evaluations will inevitably conclude that the more immigration Sweden allows in the future, the worse will be the outcomes for its public finances. Yet this conclusion is not useful for the question, because it does not say anything about the scope for strengthening public finances through an increase in certain more narrowly defined types of more productive labor immigration, perhaps in forms that did not even exist historically.

Hence what we really want is an assessment of the limits to how positive outcomes are possible. A good way to try to get to this would be to evaluate the consequences on public finances of the most productive and economically beneficial immigration that would reasonably be possible for a country to attract *on a large scale*. For example, calculating the consequences for public finances of the immigration of the average engineer on an H1-B visa in the United States would probably not be very informative. Those immigrants are too productive. There are obvious limits to how many more of them any country could reasonably attract (see further in Chapter 8). Hence although the average immigrant in this group obviously makes a greatly positive net contribution to public finances, it will hardly be possible to multiply that contribution per immigrant with a large enough number of future immigrants to make a real difference for public finances in total.

This is where the evaluations of the consequences of Eastern European migration become informative. These evaluations showed positive net contributions, yet these were small. And in this case, anyone who could get a job was already allowed to migrate, while those who could not were not. Hence this migration cannot be importantly scaled up further, unless receiving countries would do something like paying people to migrate (which obviously would not create a positive effect for public finances).

In other words, if it is to be possible to make a really significant positive impact on public finances through increased immigration, there needs to exist a large group of potential migrants somewhere outside of the Western world who are not allowed to immigrate today, yet who—if they were—would be on average significantly more productive than what these Eastern European immigrants in the United Kingdom and Sweden have been. It appears unlikely that such a group would exist. The Eastern European migrants in this case had considerable advantages with respect to their potential productivity in the receiving countries. They were quite highly educated and there was a high degree of linguistic and cultural similarity between their home and destination countries.

It thus appears reasonable to interpret the consequences of this migration for the receiving countries' public finances, as most likely a small exaggeration of how positive results per migrant would be possible to obtain at a large scale. And as the estimated positive effects per migrant were small, we should conclude that it will probably be difficult for a Western country to use more immigration as a means to make its public finances considerably stronger.

Refugees. As we saw in the previous chapter, and for reasons that are easy to understand, the immigrants who have the weakest labor market performance, and the highest dependence on public income support, tend to be refugees. Therefore, these are also those immigrants whose immigration we expect to have the most negative consequences for public finances. There have been a few empirical evaluations of the consequences of refugee immigration for public finances. They are all from the country that had the highest refugee immigration per capita in the latest decades, that is, from Sweden. This section is based on the latest and most detailed among these (which I wrote).[29]

The study uses data from 2015. In this year, people who had at some point immigrated as refugees or family members of refugees made up an estimated 7.0 percent of the Swedish population. They were underrepresented on the revenue side of public finances, paying an estimated 5.1 percent of revenues, while they were overrepresented on the cost side, being the target of an estimated 7.4 percent of costs. In total, their estimated net cost for public finances in 2015 amounted to kr.(kronor)41.5 billion (kr.10 ≈ €1), which corresponds quite exactly to 1 percent of Swedish GDP in the same year.

The study also estimates how annual net contributions to public finances from the average refugee who immigrated in 2015 are expected to develop over time. The results are shown in Figure 5.1.[30] It shows large negative net contributions from the average refugee during their first few years in Sweden, when we also saw in Figures 4.13 and 4.14 that refugees' average incomes

---

[29] Ruist (2020).

[30] Figure 5.1 is based on the Swedish version of the article (Ruist, 2018a). The English version (Ruist, 2020) shows different predictions for refugee groups with stronger and weaker historical labor market performances. The numbers in Figure 5.1 are given by taking the average between these two.

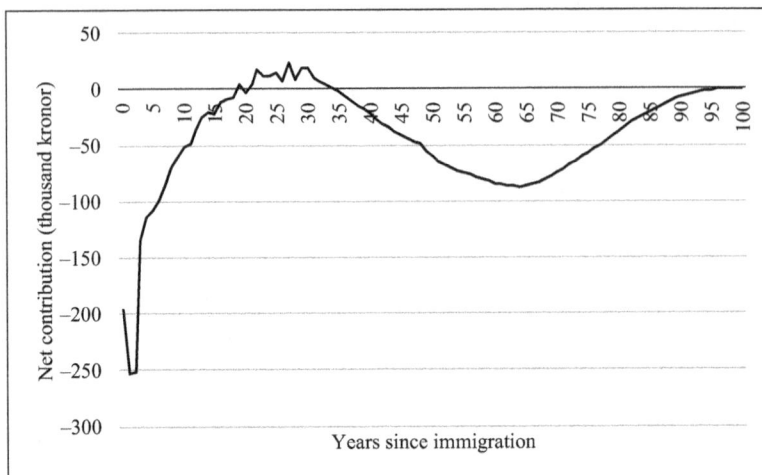

Figure 5.1 The average refugee's estimated net contribution to Swedish public finances per years since immigration.

are very low and when large resources are spent on education and integration programs for the newly arrived. As these programs are phased out after a few years, and as we saw steep income increases for refugees over time in Chapter 4, we also see in Figure 5.1 that the net cost for public finances decreases rapidly after the refugee's first few years in the country.

After approximately 20–35 years in the country, the annual net contributions of the average refugee are expected to be positive. But these will be far from large enough to cover the large deficits of the earlier years, and also those that are to come later, as larger shares of refugees reach old age. (Toward the end, the curve approaches zero as fewer will still be alive.)

Like other migrants, current refugee migrants are mostly young, and the average refugee immigrant who arrived in 2015 is expected to live for an additional 58 years in Sweden. If we distribute the total accumulated net cost from Figure 5.1 over those 58 years, the net cost of the average refugee will amount to kr.74,000 in the average year. This corresponds to 40 percent of the public sector's yearly revenues per capita, that is, it is a quite significant amount.

The study also uses some of its more detailed results to produce a rough estimate of what it would cost public finances in the EU to receive the entire international refugee population that existed in Asia and Africa in June 2018, that is, 13 million refugees. Doing this would increase the population of the EU by 2.5 percent. It would be expected to imply a net cost for public finances corresponding to not more than 0.6 percent of the total GDP of the EU per year, if we distribute it over the same 58 years as above. This is thus considerably below Sweden's estimated net cost of its entire refugee population in 2015, which was 1.0 percent of its GDP. If also the rest of the Western world contributed the cost would of course be even lower. In other words, its effect on public finances is not a very strong argument against higher refugee immigration.

However, as Figure 5.1 shows, this average over 58 years masks that the costs are considerably higher in the earliest years. Yet the recent Swedish experience shows that costs are indeed fully manageable also in a corresponding peak. A refugee immigration corresponding to 2.5 percent of the population is quite exactly what Sweden experienced in the four years 2014–17 together. Within these four years, Swedish refugee immigration rose gradually, and Figure 5.1 shows that the net cost for public finances is the highest in the years right after arrival. In other words, the net public cost of this immigration was most likely at its peak in the years 2016–18. And in spite of this, Swedish public finances made surpluses in each of these three years. Certainly, these surpluses could have been even larger if this high refugee immigration had not been. Yet the fact that surpluses were made at all shows that it is fully possible to manage the fiscal costs of refugee immigration of this magnitude also at their peak levels.

A more general version of the same point can also be made. Sweden has had higher refugee immigration than other countries for a long time, and by the end of 2017 more than 8 percent of the country's population was estimated to have once arrived as refugees.[31] The corresponding shares are far lower in most other European (or Western) countries, and would remain so even if other countries increased their shares by 2.5 percentage points, as in the example above. Certainly, this high accumulated refugee immigration has implied high accumulated net costs for Swedish public finances. Yet obviously, these have not been too high to prevent Sweden from having among the strongest public finances in Europe over the last 15–20 years.

Final words, public finances. The effects of immigration on a country's public finances look very different for different groups of immigrants. Some groups perform strongly on the labor market and have a positive impact on public finances. Others have weaker economic performance and bring net

---

[31] Ruist (2018a).

costs. Yet it seems to be difficult for these effects to become very large in either direction. The migrant groups that bring strong positive effects per capita can probably not grow large enough for their total effects to really matter at the aggregate level. The negative effect of the most costly type of immigration, that is, that of refugees, seems to have a potential to grow larger. Yet it has been shown to be at least fully manageable also at its historical peak levels, which were far higher than typical levels.

Chapter 6

CONSEQUENCES FOR SOCIAL COHESION

Humans have always lived together in societies: organized entities that are kept together and made functioning through formal rules and social codes. Throughout almost the entire history of our species, these societies have included a few tenths, or maybe hundreds, of individuals. Today, they have grown to include millions. This change has required new methods for keeping societies together, and for making all the people who constitute a society feel that they belong to and want to contribute to it although they know very few of its other members.

Different societies have had different degrees of success with this and in different ways. There are several theories about which factors are most conducive to success. Among these, two in particular may be affected by immigration: shared identity and perceived justice.

It is a quite basic psychological insight that shared identity is conducive to cohesion and collaboration. The more we recognize and can identify with in each other, the greater the feeling of solidarity with each other becomes and the more natural it feels that we are a unit that can or should work together for our common good, combining our strengths and sharing our risks.[1] When we speak about identity in this context, we often use the word *ethnicity*, which approximately denotes a common identity with which a group of people identify. (Ethnicity does not mean biological ancestry, although many of these group identities are to some extent founded on shared biological ancestry.) Closely related to this is the word *culture*, which we can define loosely as shared elements of worldview, attitudes and behaviors among a group of people. Common cultural elements are often important ingredients in strengthening the identification with an ethnicity.

The perception of justice in a society depends both on formal rules and institutions and on how these are implemented in practice. This is both about the *social contract*—that is, what society formally offers to its members and what

---

[1] Miller (1995).

it requires from them in return—being perceived as a decent deal, and about these formal rules being perceived as equal for all, and not undermined in practice, for example, by discrimination or corruption.[2]

It is also important for the perception of justice that economic inequality is not too big. Different people have different opinions on exactly what is "too big." However at some point, when too many—according to their own values—perceive the difference between rich and poor as too great, and the opportunities of the poor—or at least of their children—to one day become rich, as too small, it becomes difficult to create feelings among the rich and the poor that they belong together and want to work together for their common good. At that point, it may, for example, be perceived as morally justified for the poor to steal from the rich, the rich may isolate themselves, and politics may develop more toward a conflict between group interests with less room for prioritizing a common good.[3]

People are thus generally more content with the society in which they live, if its laws are fair on paper and in practice, if there is a certain degree of economic equality, and if they can easily identify with each other's values and behaviors. This tends to make society function better.[4] Migration has the potential to challenge these factors. It almost always increases the ethnic and cultural diversity, and most often also the economic inequality, in the receiving country. In addition, it often creates a connection between economic inequality and ethnicity, which may further harm different groups' feelings of belonging together.[5]

Immigration may also harm the feeling of a fair social contract. It may be perceived as unfair that immigrants are allowed to come and work while natives are unemployed, or that public resources that could have benefited natives are instead spent on immigrants. It may also be more difficult to make immigrants feel that they are part of a social contract that they were not themselves part in defining.

(At the same time, it should not be ruled out that immigration may in some instances have the potential to strengthen social cohesion. Solidarity with those who are weak is one of the main functions of modern societies. As it becomes more obvious that those in the most dire need of support from others

---

[2] Rothstein (2017).

[3] Rothstein and Uslaner (2005).

[4] For additional and deeper theoretical discussions and additional references, both to the factors discussed here and other factors that may be important for social cohesion, see Banting and Kymlicka (eds.) (2017), in particular the contributions from Miller (2017) and Hall (2017).

[5] Alesina, Michalopoulos and Papaioannou (2016).

are outside of rich countries' borders, these societies may be strengthened in their self-image and internal legitimacy if they do not only support the most needy within the country but also the globally most vulnerable. Such as by giving international aid or by allowing immigration.)

This chapter is about how immigration may affect social cohesion. First, I provide an overview of what the direct impact of immigration on economic inequality and cultural and ethnic diversity may be. Thereafter, I deal with the core question about how migration affects, or may affect, social cohesion, in the form of people's attitudes to each other and to the society in which they live. At the end, I present an account of people's attitudes to immigration itself, and the political mobilization of these attitudes.

Economic inequality

Most (not all) immigration increases economic inequality in the receiving country. In this section, I present some details on what the involved orders of magnitude may be. Like several times before I show some results from the United States, because it is the most important immigrant-receiving country, and some from Sweden, in this case because it is likely to be an informative extreme case and contrast to the United States.

The upper part of Table 6.1 shows the shares of the total population aged 20–64 years in the United States that in 2015 had no wage income, had positive pre-tax wage income below the median of US$36,000 and had positive

Table 6.1 Pre-tax wage income distribution in the United States 2015, ages 20–64 years

	Natives	**Central America and Caribbean**	**Other**
Share (percent) of group with			
no wage income	24.8	28.9	26.8
wage income < median	35.8	48.6	32.1
wage income ≥ median	39.4	22.5	41.0
Group's share (percent) of total			
all	81.3	8.5	10.3
with no wage income	79.5	9.7	10.9
with wage income < median	79.7	11.2	9.0
with wage income ≥ median	84.0	5.0	11.0

Source: Own calculations using data from the American Community Survey in 2016, from Ruggles et al. (2015).

income above the median. Each column thus, above rounding errors, sums to 100 percent. Separate shares are shown for natives and immigrants, and immigrants are further divided into those from Central America and the Caribbean, that is, a large immigrant group with particularly low average incomes—and others.

We see small differences between these three groups in the shares with no wage income. These shares only vary between 25 percent for natives and 29 percent for immigrants from Central America and the Caribbean. The shares with income below the median are more different. These are 32 and 36 percent, respectively, for natives and other immigrants, but 49 percent for immigrants from Central America and the Caribbean. In consequence, the latter group also has a considerably lower share than the others with wage income above the median.

Hence we can clearly see the economic inequality between the Central American and Caribbean immigrants and the other two groups. However, in spite of this, this large immigrant group has had a fairly marginal impact on total economic inequality in the United States. This is illustrated in the lower part of the table, which shows each group's share of the total population in the age interval, of the population with no wage income and of the populations with positive wage incomes below and above the median. Hence in this part, each row sums to 100 percent (above rounding errors).

We see that the Central American and Caribbean group comprises 8.5 percent of the population but 11.2 percent of the population with positive income below the median. From this we may calculate that the total number of people in the United States who earn less than US$36,000 is only slightly less than 3 percent higher than what it would have been if the income distribution of this immigrant group had been identical to that of the rest of the population.[6]

---

[6] Calculated as shares of the factual population with income below the factual median, the values on the row "with wage income < median" would then have been 79.7, 8.5 and 9.0, that is, they would have summed to 97.2 instead of 99.9 (100 minus rounding error). The factual number is thus (99.9–97.2)/97.2 = 2.8 percent higher than the nonfactual. The difference in total inequality looks even smaller if I instead calculate factual and nonfactual Gini coefficients. The factual Gini coefficient is 0.429, and only decreases to 0.427 if I remove all Central American and Caribbean immigrants from the calculation of it. The reason why the difference is so much smaller, even hardly noticeable, in this case is because the Gini coefficient is so strongly influenced by the few with the very highest incomes. It is thus more suitable as a measure of inequality between these and the rest of the population, than for measuring variation further down the income scale, like here.

Table 6.2 Pre-tax wage income distribution in the Sweden 2015, ages 20–64 years

	Natives	**Refugees**	**Other**
Share (percent) of group with			
no wage income	13.2	33.8	26.3
wage income < median	41.2	44.2	44.1
wage income ≥ median	45.6	22.0	29.6
Group's share (percent) of total			
all	80.6	9.4	10.0
with no wage income	64.6	19.4	16.0
with wage income < median	79.5	10.0	10.5
with wage income ≥ median	88.0	5.0	7.1

Source: Own calculations using Statistics Sweden's database Linda, 2015.

Hence the difference in income distributions between the Central American and Caribbean immigrants and the rest of the population clearly contributes to economic inequality in the country. Yet more importantly so by creating a visibly ethnically defined inequality than by its effect on total inequality in the country.

Similar results from Sweden in 2015 are shown in Table 6.2. In the Swedish case, the obvious large immigrant group with on average lower incomes is refugees. Hence results are shown separately for natives, refugees and other immigrants. As in the American case, around four-fifths of the total population in the age interval are natives, one-tenth belong to the immigrant group with lower average incomes and one-tenth are other immigrants.

In Sweden, we see the largest differences across the three groups between the shares with no wage income. Among natives, 13 percent belong to this group, yet a full 34 percent of all refugees do the same. Refugees are only marginally underrepresented at wage incomes below the median (kr. [kronor] 309,000) and in consequence considerably underrepresented at incomes above the median.

In the lower part of the table, we see an image of refugees' resulting contribution to total economic inequality in the country. We see that refugees comprise 9.4 percent of the population in the age interval but exactly 10 percentage points more—19.4 percent—of the population without wage income. Hence the total number of 20–64-year-old people without wage income in Sweden is around 11 percent higher than what it would have been if refugees would have had the same income distribution as the remaining population.[7]

---

[7] Calculated as shares of the factual population without wage income, the numbers on the row "with no wage income" would then have been 64.6, 9.4 and 16.0, that is, they

These two examples, from the United States and Sweden, have focused on two immigrant groups that comprise similar shares of the total population in the respective countries. The income distribution of the immigrant group deviated more from that of the remaining population, and hence also had a larger effect on total economic inequality, in the Swedish case. Furthermore, this Swedish example is likely to be *the* extreme case in the Western world in this respect, because of the country's higher refugee immigration per capita for several decades and to refugees' particularly weak labor market perform-ance in most or all countries (see Chapter 4). It is thus quite likely that the contribution of immigration to total economic inequality is smaller in all other countries. Yet common to most Western countries is the fact that immigration creates visible inequality between ethnic groups, which may easily contribute to creating a feeling of distance and difference between natives and certain groups of immigrants.[8]

Crime. Closely related to the lower average incomes in some immigrant groups is the higher prevalence of crime in the same groups. One example of this is shown in Figure 6.1, which shows the shares of different population groups in Denmark who were convicted of more serious crimes (including violent crimes, burglaries and sexual crimes) in 2016. Separate shares are shown by age group, sex and three categories of origin: natives with two native parents ("native"), immigrants from non-Western countries ("gen 1") and natives with at least one parent who was born in a non-Western country ("gen 2"). (These three groups do not sum to the total population as Western immigrants and their children are not shown.) Non-Western immigrants in Denmark are mostly refugees and their family members, and have consider-ably lower average income levels compared with natives.

The figure shows that among 20–24-year old men, that is, the category with the largest shares convicted of crime, this share was more than twice as high among non-Western immigrants as among natives with two native-born parents: 3.6 compared with 1.5 percent. Among natives with at least one non-Western immigrant parent the share was even higher: 5.7 per-cent. The crime rate decreased steadily with age in all groups of men, but the overrepresentations of non-Western immigrants and their children were similar in all age groups. The corresponding groups were overrepresented

---

would have summed to 90.0 instead of 100.0. The factual number is thus (100–90)/ 90 = 11 percent higher than the nonfactual. The Gini coefficient is 0.313 in the full sample, and 0.298 if the refugees are removed.

[8] Alesina, Michalopoulos and Papaioannou (2016).

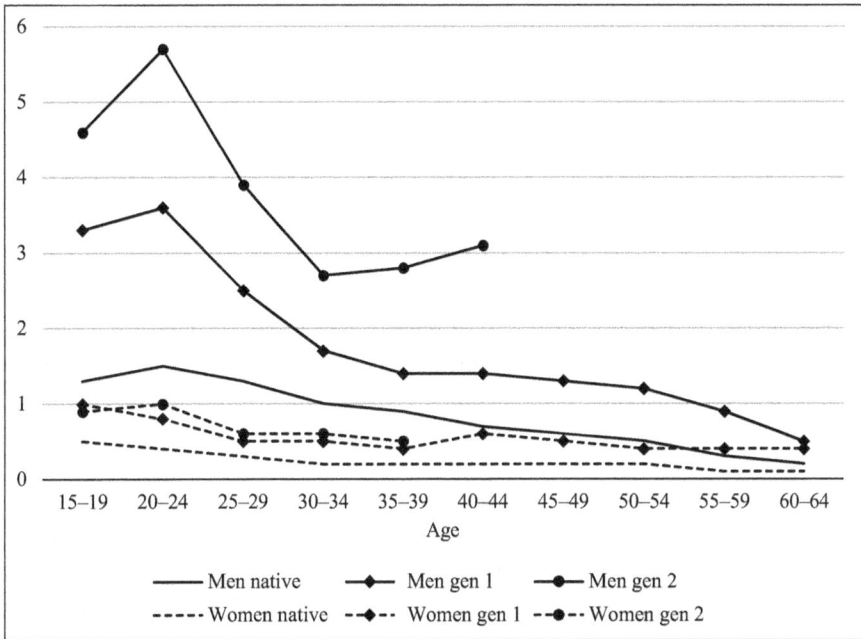

Figure 6.1 Shares (percent) of the total population in Denmark that were convicted of serious crimes in 2016, by age, sex and origin.

Source: Statistics Denmark (2018).

also in female crime rates but to a lesser extent. The total number of female criminals was also merely around one-third of the total number of male.

In total, non-Western immigrants and their children comprised around 8 percent of all men in the country but 23 percent of all men who were convicted of more serious crime. If the age-adjusted crime rate of all these men would have been only one-third as high, that is, approximately similar to that among native men with two native parents, the total number of men convicted of such crime would thus have been 15 percent lower. In other words, the overrepresentation of this group had a clearly visible effect on the total number of criminals in Denmark.

The overrepresentation of certain immigrant groups in crime statistics should not be surprising. Lower and less-secure socioeconomic status typically contributes to higher crime rates.[9] This is clearly seen among Denmark's refugee-dominated non-Western immigrant population. But even more

---

[9] Hällsten, Szulkin and Sarnecki (2013).

vulnerable, economically and most certainly also psychologically, are immigrants who live illegally in a country. A study of data from Italy in 2009 shows that such immigrants were strongly overrepresented among those arrested for serious crimes. Illegal immigrants were estimated to comprise around 2 percent of the total population residing in Italy, yet they made up a full 50 percent of those who were arrested for burglaries and 27 percent of those who were arrested for car theft. This major overrepresentation in theft of property is easy to understand, considering that these people lack legal means to earn their living in the country. Illegal work and theft are hence their only options. However, the precarious situation of the group is also visible in its comprising 17 percent of all those arrested for assault and 23 percent of all those arrested for murder.[10]

Unfortunately, there is no information on how many of those who were arrested were also in the end convicted. Hence we cannot say to what extent the numbers are inflated by any possible tendencies among the police to arrest illegal immigrants too often. But if the numbers are representative also for actual crimes committed, the conclusion becomes that illegal immigration has had a very considerable effect on the total prevalence of these serious crimes in the country.

Ethnic diversity

Immigration almost always brings increased ethnic and cultural diversity. In European countries that were virtually mono-ethnic before 1950, today between 5 and 15 percent of the populations were born outside of Europe (see Chapter 2) and a few additional percent are native-born with non-European parents. The United States, Canada, Australia and New Zealand have longer histories of more diversity, most of all in the form of people from different parts of Europe, and have during the last 50 years also received large populations of Asian or Latin American origins.

The diversity in ethnic identification and cultural expressions that is created by immigration may sometimes disappear quite quickly and some-times remain to a large extent for several generations. We talk about different paces of "assimilation," or "integration." Without going into the details on exactly how these terms may be defined, and what may differ between them, they approximately describe the process of a group of people becoming more similar to the rest of the population in the country in their culture and their identification. The word "assimilation" is probably somewhat more common

---

[10] Pinotti (2016).

in the United States and "integration" somewhat more common in Europe. Henceforth, I stick to the word integration.

It is not so simple to obtain a correct picture of the pace of integration among a group of immigrants and their descendants in a country. If one just looks around, the picture that one gets is often misleading, because those who are less integrated stand out considerably more than those who are more integrated. To obtain a more accurate picture one needs to study representative samples. But it is also difficult to make such formal studies capture what we want them to capture. Culture and ethnicity are complex and partly intangible phenomena, which are difficult to assess, for example, in surveys and interviews. We can capture small parts of them in surveys of, for example, what language people speak at home, how they answer questions about personal values, or their degrees of residential segregation from the rest of the population.[11]

However, what many researchers consider the "ultimate" measure of ethnic and cultural integration is the formation of couples and families.[12] The choice of a partner is so important to almost everybody, that we can expect whether a person chooses someone else from the same ethnic minority or not to convey useful information about the strength of their ethnic identification and culture. When a person from a minority chooses to have a family with someone from the majority population, we learn that these two individuals did not think of their difference in backgrounds as a too big obstacle for taking this life-defining step together. We also learn that the children of this minority person will likely grow up with strong influences from the majority culture at home and hence these children are likely to become strongly integrated even if the parent from the minority was not.

The scope for studying couple formation among actual first-generation immigrants is limited, because so many of these formed couples already before migrating. For third and later generations of immigrants, there are no representative enough data anywhere that could enable accurate studies. Hence studies of couple formation typically focus on second-generation immigrants, that is, native-born individuals with one or both parents born in a foreign country. Studies of second-generation immigrants with parents born outside of the Western world most often conclude that there has been a process of integration from the first generation to the second, but that also in the second there is still quite a long way to go to full integration. In other words, not

---

[11] For reviews and additional references, see Waters and Jiménez (2005), and Alba and Foner (2015).

[12] Waters and Jiménez (2005).

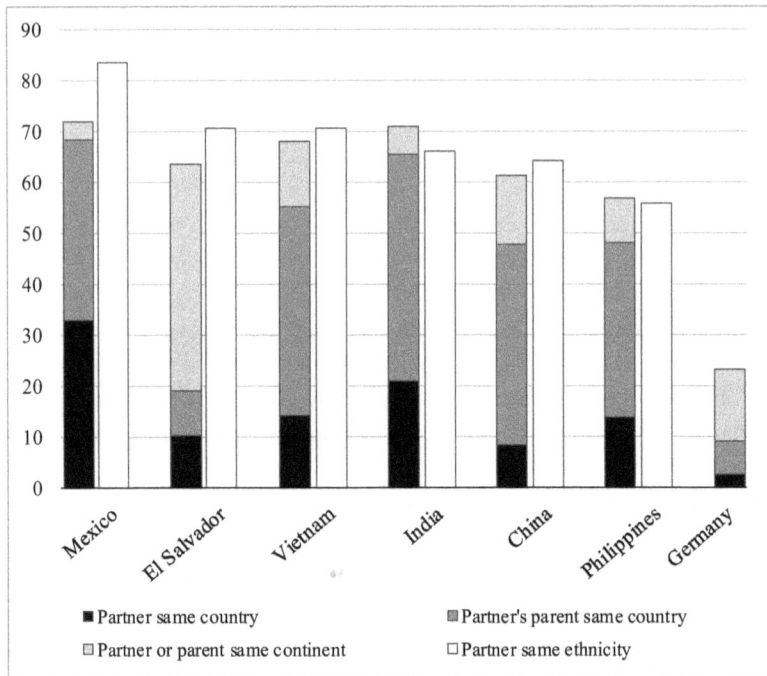

Figure 6.2 Percentage distribution of origins of partners of second-generation immigrants in the United States in 2009–18, by parents' country of origin.

Source: Own calculations using data from the Current Population Surveys in 2009–18, from Ruggles et al. (2015).

all but many second-generation immigrants form couples and families with people of origin similar to their own.[13]

An example of what the shares involved may look like is given in Figure 6.2. For native-born adults in the United States in 2009–18, who live together with a partner and whose both parents were born in the same foreign country, the figure shows information on the origin or ancestry of the partner. Information is shown for the six most numerically important countries of parents' origin, that is, Mexico, India, China, the Philippines, El Salvador and Vietnam. For comparison, information is shown also for Germany as an example of a country with a shorter cultural distance to the American majority population.

The stacked left bar for each country shows the shares that have a partner who was born in the same country as the person's own parents, the shares that have a native-born partner with at least one parent (in practice nearly always

---

[13] Waters and Jiménez (2005); Alba and Foner (2015).

both of them) who was born in the same country as the own parents, and finally the shares for which either the partner or at least one of the partner's parents was born on the same continent (Latin America/Caribbean, Asia and Europe, respectively) as the own parents.

The heights of these stacked left bars show that the majority of all six groups of second-generation immigrants of Latin American or Asian origin have formed couples with someone of ancestry similar to their own. The combined shares are also quite similar across the six groups: 57–72 percent. The internal distributions within the bars are more different, most of all between those of origin in Mexico and El Salvador. The native-born with Mexican parents had a partner of specifically Mexican origin in a full 68 percent of all cases, whereas only 19 percent of the native-born with Salvadorian parents had a partner of Salvadorian origin. On the other hand, a considerably higher share of the latter group had a partner of other Latin American origin. The difference may of course be easily explained by the fact that the group with Mexican parents is so much larger. Many of the partners of those with Salvadorian parents were also of Mexican origin.[14]

The picture looks very different for natives with two German-born parents. Only 23 percent have formed couples with someone who was, or had at least one parent who was, born in Europe, and only 9 percent have a partner of specifically German origin. This also looks similar for other Western European origins that are not shown in the figure. The difference from those of non-Western origins is most easily explained by the shorter cultural distance to the majority population in the United States. It cannot be easily explained by differences in income levels, as the median income in the group with German parents is lower than in all four groups with Asian parents, yet higher than in both groups with Latin American parents. We may also note how similar the patterns were in all the six non-Western groups in spite of their vastly different average income levels.

A limitation of the left bars is that they do not capture couple formation with third or later generations of immigrants from the same regions as the own parents. Therefore, the right bar for each non-Western country shows an alternative measure: the shares that have a partner who defines themselves as belonging to an ethnicity that matches the own parents' region of origin. These are "Hispanic" or "Asian," respectively.

These bars thus also capture partner formation with later generations of immigrants, to the extent that these still identify with the identity in question. As the bars representing India and the Philippines illustrate, they must not necessarily be higher than the left bars, as not all native-born with

---

[14] For similar results, discussion and additional references, see Alba and Foner (2015).

two Asian-born parents must necessarily identify as Asian. However for the two Latin American origins they are considerably higher, that is, indicating substantial couple formation also with later generations of immigrants. The Mexican bar in particular is very high: a full 84 percent of all native-born with two Mexican parents have formed couples with someone who defines themselves as Hispanic.

In Western Europe, it is particularly from two non-Western countries that immigration has been sufficiently high for long enough to enable studies of couple formation among adult second-generation immigrants: Turkey and Morocco. Results from a study of the origins of these people's partners are shown in Figure 6.3. The study was conducted among 18–35-year-olds in one or two of the largest cities in seven of the most numerically important receiving countries in Europe.

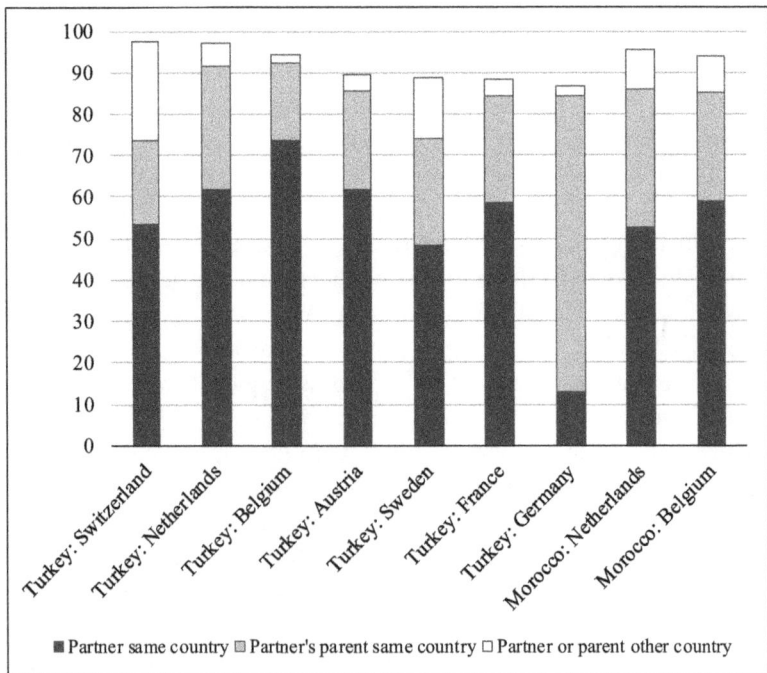

Figure 6.3 Percentage distribution of origins of partners of second-generation immigrants from Turkey or Morocco in Europe in 2007–8, by country of residence and parents' country of origin.

Source: Hamel et al. (2012).

We see, quite remarkably, that these two groups have formed couples with people of similar origins or ancestry to an even larger extent than the American groups that were shown before. The lower two fields in each bar show information that corresponds exactly to that in the lower two fields of the left bar for each country in Figure 6.2. That is the shares that have a partner who was born in the same country as the person's own parents, and the shares that have a native-born partner with at least one parent (in practice nearly always both of them) who was born in the same country as the own parents. The upper fields in Figure 6.3 show the shares for which either the partner or at least one of the partner's parents was born in any other foreign country. Hence the upper fields are not fully comparable between the two figures.

The sums of the heights of the two lower fields were 19–68 percent for the six groups of non-Western ancestries in the United States. But for these groups of Turkish and Moroccan ancestry in Western Europe they are consistently higher: 74–92 percent. The shares that have formed couples with native-born people with two native-born parents (i.e., 100 percent minus the total height of the bar) is in two cases even as low as 3 percent. Hence these results indicate very limited integration among the children of immigrants from Turkey and Morocco.

One could suspect that the limitation of this study to people who live in larger cities would create exaggerated results. As immigrants and their children on average live in larger cities more often than native-born with two native parents, it could be possible that nationally representative samples would have indicated somewhat higher integration. However in the case of the Netherlands, the results from another study that covered the country's entire population showed very similar results—both for those with Turkish-born and those with Moroccan-born parents.[15]

Out of the nine bars in Figure 6.3, eight also indicated very high shares, that is, 48–74 percent, with a partner who was born in the same country as the own parents. Presumably, many of these partners immigrated precisely for the sake of marriage, that is, second-generation immigrants found their partners abroad. The exception from this pattern is in the group of Turkish origin in Germany, where this share is only 13 percent, yet the share that formed couples with other native-born with Turkish-born parents is much higher. A simple explanation is that this is because the Turkish group in Germany is by far the largest among those that are studied here. Hence for these, the pool of people in the same country who share their ancestry is already high,

---

[15] Statistics Netherlands (2018).

meaning that it is less likely that they "need" to travel to Turkey to find suitable Turkish partners.[16]

Taken together, this overview of couple-formation patterns shows clear signs of slow cultural and ethnic integration for several major immigrant groups. The eight groups of second-generation immigrants of non-Western origins that were studied here were chosen for being the six largest in the United States and the two largest in Europe. The shares that formed couples with others of similar ancestry were higher than 50 percent in all eight groups, and much higher in several of them.

We could also see a clear difference in that integration in this respect appears to have been somewhat faster in the United States than in Europe. This result has been observed in several studies. There is no obvious explanation for it. The economic status of the two European groups is relatively low but in this they are only different from the Asian and not from the Latin American groups in the United States. A fairly popular explanation is that large shares of the two European groups are Muslims, which may—mutually—create less interest in partner formation with non-Muslim native Europeans. Another is that foreignness—although not necessarily more common per se—would be more socially normalized in the United States due to the country's longer immigration history. And hence that it would be less of a social obstacle to couple formation.[17]

Measuring integration more directly. The reason for studying couple formation here is that it serves as an indirect measure of cultural integration. By observing that ancestry has great importance for partner choice for so many second-generation immigrants, we may reasonably conclude that ancestry still plays a major role in defining the worldview and way of life for many of these people, although we cannot infer more about in exactly which ways.

Studying cultural expressions or integration more directly is more difficult, if we also want to maintain the requirement of representative samples and not fall into the trap of drawing conclusions from whatever is easiest to spot. Attempts to do this are therefore very rare. Yet I will make an attempt here to provide some more direct measures of how adult native-born children of Turkish or Moroccan parents in Europe position themselves between their parents and the majority cultures in the countries in

---

[16] Hamel et al. (2012).
[17] Alba and Foner (2015).

Table 6.3 Measures of cultural integration among immigrants and their native-born children in Belgium, the Netherlands, Germany and Austria, in 2012–16

	Foreign language (percent)	Religious	Traditional (percent)	Male employment (percent)	Female employment (percent)
Turkey gen 1	75	6.9	67	53	25
Turkey gen 2	41	6.3	62	81	54
Morocco gen 1	74	8.8	80	61	23
Morocco gen 2	16	7.8	85	71	56
Native gen 2+	1	3.5	39	83	76

Source: Own calculations using data from the European Social Surveys in 2012–16.

which they were born. I think this will have some value not least because the patterns are so stark.

Examples of traits that may roughly be described as more characteristic of Turkish and Moroccan than Western European cultures is that these place greater value on tradition and religion and have more distinct gender roles. With data from Germany, Austria, Belgium and the Netherlands, from the European Social Surveys in 2012–16, I shall try to describe how these cultural features have evolved from the first to the second generations of immigrants from Turkey and Morocco.[18]

Table 6.3 reports survey results for first- and second-generation immigrants from Turkey and Morocco, respectively, and for natives with two native-born parents. Specifically, the first generation ("gen 1") is made up of those who are older than 45 years and who immigrated before 1990. The second generation ("gen 2") is those who are 25–45 years old, and were born in the country where they reside, but have at least one parent who was born in Turkey or Morocco. The bottom row ("native gen 2+") represents 25–45-year-old native-born with two native-born parents.

The first column of Table 6.3 shows a less fluid measure of integration. It shows, for first- and second-generation immigrants, the shares (among those who live in a household of at least two persons) who do not speak one of the

---

[18] These four receiving countries were the numerically most important receiving countries of Turkish immigration from the 1950s to the 1970s. The three most important for immigration from Morocco were Belgium, the Netherlands and France. Individuals of Moroccan ancestry studied here almost all live in Belgium or the Netherlands. France is excluded from the analysis, because a considerable share of all immigrants from Morocco in this period were of French ancestry. The analysis does not use survey weights, as these are not suitable when multiple years are pooled.

country's traditional main languages (German, French, Dutch or Frisian) at home. Among first-generation immigrants we see that the vast majority, three-fourths, primarily speak a foreign language at home. We also see that this also applies to considerable shares of second-generation immigrants: a full 41 percent of those of Turkish origin speak a foreign language at home. Hence we may in turn also conclude that a significant share of the third generation of Turkish immigrants are raised in the Turkish language.

The table's second column focuses on religiosity. Its rather fluid measure is respondents' self-evaluation of "how religious" they are on a scale from 0 (not religious at all) to 10 (very religious). This survey question is of course far from perfect. But one may argue that it is equal for all, and that there should still be some valuable information in any differences between how different groups respond.

The values in this column appear to indicate very limited integration from the first to the second generation in terms of religiosity. The Turkish and Moroccan parent generations on average answered 6.9 and 8.8, respectively, on the religiosity question. The second generations give almost equally high answers, 6.3 and 7.8, while native-born of two native-born parents in the same age group on average answer as low as 3.5. In other words, the second generation appears to answer considerably more similar to their parents than to the similarly aged majority populations.

We see a similar pattern for the question of whether one sees oneself as a person who thinks traditions are important and who tries to live according to the customs learned from one's religion or one's family. The third column of the table shows the shares who responded that such a person "is like me" or "is very much like me." These shares are quite equally high among the first and second generations from each country, yet considerably lower among the native-born with native-born parents.

Gender roles are evaluated in the last two columns, through a comparison of employment rates (only for those below 65 years) among men and women. Here we see large gender gaps in employment among both first- and second-generation immigrants. Among native-born with at least one Turkish-born parent, the employment rate is almost 30 percentage points higher among men than among women. Among native-born with two native-born parents in the same age interval the corresponding difference is only 7 percentage points.

(Here it is well worth noting the difference from Figures 4.13 and 4.14. These figures showed an almost complete closing of gender income gaps in non-Western refugee groups in Sweden already in the first generation. This provides a strong hint that in the Swedish case there has also been more of integration with the majority culture's norm that work is – at least almost – as important for women as for men than what has been the case for the groups that are studied here.)

Although the measures that are reported in Table 6.3 are fairly rough, the results are quite stark. They appear to show quite clear signs of only limited cultural integration among second-generation immigrants of Turkish and Moroccan origin in Western Europe. As a rough summary of the results, this second generation in several ways appears more similar to their foreign-born parents than to the native-born majority populations.

Diversity and cohesion

Immigration thus tends to increase the ethnic and cultural diversity in a society, and often so for a long time. In other words, it often makes people in a society identify less with each other. There are several different mechanisms, which partly overlap, through which more diversity may potentially have negative effects on the cohesion and function of a society. If different groups have different values and priorities, it may be more difficult to reach agreements on laws and rules, public goods, welfare systems, etc.[19] If solidarity is felt primarily with one's own group, it may lead to conflicts between groups about how to distribute resources.[20] The nation or the state may be perceived of as less of a natural and logical unit for policy-making and solidarity.[21] Less mutual trust and understanding between people and between groups may imply less active engagement with society and its institutions, fewer social contacts and less activity in civic organizations, charity, etc.[22] It may also imply that people in different ways spend more time and money on protecting themselves and their interests from each other.[23]

How important these potential negative effects of ethnic diversity are in practice is difficult to investigate empirically. At one level, it may appear obvious beyond questioning that detrimental consequences may be very large. Armed conflicts between ethnic groups are common across the world, and countries with more ethnic diversity on average have more armed conflicts and lower economic wealth.[24] Several of the worst disasters in human history are labeled "genocides" and represent one ethnicity next to eradicating

---

[19] Alesina and La Ferrara (2005).
[20] Alesina and La Ferrara (2005).
[21] Miller (1995).
[22] Rothstein and Uslaner (2005).
[23] Alesina and La Ferrara (2005).
[24] Alesina and La Ferrara (2005).

another. Obviously, this would not have happened—at least not in exactly that form—if multiple ethnicities had not existed.

However, it is still not obvious what caused what. Do some societies have more conflicts because they have more ethnicities, or could it be that they have more ethnicities because they have, or used to have, more conflicts? Ethnicities are not cut in stone. They have evolved and changed through history. If two initially similar groups are separated for long enough they are likely to become—and to see themselves as—more different than before. If a conflict erupts between two groups, their ethnic identification is likely to be strengthened and they are likely to come to view each other as more different, or their differences as more important, than before. Correspondingly, if two groups that initially see themselves as different live together peacefully for a long time, cultural exchange, family formations between groups, etc. may erase the boundaries and make the two come to see themselves more as belonging to the same group.[25]

These processes may occur without anyone's active intent, or may be purposely influenced by policy. The creation of modern European (nation) states over the last few centuries contain several illustrations of this. To a large extent, their borders have been defined with high correspondence to pre-existing ethnical boundaries. But when they have not, rulers have in several cases worked actively to create a more common ethnic identification within the borders of a state. This has been, for example, by working to create a common language or by the creation of music or literature about true, invented, or at least exaggerated national historical challenges, achievements and heroes.[26] Similarly, ethnic differences may be intentionally mobilized and strengthened when it is in someone's interest to create a group of followers and an image of a common outside enemy.[27]

In other words, the extent of ethnic diversity in a country today may to an important degree be a result of the prevalence of conflict in the earlier history of the same geographic area. Hence the fact that countries with more ethnic diversity have more conflicts, less wealth and less cohesion must not necessarily be because the ethnic diversity caused less cohesion and more conflicts. It could also be the other way around.

More generally, ethnic identification and ethnic diversity are not exogenously given characteristics that have appeared out of nowhere. Each ethnicity,

---

[25] For a theoretical overview of how ethnicities form and change, see Ahlerup and Olsson (2012), or the more elaborate earlier version in Ahlerup and Olsson (2007).

[26] Miller (1995).

[27] Olzak (1983).

and each case of ethnic diversity, has its own history, where it was shaped by historical events and often also by rulers' and others' active intention to manipulate them.

Therefore, the methodological problems that we saw in the last chapter with providing trustworthy empirical estimates of the labor market consequences of immigration, are only the beginning of the corresponding problems when trying to pinpoint the consequences of ethnic diversity for any form of social cohesion or expression thereof. As was the case with that in immigration, the geographical variation in ethnic diversity is not exogenous. It looks the way it does for a reason (or many). But in addition to that, we cannot compare ethnic diversity in one place with ethnic diversity in another and accurately describe the difference between the two places as one where the two simply have different amounts of the same thing.

Concretely, if places A and B both receive immigrant inflows of 0.01 immigrants per capita, we may accurately describe the situation by saying that "immigration was equally high in both places." But if the population in place A consists of 80 percent ethnic group A1 and 20 percent ethnic group A2, while the population in place B consists of 80 percent ethnic group B1 and 20 percent ethnic group B2, we may be compromising a lot more on reality by thus simply concluding that "ethnic diversity is equally high in both places." The numbers alone do not reveal whether A1 and A2 are almost superfluous ethnic labels that not many people care much about while B1 and B2 have been arch enemies for a thousand years. They do not reveal how the ethnic diversity is interpreted in public discussions and in people's minds.

Furthermore, it may not be appropriate to attempt to identify deterministic causal effects on an outcome variable that plays out in people's minds. Circumstances always influence our reactions, but we also have much power to influence them with our free will. When we encounter an obstacle, we can to a non-negligible extent decide to focus on it as a problem or to shrug our shoulders and think that this cannot be so bad. Hence even if we can identify historical patterns in which some reactions are the most common to a phenomenon this may not be a valuable prediction of what the reaction will be next time around, in the same way as, for example, a historical pattern in how wages respond to immigration is likely to also be a good prediction of how they will respond next time.

Finally, empirical studies on the subject are also made difficult by our limited ability to measure the rather fluid outcome variable social cohesion, beyond the case where it deteriorates into the extreme, that is, into violent conflict, which is quite easily observed and measured. The best we can do is to measure limited aspects or expressions of cohesion, which tend to involve a great deal of simplification. The most popular empirical measures in research on cohesion are the share of people who respond in surveys that "most people can be trusted," measures of active civic engagement in associations or charities, the share of people who express their support for financial redistribution through the welfare sector, or measures of factual such redistribution, or spending on public goods such as roads, schools, hospitals, etc.[28] For any of these, it may be discussed at length (and has been—most often inconclusively) what it really measures. And one may indeed get the feeling that each of them mostly misses the point.

For all the reasons just mentioned, it is doubtful whether there is much reason to use formal quantitative empirical studies to learn about the relations between ethnic diversity and social cohesion. However, a large literature exists that tries to do just that. I will present a brief review of this literature here, before concluding that for the purposes of the present book, perhaps we can learn more from a more casual look at the world.

Some empirical studies compare levels of ethnic diversity across countries and relate these to various measures of social cohesion, conflicts or economic wealth. Yet recognizing the just-mentioned inherent problems in this, the most common strategy in this research field has instead been to focus on variation within rather than across countries. This should take away some of the problems relating to the fact that ethnic diversity in different countries are not really suitable for comparing with each other. In contrast, whatever the history of understanding or conflict between the two specific ethnic groups A1 and A2 in country A, it is in most (though not all) cases quite similar in different parts of that country. The stories and interpretations of ethnic relations often to a large extent play out at the national level and should thus, in most cases, not to a large extent bother comparisons within a country.

Hence these studies relate the local variation in ethnic diversity across different parts of a country to the similarly local variation in measures of social cohesion. Yet while this strategy may do away with one problem, it does not get to the problem that this local variation is also not exogenous but exists for a reason. It also runs the risk of missing the point. The very fact that ethnic relations are often mostly interpreted at the national level, leaves some doubt about whether we should expect the degree of *local* ethnic diversity to have a major impact on cohesion, or to be what people care most about. Or

---

[28] Alesina and La Ferrara (2005).

if it is predominantly the level of diversity at the national level that matters to people.

This empirical literature has also not delivered any firm conclusions. An overview from 2014 of (among other things) 71 studies of correlations between local ethnic diversity and social cohesion within countries roughly summarizes the findings as 22 studies identifying negative relations, 14 not doing it and 35 having mixed or unclear results.[29]

The same review also shows that negative correlations are identified considerably more often in studies that use local variation within the United States (10 out of 20 studies) than in studies that use local variation in any other country (12 out of 51 studies). This may serve as a good illustration of several of the problems mentioned, because the main component of the ethnic diversity that is studied in the United States is that between whites and blacks. The finding that a negative correlation is more often observed in the United States than in other countries thus illustrates the point that ethnic diversity is not the same thing everywhere. We know very well that white–black relations in the United States are among the most conflictual cases of ethnic relations in the recent history of the Western world. It thus appears unfair to draw conclusions from that particular case about how ethnic relations work in general.

Secondly, in this case, we have good knowledge about how nonrandom or non-exogenous the variation in ethnic diversity across the country is. It is to a large extent determined by where there was more demand for slave labor in the eighteenth and nineteenth centuries, as also today blacks in the United States mostly live in the parts of the country to which their ancestors were taken as slaves. Hence it appears potentially quite unfair to ascribe any lower social cohesion in these areas to ethnic diversity as such, rather than to the legacy of the institution of slavery.[30]

Third, related to this, in this particular case we know well that there is much variation within the country in how ethnic relations are publicly and privately interpreted, in particular, between the North and the South. Hence comparing these parts of the big country becomes quite like comparing multiple countries anyway. We said that the interpretation of ethnic relations should be

---

[29] Van der Meer and Tolsma (2014). This review also covers studies that compare countries. Earlier influential reviews are Alesina and La Ferrara (2005), and Stichnoth and Van der Straeten (2013).

[30] Acemoglu and Robinson (2012) make the related point that economic development in the former slave states did not start to converge toward those in the rest of the country before the laws and institutions that discriminated strongly against blacks were dismantled in the late 1960s.

quite similar in all parts of a country in *most* cases. White–black relations in the United States may be the best-known exception.

In sum, while there has been a lot of empirical research on ethnic diversity and social cohesion in general, it does not appear to be able to teach us very much. However, as this is a book about the consequences of migration, our primary interest here is not so much in this relation in general, as in the consequences of the often fast and large increases in ethnic diversity that have been brought about through immigration in many Western countries. In this regard, I wish to conclude with a more casual observation that I think should be at least somewhat informative on what the orders of magnitude have been so far.

History contains several examples of short or long periods of high immigration. The United States, Canada and Australia were populated by migrants in the second half of the nineteenth and beginning of the twentieth centuries. In the richest Western countries today, around 8–17 percent of the populations were born in non-Western countries (see Figure 2.5). In Sweden, 8–9 percent are refugees, which has also not least implied a noticeable increase in economic inequality and fiscal costs in the country. Most of these high percentages have been reached within less than a human lifetime. Many who live in Western Europe today were born when most of the region had virtually no non-Western immigrants at all.

I think it bears noting that these countries are still, by and large, the countries of the world where social cohesion appears to be stronger than anywhere else, with well-functioning institutions, broad support for welfare sectors and high levels of interpersonal trust. Plausibly, in certain ways social cohesion in these countries might have been even stronger if their high non-Western, or specifically refugee immigration had not been. But considering how high it still is, it appears difficult to imagine that the difference could have been huge. (Perhaps this also adds some support to the idea that some generosity toward the less well-off outside world is almost *necessary* for a society and a welfare state to maintain its high cohesion and legitimacy.)

The only example of a similarly rich country that has chosen an entirely different path with regards to allowing immigration and ethnic diversity would be Japan, which has largely barred immigration for a long time. This choice was of course not exogenous either. Yet one may still note that there is no obvious way in which its lower immigration has kept Japan far more cohesive or well functioning than countries like Australia, Canada or Sweden, which have in different ways stood out by accepting particularly high levels of new diversity.

Yet in spite of this conclusion, I set out and motivated this book by stating that immigration has had profound effects on Western societies in recent years, being a major contributing factor behind far-reaching political events that have shaken the Western world and its political landscape, that is, the European refugee crisis, the Brexit vote and the election of Donald Trump for president of the United States. Immigration appears to have contributed to a political polarization that in this sense certainly appears to have damaged the level of cohesion in these societies to a non-marginal extent.

Yet there is a crucial distinction to be made here. These three are not examples of immigration contributing to a polarization of society by increasing its diversity, as much as they are examples of (among other things, in the Brexit and Trump cases) cases of polarization over immigration *policy*. These are different things. The first is about the consequences of what society has become, and the second about defining the policies that will shape what it will look like in the future.

To see the difference, one can imagine that the supply of migrants would disappear. All refugee-producing wars would end, all Eastern Europeans would declare their unwillingness to move to the United Kingdom, all Mexicans declare their unwillingness to move to the United States and so on. This would imply the immediate end of all political polarization over how much immigration to allow and by what means. Yet it would have zero impact on current levels of ethnic diversity in Europe, or the United Kingdom or the United States.

Hence, from a casual look at the world, there is no obvious example of immigration increasing ethnic diversity to a point where social cohesion importantly breaks down. But there seem to be several obvious examples of at least some form of cohesion being importantly damaged by profound disagreements and many people's worries over immigration policy. In short, the most profound effects of all of high immigration on the receiving Western societies seem to be those on attitudes on immigration policy in these societies. Therefore, the rest of this chapter is devoted to these attitudes.

Attitudes on immigration policy

Again, immigration is polarizing. Many feel strongly for giving others the possibility to migrate, to allow them a chance to improve their standards of living or to escape from war or persecution. Yet many others are strongly against this. Immigration policy has a delicate balancing act to perform between these. In Western countries in recent decades, it has quite consistently performed it leaning toward the more generous part of the spectrum of attitudes in the populations. Irrespectively of when and in which country attitude surveys have been conducted, they have almost always shown that the population share that thinks immigration is too high is larger—often many times larger—than that which thinks it should be higher.

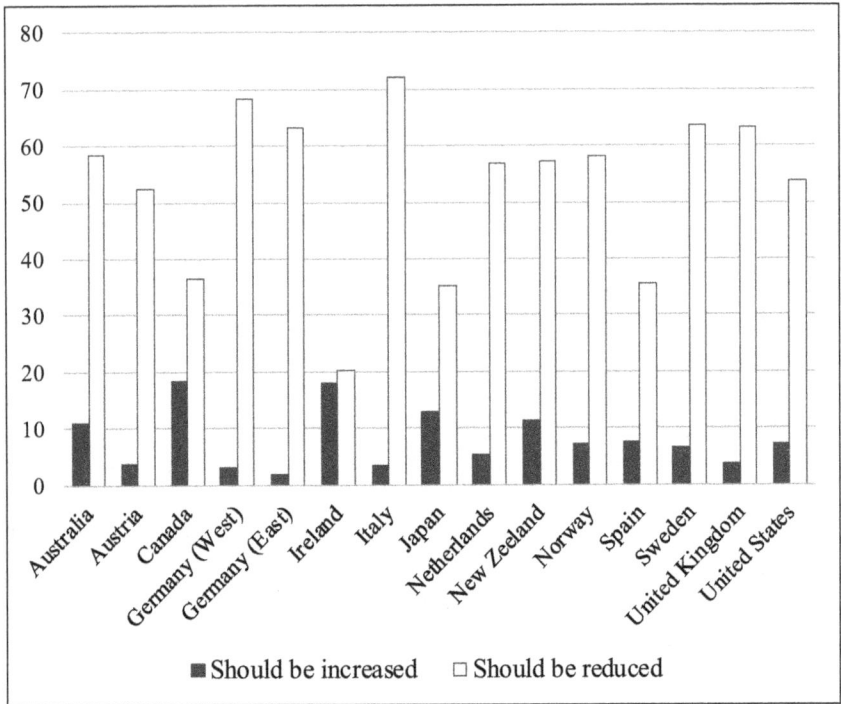

Figure 6.4 Respondent shares (percent) by country in 1995 who thought immigration to their country should be increased and reduced, respectively.

Source: Own calculations using data from the International Social Survey Program in 1995.

Two snapshots from the International Social Survey Program (ISSP) illustrate this well. First in 1995, people in many countries were asked in this survey whether they thought immigration to their country should be increased, reduced or remain the same as it was. Figure 6.4 shows the shares in the Western countries that participated in that year that preferred increases or reductions. We see that the response "should be reduced" was more common than "should be increased" in all these countries, and with a large margin in all of them except Ireland (where at the time immigration was so low it could not be reduced much further—a big difference from what has been the case in the country since). In five out of fifteen countries, "should be reduced" was even more than ten times as prevalent as "should be increased."

Hence in 1995, if Western governments would have substantially reduced immigration, the share of their voters that would have been pleased would most likely have been bigger than the share that would have been displeased. But overall, they did not do this. Immigration policy did not generally become

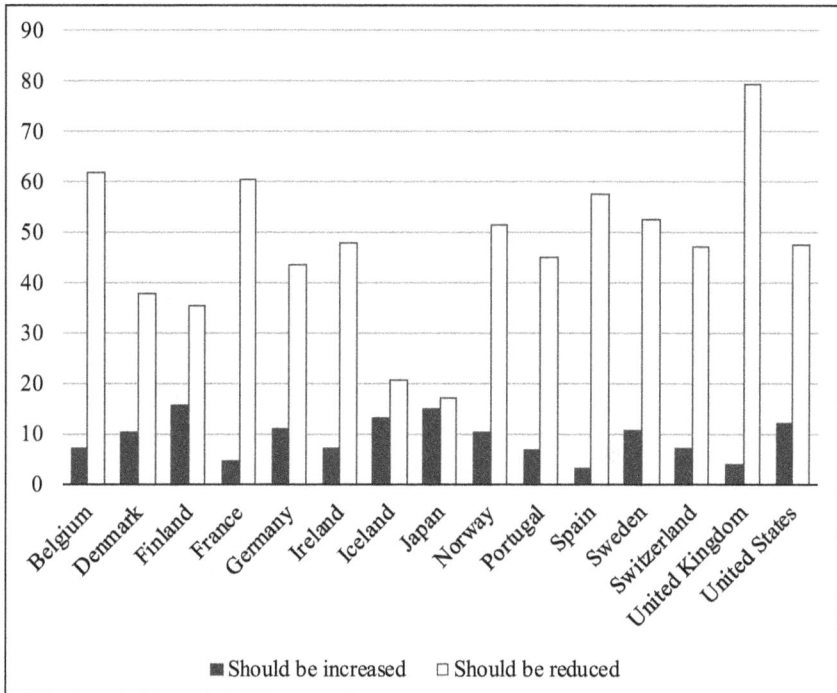

Figure 6.5 Respondent shares (percent) by country in 2013 who thought immigration to their country should be increased and reduced, respectively.

Source: Own calculations using data from the International Social Survey Program in 2013.

less generous over the following decades. And ISSP surveys continued to show similarly unbalanced opinions in the populations. The corresponding results from the latest survey in 2013 (i.e., before the European refugee crisis, at a time when immigration policy discussions in Western Europe were still mostly about immigration from Eastern Europe) are shown in Figure 6.5 (the sample of participating Western countries were partly different in these two years). The pattern looks very much like that in 1995, with similarly large dominance of the willingness to reduce immigration over that to increase it (and with the United Kingdom standing out in an illustration of its special take on immigration from Eastern Europe).

Two lessons can be learned from these patterns. First, across the West, political leaders have for a long time chosen more generous immigration policies than what most of their voters appear to have preferred. Second, and no less important, for a long time they have gotten away with it. The preference for more restrictive immigration policy that has consistently been observed in surveys has to a large extent been mostly latent. People have responded in surveys that they would prefer change yet they have in most situations not strongly demanded it. They have not ousted their immigration-friendly governments to put most restrictive ones in place. Populations did not become more content with policies between 1995 and 2013.

Smaller population shares have tried hard to demand change. Political parties with reducing immigration as the dominant item on their political agendas have sprung up, and gained parliamentary seats, in most Western countries. Yet these parties have mostly been kept from formal influence, and even when they have been given some formal influence actual immigration policy has remained at least mostly the same.[31]

It is thus clear that not completely adhering to the popular will "worked" for a long time. Yet one also easily understands that there was some instability in this situation and that there existed a potential for change if the circumstances changed on the ground. Anti-immigration parties received consistent and sometimes really high electoral support. In several cases they would probably also have received considerably more support for longer periods if they had not imploded due to factional infighting. Most of the populations appear to have had at least a weak preference for reducing immigration. And smaller parts of them also seem to have preferred vast reductions. In the European Social Survey, respondents have consistently been asked to what extent they think people from poorer countries outside of Europe should be allowed to come and live in their country. One of the four possible answers have been the extreme "none" (the other three have been the more blurred and language-sensitive "few," "some" and "many"). Generally, significant population shares have chosen this extreme response alternative. The shares who did so in 2012 (i.e., the last survey year before European refugee immigration increased substantially) are shown in Figure 6.6. Among Western European countries, they range from as little as 1.5 percent in Sweden to 22 percent in the United Kingdom.

The figure also includes Eastern European countries, to give an illustration of the large general difference in attitudes to immigration between Eastern

---

[31] Denmark presents a quite interesting example, where a political party—Dansk Folkeparti—that is strongly hostile to immigration has had formal political influence most of the time since the early 2000s. This has led to visible, but to a large extent mostly symbolic, changes to the country's immigration policy. We see in Figure 6.5 that the population share that preferred reduced immigration was still much higher than that which preferred an increase in 2013 also in Denmark. Yet the share that was quite content with the present level (100 percent minus the combined height of the two bars) was also as high as 50 percent, that is, higher than in all other countries in the figure except three that had very low immigration at the time.

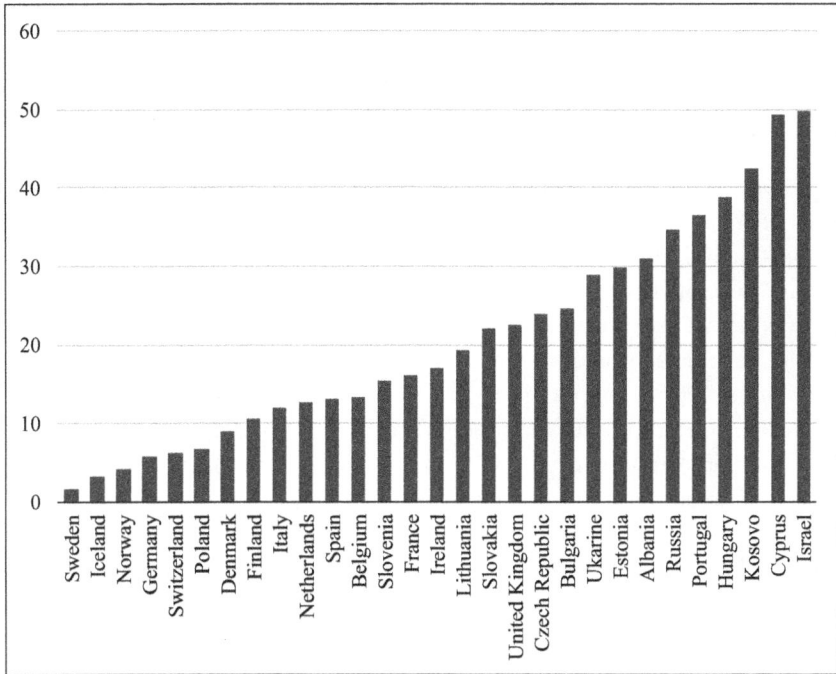

Figure 6.6 Respondent shares (percent) by country in 2012 who thought their country should have no immigration at all from poorer countries outside of Europe.

Source: Own calculations using data from the European Social Survey in 2012.

and Western European countries. The shares preferring no immigration at all from poorer countries outside of Europe are generally very high in the East. Before the refugee crisis, this vast opposition to immigration in these countries was not very high on their political agendas as their immigration was typically very low. But when this changed with the inflow of refugees a few years later, the populations in these countries responded with much outrage, which is not surprising given what their attitudes seem to have been already when they had almost no such immigration.

Exactly when and how resistance to immigration is mobilized into a more important political force is obviously complicated, and seems to look quite different in different cases, depending on the circumstances of the particular case and the particular mobilizing political party or movement. Over the last decades, electoral support for anti-immigration parties across Europe has risen and fallen in ways that have often not been possible to explain by simple

factors such as changes in immigration patterns or people's attitudes to immigration. Put simply, *mobilization skills* seem to have mattered much in many
cases. Sometimes in the form of a single charismatic leader who has succeeded
in interpreting the current public mood and hit the "right" strings at the right
time, and without whom the party has later been shown not to be able to
mobilize many voters. In short, there has been much variation in the degree
of political mobilization of resistance to immigration, which has been difficult
to explain and summarize in general patterns beyond the case specific.

However, the European refugee crisis in 2015 was a profound enough event
to provide an exception. In a short time, limiting or reducing immigration
rose to become a very important political priority for many European voters.
Traditional parties reacted and sharpened their messages and policies, and
electoral support for anti-immigration parties increased across the continent.
For example, support for the German Alternative für Deutschland almost
tripled between the Bundestag elections in 2013, when they received 4.7 percent of all votes, and 2017, when they received 12.6 percent. Candidates from
the Freedom Party (FPÖ) and Front National finished second in the presiden-
tial elections in Austria in 2016 and France in 2017. In Italy, the Five Star
Movement and the League together received more than half the seats in both
chambers of parliament in 2018.

Considering how broad this increase in the support for anti-immigration
parties and restrictive policies has been, it is difficult to deny that the refugee
crisis must have been a major contributing factor. Yet again, as I emphasized
in Chapter 2, to understand why and how it did so one must probably look
beyond the size of the inflow. Refugee immigration in the EU in the peak year
2016 corresponded to only 0.14 percent of its population. Refugee immigration
in 2008–16 combined corresponded to no more than 0.37 percent. This is not
high immigration by any reasonable standard. On the other hand, the refugee
crisis stands out in that it showed European populations how unable the continent was to control its refugee immigration, creating uncertainty about future
inflows.

If this significant lack of control is a major part of the explanation for the
European people's powerful reaction to this event, one should also be careful
with the labeling of this reaction. It is not necessarily correct to say that the
refugee crisis has made Europeans "more negative to immigration." Maybe
it has only made them care more about effectively controlling immigration.
Their preferred levels of immigration have not necessarily decreased. It may
be only that, after seeing what was possible in 2015, they now increasingly
think that stricter policies are needed to ensure that actual immigration does
not rise above those preferred levels.

We can observe something in attitude surveys that can be interpreted in
this direction. Figure 6.7 shows, for the 13 Western European countries that

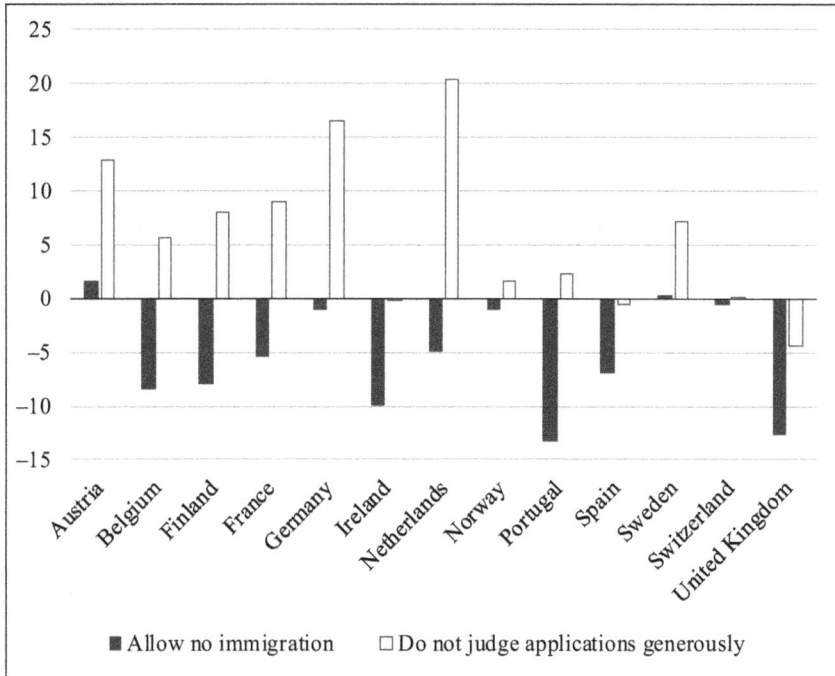

Figure 6.7 Changes in percentage points 2014–16 in respondent shares who think no immigration should be allowed from poorer countries outside of Europe, and that the government should not be generous in judging people's applications for refugee status.

Source: Own calculations using data from the European Social Surveys in 2014 and 2016.

took part in the European Social Survey in both the autumn of 2014 and the autumn of 2016, that is, one year before and one year after the most intense phase of the refugee crisis, how two different immigration-related attitudes changed over the period in between. One attitude is the same as that studied in Figure 6.6, that is, the preference for no immigration at all from poorer countries outside of Europe. The second is specifically about refugee policy. It measures the shares responding that they "disagree" or "disagree strongly" with the statement that "the government should be generous in judging people's applications for refugee status."

The figure shows the changes in percentage points in 2014–16, by country, in the shares giving each of these two responses. And it shows completely opposite trends for the two. The shares who did not think applications should be judged generously increased considerably over these two years, illustrating the increase in the preference for stricter refugee immigration policies. Yet among the same individuals, the attitude that no immigration at all should be allowed from poorer countries outside of Europe became considerably *less* prevalent over the same time period. Possibly, we might even dare to interpret also this as an impact of the refugee crisis. Perhaps this new situation opened the eyes of many Europeans to the needs of the world's refugees, and increased the prevalence of the attitude that at least some of them should be allowed to come to Europe. Yet at the same time, the same events showed that existing policies may create uncontrolled inflows, and hence increased the support for more restrictive policies.

This is a possible interpretation, although it is not obvious that it is true. However, whether one finds it plausible or not, a more unambiguous lesson from Figure 6.7 is that we should not say that European populations have become unambiguously "more negative to immigration" after the refugee crisis. The picture appears to be more multifaceted than that.

Final words

Immigration to the Western world almost always brings increased ethnic and cultural diversity, and so for a long time. It also often brings increased economic inequality and prevalence of crime. These features may potentially reduce social cohesion in receiving societies, and in turn the functioning of these societies.

Formal empirical research has not provided any good answers to how important such effects are, or have normally been. Yet a casual look around the Western world appears to indicate that they have at least not been all too large thus far. Several countries have had high immigration, and have gone from being almost mono-ethnic to having large population shares born in other continents over merely a few decades. These countries still deserve being labeled as at least as cohesive and well functioning as any other on the planet. Quite likely their cohesion has been to some extent negatively affected by high immigration, yet it appears not so to a very large extent.

In any case, resistance to immigration is widespread in the West. Popular support for less immigration is almost always higher, and often very much higher, than support for more immigration. In that sense, immigration always exists at voters' mercy. If it grows too high, or is perceived as being too much out of control (and hence potentially too high in the future), reducing it, or at least bringing it under control, may become an important political priority for many voters. To what extent Western countries succeed in controlling immigration, and showing their populations that they do so, therefore appears very important for their future development. Whether and how this may be possible will be discussed in Chapter 8.

Chapter 7

CONSEQUENCES FOR POORER SENDING COUNTRIES

This book is mostly about how migration from the rest of the world to the West impacts on the countries that receive the migrants. The policy decisions that directly influence this migration are mainly taken in the receiving countries. Hence, they are most strongly influenced by information about the impact of migration on those, and therefore this is also what the book primarily aims to discuss. However, migration may also have important consequences for the—most often poorer—countries that migrants leave. It may offer a potential route to economic development, through the opportunities it provides for the migrants themselves, through the money these remit to their relatives, and perhaps also by helping to create networks and integrate the home countries into the global economy. On the other hand, emigration might also in some cases be an obstacle to development, because talented and educated individuals that poor countries may sorely need for their own development leave them. This chapter discusses these aspects of this migration.

The most obvious and sizeable economic effect of migration from the rest of the world to the West is the income effect it has for the migrants themselves. There exist a few studies of their magnitude. (Notably, we do not learn much about them by simply studying average incomes in sending and receiving countries, because migrants' and others' average incomes may be very different in both these places.) In one of these, immigrants who had obtained permanent residence permits in the United States in the summer of 1996 were asked a few months later about their current income and about their income at the last employment they had before migrating. The purchasing-power adjusted annual incomes of these migrants (whereof 70 percent were from Latin America and Asia) were on average around US$10,000 (or 68 percent) higher after comparing with before migration for men and US$6,000 (or 62 percent) higher for women. Again, differences were large across different migrant groups. For men who immigrated on employment visas, the average increase in annual income was US$27,000. At the same time 28 percent of men and 27 percent of women earned less in the United States than what they had done at their last job abroad.[1] Notably, all these numbers only capture income changes over a relatively short time. On average, the immigrants in the study had been in the United States for around three years. As we saw in Chapter 4, many migrants who have been in a receiving country for such a short period of time have large further income increases ahead of them.

Another study followed migrants from Tonga, who had won residence permits in New Zealand's annual lottery of 650 such permits to people from Fiji, Tonga, Kiribati and Tuvalu. Shortly after immigration (14 months at the median) these migrants earned on average the equivalent of approximately US$200 (or 263 percent) more per week (which translates to US$10,000 per year, that is, quite similar to in the previous study) than other Tongans who participated in the same lottery, but lost, and were thus still in Tonga.[2] Also these migrants were likely to have further large increases ahead of them.

We may use these numbers to produce a very rough estimate of the total income effect that has been realized by the migration of all currently living migrants from the rest of the world to the West. If the average migrant already shortly after migration had increased their annual income by around US$10,000, it seems quite reasonable to assume that the average across all living migrants in the West would be an increase of US$15,000 compared to what they would have earned per year if they had stayed in the home country. (For comparison, we saw in the last chapter that the median annual labor income in the United States in 2015 among those with positive labor income was US$36,000.) Multiplying this number with 90 million migrants we obtain an estimated total income increase of almost one and a half trillion dollars per year. That is approximately the equivalent of the GDP of Canada (which has 37 million inhabitants).

This is of course a very rough number with a large error margin. Yet I think it is useful for giving a sense of orders of magnitude. It may, for example, be compared with the annual flow of international aid to low- and middle-income countries, which was around US$140 billion in 2016.[3] This comparison thus indicates that people who were born in low- and middle-income countries on average earn a full 10 times more per year because some of them have migrated to Western countries, than what they receive in aid

---

[1] Jasso et al. (2000).

[2] McKenzie, Gibson and Stillman (2010). Also these "randomly" chosen migrants are far from a representative sample of the total population of their home country. Also after winning the lottery, only those with a job offer in New Zealand are allowed to migrate. And while still living in Tonga, the future migrants who were followed in the study earned on average almost twice as much as the rest of the population in the country.

[3] Source: OECD. The total official aid flow was US$158 billion, whereof 15 billion were used for costs relating to refugee immigration in donor countries.

from mostly the same countries.[4] And furthermore they do this with the additional advantage that this money was not transferred from the populations of Western countries. Instead it corresponds to an increase in global GDP. (This follows from the conclusion in Chapter 5 that migration does not have a long-term impact on average wages—and hence on worker productivity—in the receiving countries.)

However, one easily obtains a misleading picture by calculating an average over something that is very unevenly distributed. And this large income gain from migration is indeed very unevenly distributed over the populations of the sending countries. It accrues entirely to the small minority of about one and a half percent who are the migrants. These, furthermore, are more often from middle-income countries than from the low-income countries that receive most of global aid (see Figure 3.2). And they also more often come from the wealthier strata within countries.

The distribution of the total migration-associated income increase becomes at least somewhat more even though, if we also consider that many migrants share part of their income in the form of *remittances*, that is, money that they send to others—almost always relatives—in their home countries. Most of this chapter is about these remittances: their size, who sends them, who receives them and some about how they are used. This is followed by a short section on the presumed negative consequences of the emigration of highly educated people from poorer countries, that is, what is commonly labeled *brain drain*.

Remittances

Migrants' remittances have received much positive attention in the last 10–20 years. It is popular to report how sizeable they are and how much they have grown over only a few decades. The numbers that are then reported are those that are based on the estimates of the World Bank. These say that the total value of all remittances worldwide in 2016 was US$570 billion, whereof US$410 billion flowed to low- and middle-income countries. Hence, according to the often-made comparison based on these estimates, these countries received around three times as much in remittances as they did in international aid. Which is an important increase from 20 years earlier when the two flows were estimated to be approximately equally large.[5]

It is unfortunate though that these estimates have been published and so often repeated. Because in reality, we know little about the magnitudes, and

---

[4] For more elaboration on measuring income development over people who were born in a country, instead of over people (still) living in it, see Clemens and Pritchett (2008).

[5] Source: World Development Indicators, the World Bank.

even less about changes over time in international remittances. Countries'
national accounts do not reveal which financial flows are remittances. Instead,
the numbers that the World Bank reports are roughly estimated, and presumably exaggerated, as the sum of two national accounts components: the
salaries of temporary migrants and expatriate workers, and transfers between
two private persons in different countries.[6]

The first of these two components does not conceptually correspond
to the normal definition of a remittance, that is, money that is sent to the
home country by a migrant. Instead it is money that temporary migrants and
expatriates might bring with them when they return to the home country—
presumably for their own consumption—yet only to the extent that they have
not already spent it in the country where they earned it while working there.[7]
And the second component includes all transfers between two private persons
whether the sender is a migrant or not.

Results from surveys. The only data sources that really identify flows of
money as actual remittances are surveys. Yet these are few and seldom based
on fully random or representative samples of migrants. An important exception that gives us valuable information is the supplement module on migration of the Current Population Survey in the United States in August 2008.
(Fortunately, the study was conducted the very month before the bankruptcy
of Lehman Brothers started the financial crisis. A study of remittances in the
following period, when many immigrants lost their jobs, would have given far
less generalizable results.)

In this survey, immigrants were asked about how much money their household had sent abroad during the previous 12 months. The responses from
immigrants from low- and middle-income countries are summarized in
Table 7.1. Of all these migrants, 24 percent lived in a household that had

---

[6] International Monetary Fund (2009).

[7] According to World Bank statistics, the four countries in the world that received the largest inflows of remittances as share of GDP in 2016 were Nepal, Haiti, Kirgizstan and
Tadzhikistan, with inflows corresponding to 27–32 percent of GDP. Three of these four
have large flows of seasonal and other temporary migration to India (Nepal) or Russia
(Kirgizstan and Tadzhikistan). Hence from these statistics, we do not know whether or
not most of this money was actually spent abroad. Afghanistan, which is one of the
poorest countries in the world, and has had quite high emigration, reportedly had more
than twice as large outflows as inflows of remittances in 2008 and 2009. This does not
seem realistic, yet may be explained by the large number of expatriates working in the
country at the time, for the UN and various aid organizations, often earning very high
salaries. These salaries, which are not financed by funds that were sourced in Afghanistan,
are counted in these statistics as remittances from Afghanistan to the expatriates' home
countries.

Table 7.1 Remittances from immigrants from low- and middle-income countries in the United States during 12 months

	Share remitting (percent)	Average remittance	
		(dollars)	(percent of income)
All	24	638	2.3
Household income ($/year)			
0–12,499	23	492	6.9
12,500–29,999	28	576	2.9
30,000–59,999	31	611	1.5
60,000–	26	1,045	1.1
Region of origin			
Mexico	29	755	3.4
Latin America/Caribbean	24	478	2.2
Asia	18	654	1.2
Africa	29	574	2.4
Years since migration			
0–4	32	1,223	6.0
5–8	29	941	3.6
9–18	28	681	2.0
19–28	24	440	1.1
29–38	17	330	0.9

Source: Own calculations using data from the Current Population Survey in 2008, from the US Census Bureau.

remitted any money in the previous 12 months. Calculated over all households (i.e., including the non-remitting), the average household had remitted US$638, that is, 2.3 percent of its income. The probability of remitting at all was quite independent of household income. Households with higher income on average remitted more money though, yet at the same time a smaller fraction of their total income.

Looking separately at four large groups of immigrants defined by their regions of origin, we see some modest differences in remittance patterns. Immigrants from Mexico had the highest share of remitters (together with immigrants from Africa), the highest average remitted sum and the highest average share of household income remitted. Immigrants from Asia were the least likely to remit at all and on average remitted the lowest share of household income. However, as their average incomes were higher than those of the other groups, their average sum remitted was still the second highest in the table.

Looking separately at immigrants by how many years they had been in the United States (only for immigrants who were at least 18 years old when they immigrated), we see clearly, by all three measures, that immigrants remitted less the longer they had stayed in the country. This should not be surprising, as a reflection of ties to the home country becoming weaker over time.

Even adults who immigrated as children remitted considerable amounts. Those who were at least 30 years old when surveyed, yet below 18 when they immigrated, on average lived in a household that remitted US$437 (not shown in the table).

Surveys from other countries tend to cover less-representative samples, yet mostly indicate similar remittance patterns. One study from 2011 summarized 14 surveys from receiving Western countries, whereof 12 contained information on remittances to low- and middle-income countries in the previous year. Three of these were based on at least somewhat representative samples of immigrant populations in countries other than the United States. The average immigrant from a low- or middle-income country who lived in Spain in 2007 lived in a household that remitted US$932. (All sums from this study are in 2003 US dollars.) The average immigrant who lived in Germany in 2000 (in a household that could be linked to a household in West Germany in 1984, as this was a panel survey that started in that year) lived in a household that remitted US$397. The average immigrant who lived in Australia in 1997, and had moved there between September 1993 and August 1995, lived in a household that remitted US$316. In total, the study produced a rough combined estimate saying that the average immigrant from a low- or middle-income country, who lived in an OECD country, lived in a household that remitted US$734 in one year.[8] This comes very close to the more certain estimate of US$638 from the Current Population Survey in 2008.

We may use the number US$638 to make a comparison with the World Bank's estimates of total remittance flows. The average household in the survey contained 2.63 immigrants. Hence the amount remitted per migrant in one year was US$243. In 2008, there were nearly 80 million migrants from low- and middle-income countries living in the West. Multiplied by US$243, this would give slightly less than US$20 billion in total remittances. The World Bank's estimate of remittances to low- and middle-income countries in the same year was around US$300 billion. If we, quite conservatively, assume that at least US$200 billion of these came from the West (quite significant sums are also remitted from Gulf States), the estimate based on the Current Population Survey is still only one-tenth as high. It would thus imply that in that year,

---

[8] Bollard et al. (2011).

low- and middle-income countries in total received only one-fifth as much in remittances as in international aid, instead of around twice as much.

Conversely, for the World Bank numbers to be true, the average household, including those not remitting, needs to have remitted around 20 percent instead of slightly more than 2 percent of its annual income. If we still accept that only around one-fourth of all households remitted at all, this would imply that those who did remit, remitted around 80 percent of their income. This is of course not possible.

Hence, it appears to be a good idea to stop repeating the claim that remittances are much larger than international aid. If we hear it often enough, we might conclude that aid has become less important and then cut down on it for that reason. Yet the claim is very likely not true—not even when referring to the large and diverse receiving group that we call "low- and middle-income countries," and within which average incomes are more than 10 times as high in some countries than in others. And it is most likely even less true if we focus on the very poorest countries. These receive most of the aid flows. But most remittances flow to the countries that have sent the largest numbers of migrants. And as we saw in Chapter 3, these are middle-income countries and not the poorest countries.

The receivers of remittances. For much the same reason, remittances seldom reach the poorest people within a specific country. As we also saw in Chapter 3, the most likely reason why more people migrate from middle- compared to low-income countries is that migration itself requires some economic resources to cover the initial costs. We also saw that people with college degrees, which make up very small shares of the populations in most low-income countries, are for the most part considerably more likely than others to migrate to the West. Thus presumably, families that already have some wealth and socioeconomic status should be more likely to become beneficiaries of remittances compared with poorer families in the same country.

To directly study this, we need surveys that have collected information on remittances received in households in emigration countries. Also in this case, surveys are few, and surveys based on representative samples of the population in a country are even fewer. One of the best exceptions is the Migration Household Survey in Nigeria 2009. I use results from this survey to show incoming sums, their distribution across the Nigerian population and some about how they are used.

A summary of inflows into Nigerian households of remittances from relatives in Europe and North America (most often the United States or the United Kingdom) is shown in Table 7.2. Out of all households in the country, an estimated 5.4 percent had received at least one remittance in the past

Table 7.2 Remittances to Nigerian households from Europe and North America during 12 months. The first two rows are calculated over all households in Nigeria, the remaining five over all remitting individuals

Share receiving remittance (percent)	5.4
Average remittance (naira)	15,600
Share (percent) of senders who are	
partner	3
son/daughter (including in-law)	51
sibling	21
grandchild	18
other	7

Source: Own calculations using data from the Migration Household Survey in Nigeria in 2009.

12 months when the survey was conducted. Calculated over all households, that is, including those that received no remittances, an average household received remittances amounting to ₦(naira)15,600 (around US$100) from Europe or North America in the past 12 months. As the average household had 6.9 members, that is around ₦2,300, or slightly below US$20, per person. Adding remittances from other African countries, the average person in Nigeria received ₦2,500 in remittances. This result implies that the total inflow of remittances into Nigeria in this year corresponded to 1.5 percent of the country's GDP. (This is around one-seventh of the World Bank's estimate of 10.8 percent of GDP in the same year. Hence survey results in both sending and receiving countries paint similar pictures of by approximately how much the World Bank's estimates are exaggerated.)

The table also summarizes how the senders of remittances were related to the "heads" of the receiving households (most often their oldest male member). We see that 51 percent of all remitters were children (including children-in-law) of the household head, 21 percent were siblings, 18 percent were grandchildren and only 3 percent were partners of the household head.

We may also investigate how remittances were distributed across households of different socioeconomic status in Nigeria. We cannot do what we would ideally want to do, which would be to correlate remittances with household wealth *before* the flow of remittances started (as current wealth will be partly due to the remittances). Yet we can obtain a fairly good picture of the socioeconomic distribution of remittances by studying the education levels of the parents of remitting migrants. These levels have most likely seldom or never been affected by remittances. Remittances are quite often used to finance the education of younger relatives, but not of parents. Hence parents' education

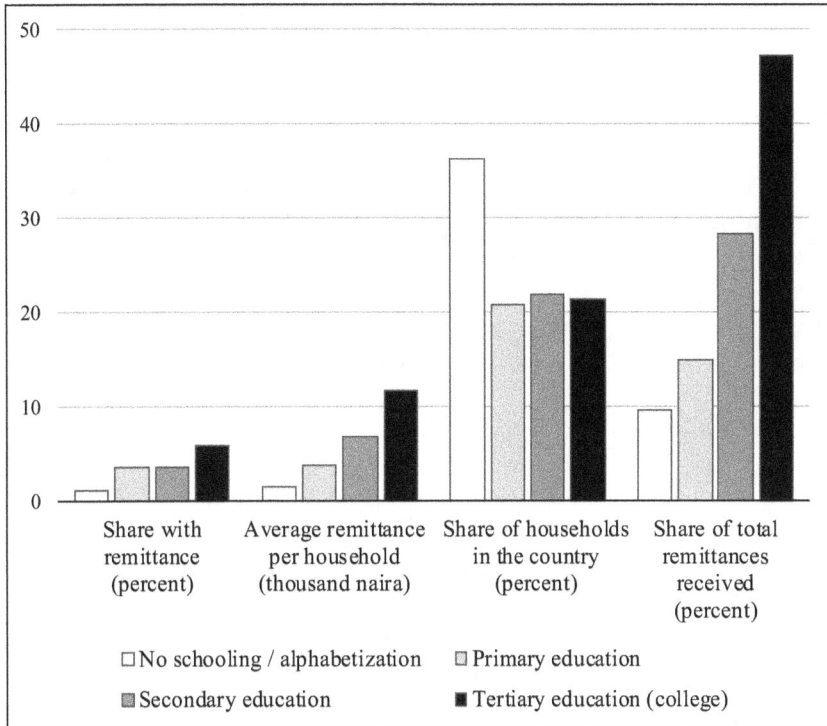

Figure 7.1 Distribution of remittances from Europe and North America to Nigeria during 12 months, from children of 40–60-year-old household heads, by education level of the household head.

Source: Own calculations using data from the Migration Household Survey in Nigeria in 2009.

levels should be mostly the same as what they were before a household started to receive remittances.

Therefore, we look at households where the head is 40–60 years old, and only at whether and how much they have received in remittances specifically from the head's children (or children-in-law). Figure 7.1 shows clear correlations between the prevalence and size of remittances and the education level of the household head. Only 1.1 percent of all households where the head had no schooling had received any remittance, yet the same was true for 5.9 percent of those where the head had tertiary (college) education. The average sum received over the last 12 months, estimated over all households in each category, was almost 10 times as high in the group with the highest as in the groups with the lowest education: ₦11,700 compared with ₦1,400.

The two groups of bars furthest to the right in the figure illustrate the distributional impact of this. In 36 percent of all households in the country where the head was 40–60 years old, the head had no schooling at all. Yet these 36 percent of households only received 10 percent of the sum of all remittances. And almost half of the sum of all remittances reached the 21 percent of all households where the head had tertiary education.

Remittances thus have several layers of mixed distributional consequences. They transfer money from high-income countries to low- and middle-income countries. Yet they contribute to increasing income inequality between low-income countries on the one hand and middle-income countries on the other. And they also contribute to increasing income inequality within countries.

Utilization of remittances. The Nigerian Migration Household Survey also included questions about how households had spent their remittances during the last 12 months. One may certainly discuss whether it is possible to say what a specific part of household income was used for. But presumably the responses are informative about what expenses the household thinks were enabled by the remittances, that is, would not have happened otherwise. Out of the total sum of stated remittance expenditures, 26 percent were on building, repairing or buying houses, 18 percent on education, 16 percent on business, 11 percent on purchase of land and 9 percent on purchase of food. This illustrates the common result from various studies, that remittances are used for many things. They enable both basic consumption, such as on food and housing, and productive investments in business and education. Hence most likely they contribute significantly both to improved living standards in the short run and economic development in the longer.[9]

One study from the Philippines showed that when the value of remittances increased suddenly and unexpectedly, due to large exchange rate movements in the Asian financial crisis in 1997, the remittance-receiving households that gained from the unexpected change thus increased their expenses on productive investments in business or education considerably more than on direct consumption.[10] This does not imply that remittances are more important for investment than consumption generally though, as in this case it was a matter of households receiving more money than they had expected. It appears likely that money that households needed to cover their more basic consumption needs would have been sent by their migrant relatives regardless of the exchange rate movements.

---

[9] For a broader overview of the aims with and utilization of remittances, see Yang (2011).
[10] Yang (2008).

Finally remittances, or more correctly the existence of a migrant relative who can remit if necessary, plays an important insurance role for many people in low- and middle-income countries. Another study from the Philippines showed that when household income decreased for an unexpected reason, that is, lack of rainfall in the dryer season, on average 60 percent of the implied income loss was covered by increased remittances in those households that had a migrant relative abroad.[11]

Brain drain?

So far, seen from the perspective of the poorer, I have only covered positive effects of migration from poorer to richer countries. Yet when this migration is discussed from the perspective of these countries, there is also often a potentially important negative aspect included. This is the risk that a country will lose too many of its most-gifted and educated citizens, whose skills they would have needed for their own economic development. This is popularly labeled the risk of *brain drain*.

The population shares that have college degrees are very low in many low-income countries, and at the same time the emigration rate among these few is often very high. Figure 3.6 showed that the emigration rate among those with college degrees was over 60 percent in as many as 18 countries (although all of these are very small countries). Several of these had very few college graduates to begin with. In Guyana and Haiti, where the emigration rates of college graduates were estimated to be higher than 80 percent, less than 1 percent of the resident populations have such degrees. In Guyana, it is even less than 0.5 percent, as is also the case in Zimbabwe, Mozambique, Guatemala, Malawi, Tanzania and Zambia,[12] where the estimated emigration rates of college graduates in Chapter 3 were 27–56 percent. In other words, certain countries in the world have managed to provide higher education only to very small shares of their populations, and subsequently large shares of these small groups have left these countries for North America or Europe where the economic return to their education has been much higher.

It has been like this for a long time. Emigration rates of college graduates from low-income countries have been quite stable for several decades,[13] and for equally long they have been discussed as a potential obstacle for these countries' development. Partly this is a question about productivity: innovation and corporate and political governance requires educated people. Partly

---

[11] Yang and Choi (2007).

[12] Source: Barro and Lee (2013).

[13] Brücker, Capuano and Marfouk (2013).

it is about public finances: providing college education is expensive and typically places a significant burden on poor countries' public finances. It is simple to conclude that it is unfair that these countries should have to use their limited resources to educate people, only for the benefit of North America or Europe who could easily have paid those costs.

It is obvious that these factors may create potentially important negative consequences. Yet there is far from any consensus that the negative effects for poor sending countries of the emigration of college graduates would outweigh the positive. There are also several arguments about why the positive consequences could be more important.[14]

One of these, which I already covered, is remittances. Emigrants send money to their home countries, and as we saw, those with college degrees on average send more than those without.[15]

Another is that home countries may benefit from the skills and networks that migrants acquire abroad. Migrants may contribute to international trade with, investments in, and knowledge transfers to the home country, either from their foreign destination, or later in life after returning to the home country.

A third is that many highly educated emigrants plausibly never would have emigrated if they actually had opportunities to contribute economically or politically to development in the home country. Most people prefer to live where they grew up. The fact that these people emigrated anyway should perhaps be taken as a sign that there are structural problems in the home countries that prevent them from becoming useful and contributing to economic development.

A fourth argument is that high emigration of college graduates does not necessarily have to lead to fewer college graduates in the country in the long run. This depends on to what extent college education in the home country is limited by people's own willingness to acquire education and possibilities to afford it, versus the amount of public resources that is spent on it. If the answer is predominantly the former, the prospect of potential future emigration may lead more people to acquire college education. And eventually, not all of these will emigrate. (This does not take away the objection against the home country having to foot the bill though.)

Discussions about potential brain drain typically focus a lot on theory, that is, on discussing which of the above-mentioned positive and negative potential effects of highly educated emigration are reasonably the most important. Yet there is not much in the way of empirics to guide us in making conclusions

---

[14] For a theoretical and empirical overview, see Gibson and McKenzie (2011).

[15] This result also holds in general across the surveys reviewed by Bollard et al. (2011).

about this. In short, we have very little certain knowledge about whether we ought to conclude that this emigration is a mostly good or a mostly bad thing. I have already emphasized in several parts of this book that our knowledge about the consequences of migration is limited. But the effects on the sending countries of highly educated emigration may well be the one question where we know the least. On several other issues, we can at least provide some sort of bounds as to what effects may look like, or what they have looked like so far in history. But on this topic we cannot reasonably rule out neither that the net effect is strongly positive, nor that it is strongly negative.

It appears however that questions about brain drain have received somewhat less attention in the last 10 or 15 years, compared with before. Although no clear evidence has been presented that there is not much reason to be worried, it appears that we are in fact a little less worried today than in the past. I can see some potential explanations behind this.

One is the dramatic increase in estimated remittance flows. This has clearly had a positive influence on many people's views on highly educated migration. (Probably somewhat unfairly though, as I just emphasized that these estimates are likely to be greatly exaggerated.)

Another is that we consistently observe rising education levels also in most of the poorest countries. Hence if it was feared, some decades ago, that their emigration would increase too much for such increases to be possible, we have now seen clearly for a long time that this has not been the case.

Finally, a number of success stories, with the growth of the Indian information and communications technology sector as the prime example, have shown highly visible examples of highly educated migrants contributing to knowledge transfers to, and economic development in, their home countries. However, while sometimes highly visible, such stories actually appear to be quite rare. A comprehensive study of emigrants with exceptional study results in their home countries showed that most of these were not much engaged in trade with, investments in, or knowledge transfers to their home countries.[16]

There is one major exception though from the claim that perhaps worries about brain drain have in general decreased. This concerns the effect of emigration on health sectors in, most of all, certain countries in sub-Saharan Africa. Physicians and nurses are among the categories of highly educated workers whose skills are easily transferable across countries (compare, e.g., with lawyers), and for whom migration from poorer to richer countries may

---

[16] Gibson and McKenzie (2012).

therefore be particularly attractive. Hence in certain cases, these health professionals have had very high emigration rates. One study estimated the shares of all working physicians and nurses who were educated in each country in Africa, who were in 2000 working in any of the nine most numerically important destination countries of highly educated emigration from African countries. (These were Australia, Belgium, Canada, France, Portugal, South Africa, Spain, the United Kingdom and the United States.) For physicians, the share was above 20 percent in 41 out of 53 countries, over 40 percent in 25 and over 60 percent in 6 countries. The corresponding numbers for nurses were lower yet still high: 17, 7 and 4 out of 53 countries. The emigration rate of nurses in Liberia was even a whopping 81 percent.[17]

There exists no unambiguous empirical evidence that the high emigration of physicians and nurses harms health provision in African countries or to what extent. One study with the provocative name "Do visas kill?" concluded that countries from which more physicians have emigrated per capita do not have fewer physicians per capita still in the country, and also do not perform worse on different indicators of population health.[18]

However such results should be read carefully, as many factors may disturb comparisons between countries, and how many physicians were educated in different countries in the first place was of course not randomly distributed (see again Chapter 5 on exogenous variation). And it is probably most fair to say that the "anecdotal evidence," that is, the collection of stories about health sectors in these countries, which are also in many cases heavily burdened by Aids, struggling with the impact of emigration—is vast. It is also quite common sense. Training physicians is even more expensive and time con-suming than most other college education. It appears unlikely that the poorest countries would devote their very limited resources to train more than what they sorely need and can employ. And when these few move, it takes a long time to train new ones to replace them.

Against this, one may in turn object that rich countries can easily pay—and do so—for the physicians they "steal" from Africa. One estimate that has received a good deal of attention concludes that the total cost of educating all currently (2013) living physicians who have migrated from Africa to the OECD corresponds to at most three weeks of aid flowing in the opposite dir-ection, and probably less.[19] But then again, this makes little difference if it is not limited financial resources as much as lack of other forms of capacity that

[17] Clemens and Pettersson (2006).
[18] Clemens (2007).
[19] Clemens (2013).

makes it difficult for poor countries to importantly scale up the numbers of physicians that they train.

Final words

Migration creates change most of all for the migrants. Most people who move from low- and middle-income countries to high-income countries thereby obtain large income increases. Roughly estimated, people who were born in low- and middle-income countries on average earn a full 10 times as much from some of them having migrated to the West as they do from Western aid. This average does not benefit most of them at all, and seldom benefits the poorest, but still shows an interesting order of magnitudes.

The impact of this migration on people still in the sending countries also appears to be mostly positive. This is most obviously so because of the financial remittances that many migrants send to their relatives. These create important income increases for many more than the migrants themselves. Yet they too are very unevenly distributed across the populations in low- and middle-income countries, reaching the somewhat wealthier more often than the poorest.

Therefore, one should not view remittances as a substitute for aid, as is seldom done explicitly, yet I think often implicitly with the frequent emphasizing of remittances amounting to much larger financial flows than aid. I have shown in this chapter that in reality aid is probably much larger. And aid also reaches, or at the very least tries to reach, the poorest to a considerably higher extent.

Chapter 8

FUTURE MIGRATION

There are many concerns and worries over immigration in the West. It is one of the political issues that seems to create the most worries in this part of the world today. In three recent cases, the negative reactions to immigration have been particularly powerful and politically far-reaching. Resistance to immigration from Eastern Europe appears to have been a major component behind the British decision to leave the EU. Resistance to illegal immigration, most of all from Mexico, appears to have been a major component behind the election of Donald Trump to the presidency of the United States. And resistance to refugee immigration has created animosity and inability to reach agreements between countries in the same EU that only a few years earlier was so successful in compromising even on the intricate problems of its debt crisis.

These are examples of three quite different forms of migration. One is refugee migration, one is illegal economically motivated migration, and one is legal economically motivated migration. However, they share one aspect: they all represent recent cases where people have felt that the countries they live in do not have the ability to control their immigration.

How this factor unites these three cases, in spite of their differences, may indicate something important. Possibly it indicates that most people do not see very important problems with the immigration that has happened until now. Instead, it may first of all be the lack of control that has made resistance rise to these proportions.

Lack of control may of course constitute a problem in itself. People's respect for the politicians in charge is reduced when these fail to implement policies that create the results they were elected to create. However, the really important problem with lack of control over immigration is of course that it creates worries about future immigration.

Therefore, this last chapter is about future migration. It aims not to predict what future migration will actually look like. That will depend to a large extent on policy decisions made in the West, and predicting those does not appear to be the most useful thing to do. Instead, the aim is to characterize the setting for those decisions. First, to investigate if we may predict how people's will-ingness to migrate will develop, that is, approximately how many will want or try to migrate in the future, if the laws and mechanisms that regulate this remain approximately the same as they are today. Second, to investigate what scope Western countries have to decide how high their immigration shall be. So far, they have clearly not been completely successful with this. It is estimated that approximately one-fourth of all non-Western immigrants in the United States do not have permission to be in the country.[1] And almost all of Europe's (and significant parts of other Western countries') refugee immigration involves illegal entry. (Legal status is given later, when asylum is applied for, which gives legal status during the asylum process, and when it is granted.)

Most of the chapter is thus about the future development of migration that Western countries are generally concerned about keeping low. Yet it also covers migration that the same countries typically want to be as high as pos-sible, that is, that of highly skilled and productive professionals who often work in the science and technology sectors, and how successful different policies seem to be in attracting such.

Recent trends

To enable a better discussion of future migration, we begin by looking at trends in the recent past. We then see that, depending on how we measure it, migration from the rest of the world to the West has either been stable or decreased over the last decades. The accumulated number of migrants has increased but not the pace of migration. This can be seen in Figure 8.1, which shows how the accumulated number of migrants from the rest of the world in the West (current EU, Iceland, Norway, Switzerland, Canada, the United States, Australia and New Zealand) has changed in 1990–2017. It has increased quite steadily by on average approximately two million migrants per year, and hence in these 27 years more than doubled from 40 to 92 million. Throughout the period, the United States has hosted quite exactly half of all migrants.

The number of migrants has thus also increased steadily when measured as a share of the total population in the West. This increase has been on average nearly one percentage point every five years, from 5.1 percent in 1990 to 10.0 percent in 2017. It has thus steadily become more obvious to people in Western countries that these are countries of immigration, with increasingly

---

[1] Krogstad, Passel and Cohn (2019).

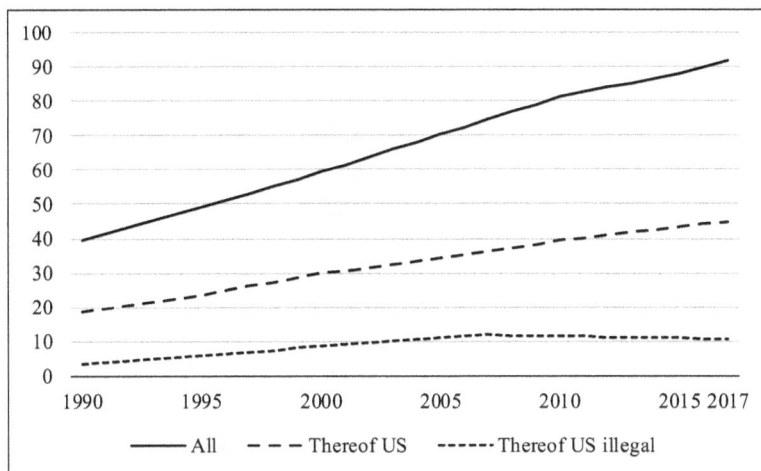

Figure 8.1 Number of migrants (millions) from the rest of the world in the current EU, Iceland, Norway, Switzerland, Canada, the United States, Australia and New Zealand, 1990–2017.

Source: "All" and "Whereof US": United Nations Global Migration Database. "Whereof US illegal": Krogstad, Passel and Cohn (2019).

multiethnic populations. This may understandably have contributed to the rise of immigration as a question of political importance.

The pace of net migration is approximately represented by the slope of the solid line in Figure 8.1. (More exactly, this slope represents net migration minus the number of deaths of migrants. However, the latter has been comparably low throughout the period, because historical migration was much lower and therefore relatively few migrants are old.) It has been quite stable throughout the period, yet appears to have decreased somewhat after around 2010, from on average 2.1 million people per year in 1990–2010 to 1.5 million per year in 2010–17.

Finally, if we measure net migration as a share of the total combined population of the sending countries, that is, the net emigration rate, we see a more distinct fall in migration after around 2010. The bars in Figure 8.2 show the change in the number of migrants in the West per year over five- or seven-year periods, expressed as percentages of the total population in the rest of the world at the beginning of each period. In each of the first four periods, that is, 1990–2010, this approximate annual net emigration rate was consistently around 0.04 percent. Yet in 2010–17 it was only 0.024 percent.

Much of this decrease is driven by that in illegal net migration from non-Western countries to the United States, which could also be seen in Figure 8.1.

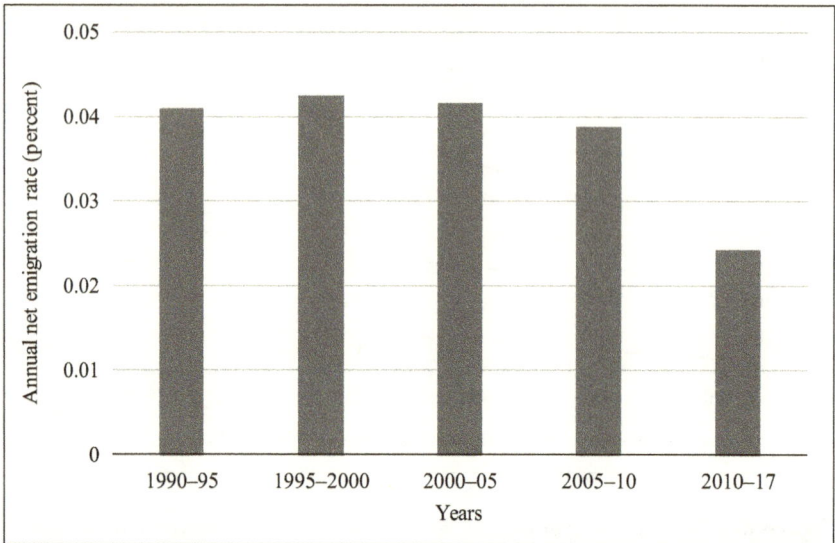

Figure 8.2 Approximate average annual net migration to the West per period, as percentages of the total population in the rest of the world at the beginning of each period.

Source: Numbers of migrants in the West: United Nations Global Migration Database. Population in the rest of the world. World Development Indicators, the World Bank.

The population of illegal immigrants in the United States is estimated to have peaked in 2007.[2]

We may say that what future migration will look like will depend on four things: how many will want to migrate if they are allowed to, how many will be allowed to, how many will want to migrate even if they are not allowed to, and how many of those will succeed. The first two among these require no discussion. It is obvious that the number who would want to migrate if they were allowed to is far higher today than the number who actually are allowed to do it, and with all likelihood it will remain so in the foreseeable future. In other words, there are few questions to ask about the size of future legal migration. It will be as high as the receiving countries decide they want it to be.

The more open question that warrants a longer discussion is about the size of future illegal migration. It is useful to separate this discussion into two

---

[2] Krogstad, Passel and Cohn (2019).

parts: how many will want or try to migrate illegally if we assume that immigration laws and their implementation will continue to look approximately like they do today, and what scope receiving countries have to influence illegal migration by their policies.

Developments in underlying driving forces

Beginning with the first, there is not much to say here by way of predicting the future development of underlying driving forces for illegal *refugee* migration, that is, refugee migration where entry is illegal. On this matter, let us simply express our collective hopes that the very recent global peak that has been created most of all by the war in Syria shall remain a peak and not be the beginning of an increasing trend.

There is more to say about likely future developments in underlying driving forces for illegal migration that is economically motivated. To do this, we may look at four factors that may change over time, and which we saw in Chapter 3 may importantly influence the size of migration: the expected income increase from migration, the costs of moving and of maintaining relations with the home country, the number of young adults in the population, and the number of previous migrants from the same origin in the same destination.

Future changes in expected income increases from migration will most likely contribute to a lower future willingness to migrate. More and more countries make the transition from being low-income countries to being middle-income countries, while few make the opposite transition. If this process continues, it should imply better income prospects at home for more people, and hence that fewer will have reason to expect really large income increases if they migrate to a Western country.

Yet future cost developments are likely to work in the opposite direction. Costs of travel and communication may fall further as they have done throughout modern history. Also, higher incomes at home would imply that more people will be able to afford the costs. It appears quite unlikely though that future cost decreases will have more than a modest impact on the total willingness to migrate illegally. This is considering the enormous cost decreases that have happened over the last few decades, and the millions of people that have simultaneously risen out of poverty, without resulting in any increase at all in illegal net migration.[3]

---

[3] The costs of international flights and phone calls are only fractions of what they were a few decades ago. Internet communication has spread globally. The global population was around four and a half billion in 1980, and a full 40 percent were living below the poverty line at US$1.90 per day in 2011 dollars. Today the global population is

Future changes in the numbers of young adults in populations outside of the West will most likely contribute to lower willingness to migrate. We saw in Chapter 3 that the populations of Latin America and Asia were considerably younger in 1970, and also in 1995, than what they are today when most of these regions have completed their demographic transitions. This may be an important explanation behind the fall in illegal net migration, mostly from Latin America, to the United States in the last decade. And, as Asian and Latin American populations are expected to become even older in the future, we may expect this to contribute to even lower future willingness to migrate illegally, in particular to the United States. Africa on the other hand has a different demographic trend. Its population is still young and growing fast and is expected to remain so for many years ahead. Demographic trends may thus contribute to increasing future willingness to migrate, also illegally, out of Africa.[4]

Finally, processes where migration makes more migration easier can of course nothing but contribute to more willingness to migrate in the future, as the accumulated number of migrants in the West keeps increasing. It is important to understand though, that this effect will not necessarily be huge. Some of the results that were shown in Chapter 3 can easily be interpreted as hinting that it may easily become very big. We saw patterns where previous migration had an influence on later migration for a long time. If people started to move from A to B, and from C to D, yet not from A to D, or C to B, these patterns often remained to a large extent among later migrants from A and from C, respectively, also long after the initial cause of the pattern had disappeared.

These stark patterns easily lead to thoughts of migration increasing exponentially: more migrants lead to more migrants, which lead to even more migrants. As only one and a half percent of the population of the rest of the world has yet moved to the West today, one may thus easily imagine that global—illegal—migration is only just about to start picking up the pace, and that in the future the West will be overwhelmed by huge immigration, whether it permits it or not.

Such reasoning is not uncommon.[5] Yet the result that migrants concentrate geographically does not necessarily imply that the number of earlier migrants

---

seven and a half billion, with only 10 percent below the same poverty line (the picture is similar if we use different poverty lines). Source: World Development Indicators, the World Bank.

[4] Hanson, Liu and McIntosh (2017). Global population forecasts are regularly published by the UN organ DESA.

[5] See, for example, Collier (2013).

affects the *total* inflow of new migrants into a place to any large extent. All it says for certain is that previous migrants often have a large effect on *who* migrate *where*. Even if we imagine that the total inflow of migrants into a place is entirely driven by labor demand in that place, with no causal role for the number of previous migrants, we could still get persistent patterns of migrant concentration like those that were shown in Chapter 3.

We saw then that a major reason for this migrant concentration is that information about local income opportunities flows from previous migrants to their friends and relatives at their place of origin. Hence if, for example, new income opportunities arise in a place with many previous migrants from Ireland, this information is likely to flow more efficiently to Ireland than to other foreign places. These opportunities will then most likely be met by more migration from Ireland. The fact that more migration happens is still entirely because of the labor demand at the destination. The presence of previous migrants only determines from where new migrants appear to fill this demand. If there had been no previous migrants from anywhere when the new income opportunities arose, information about them would eventually have attracted migrants from somewhere anyway. But the presence of previous migrants made it happen faster and from a certain place.

Hence the patterns that were shown in Chapter 3 do not necessarily imply that immigration creates much more immigration in total. Most likely it does in many cases create at least *some* more. But importantly, there is no single case in history where this mechanism—or any other—has created something like a sustained exponential development of a migration flow—whether legal or illegal. In an early phase when a migration flow is still very small, an exponential development is not uncommon (it does not require very much to double a small number). Yet after some time, as we saw repeatedly in Chapter 2, migration flows tend to stabilize, and eventually drop. Either because labor demand at the destination drops, or because most potential migrants have already moved, or because economic conditions at home have improved (perhaps partly due to emigration).

Summing up, the combined picture of plausible future developments in underlying economic driving forces for migration to the West is mixed. Among four important factors considered, two are likely to contribute to an increase in the willingness to migrate and the other two to a decrease. Recently, those that work toward a decrease appear to have dominated. Most of the illegal economically motivated migration to the West is to the United States, which is also where the best estimates of its size exist. Since 2007, the total number of illegal migrants in the country is estimated to have decreased by almost two million, or around 14 percent.[6]

---

[6] Krogstad, Passel and Cohn (2019).

How effectively can migration be controlled?

We turn now to the receiving countries' scope to limit their illegal immigration. So far, both the EU and the United States have obviously failed importantly with this. Millions of migrants have passed unseen across their borders. Their incentives to migrate have been too strong for walls or even the risk of death in the sea or the desert to stop them.

However, the partly failed methods for preventing illegal border crossings on both sides of the Atlantic have been mostly about guarding the borders, through walls, patrols, etc. They have been little about changing people's incentives to overcome all these things. These incentives have remained mostly unchanged, and this is why migration has continued in spite of all the efforts to stop it.

Incentives explain why it is the United States that receives such a vast majority of the West's illegal economically motivated immigration. The United States has for long provided ample opportunities to find employment, also for those without residence permits, at conditions that have been deemed by many as considerably better than what has been available to them in their home countries, such as Mexico. Illegal employments are considerably more common and less monitored in the United States than in other Western countries. Likewise, if we compare European countries, illegal immigration for economic reasons appears to have been higher in the United Kingdom, Spain and Italy, where monitoring of illegal employments is somewhat more slack, and lowest in the Nordic countries where it is very strong.[7]

Even if income levels in a country are high, illegal economic immigration remains low if illegal employments are effectively controlled. No large migrant group, refugees excluded, has at any point in history moved to mass unemployment in a far-away country. Several large refugee groups have done so. By their refugee status, these have been entitled to social security and hence they have survived also without employment. Throughout modern history, many economically motivated migrant groups have moved to hard work and low salaries far away. But never to mass unemployment. There is simply no reason to do that.

In Europe on the other hand, the most important incentive for illegal entry has been the right to asylum. Any person (with the limitations that were explained in Chapter 2) who manages to enter a country, and can prove fear of persecution in the home country, has the legal right to remain, the right to work and the right to welfare benefits. This is considerably more attractive than the conditions under which millions of refugees live, for example, in

---

[7] Kovacheva and Vogel (2009).

Turkey and Lebanon. Hence millions have made the move, in spite of the dangers.

Hence although in different ways, the failures to control external borders on both sides of the Atlantic show that walls—physical as well as abstract—are not very effective, if there are strong enough incentives to climb them. And in recent history, little has been done to change the most important among these incentives.

What the United States could most importantly do differently from today in this respect is obvious. If it did what almost all other Western countries have long done to control and monitor illegal employments, there is little reason to expect that it would have more illegal economically motivated immigration than what those other countries do.

If anything, the recent European experience even indicates that when illegal employments are effectively controlled, limiting people's rights to cross borders may even be superfluous. The average income gap between Mexico and the United States is quite similar to that between Romania and Bulgaria on the one hand, and several Western European countries on the other. Since the EU accession of Romania and Bulgaria in 2007, no border controls prevent their citizens from traveling freely, for example, on holiday, to Western Europe, that is, what Mexican citizens cannot freely do to the United States. For a Bulgarian citizen who wants to work illegally in a Western European country, crossing the border into that country is not an issue. Still, as there are not many such illegal jobs available, Bulgarian citizens do not do this at rates anywhere near those at which Mexican citizens have done it into the United States in recent decades.

Much could be done also about refugees' incentives to cross borders illegally and in ways that put their lives in significant danger. The historical contingencies that have led to the current situation where refugees have strong incentives to do this were explained in some detail in Chapter 2. Because of how it has developed out of a framework that was only intended to provide a solution to one particular situation more than 70 years ago, the international right to asylum in practice places unlimited obligations upon countries to care for all refugees who reach their territories. If all refugees in the world decided and managed to set down their feet in Austria, Austria alone would be obliged to receive them all.

It is quite understandable that potential receiving countries are not happy with this, and that it makes them nervous. However, as I emphasized in Chapter 2, they took a fateful turn in how they chose to respond to this problem when it became apparent in the 1980s. Instead of changing the unlimited legal obligations, they left these intact and took to strong measures to prevent refugees from reaching their territories to claim their universal rights. Because of the same historical contingencies these rights could not be claimed from a distance. Huge incentives have thus remained for refugees to travel to Western countries, in particular to Europe. Many keep succeeding with this, yet Europe has made the routes so dangerous that tens of thousands have also perished on the way. It is a situation that is beneficial to no part and with which no one is happy.

Yet it could be changed. But to enable this, the West needs to admit that the refugee convention and the international right to asylum is not the central pillar of any conceivable truly humanitarian approach to refugee movements, but a historically contingent product that is unfit for today's realities. If the international response to refugee movements would be created from zero today, it is almost inconceivable that it would look something like it.

Only if the refugee convention and the international right to asylum in their current forms were removed would it be possible to create an alternative that could put the receiving countries in control and calm their worried citizens, remove all incentives for refugees to dangerously cross the Mediterranean Sea, relieve Europe of the need to make compromises with African and Asian dictators to make these hold migrants back, and allow Europe to select which refugees to receive, instead of (like today) letting this selection happen by only some refugees being resourceful enough to manage to pass all the obstacles that have been put in place to keep them out. All these things would be possible, if the current unconditional (in practice) right to asylum in the refugee's country of choice was removed and the rich Western countries instead gave themselves the legal right to cap their refugee immigration.

Such a right to cap refugee immigration would of course not apply to refugees who are about to cross the border out of the country where they are persecuted. It would only apply to refugees who are already out of that country (which is the case for almost all refugees today before they reach Europe). It would not prevent refugees from leaving the home countries where they are persecuted. But it would create a system for an orderly distribution of refugees across multiple receiving countries, that is, for burden-sharing between receiving countries—once they have done so. If refugees escape, for example, from Syria into Turkey or Jordan, it would be about changing the means by which some of these refugees are eventually allowed to end up in Europe. If Austria was allowed to cap its inflow, any number of Syrian refugees in Turkey could apply for resettlement in Austria. Yet only the number that Austria decided would be granted this permission.

Partly as a side note, it is even likely that if Europe brought its refugee immigration under control in this way, its resulting immigration would become higher. As I showed in Chapter 2, while Europe has for a long time been busy struggling to keep refugees out, other Western countries that have been more in control have voluntarily admitted similar and often even higher numbers of refugees per capita. It may be a lot easier to be generous when one is in control of the situation and does not face important uncertainty about the consequences of generosity.

A country being wealthy is not in itself incentive enough for people to want to migrate to that country. There must also be a way for prospective migrants to obtain a share of that wealth, legally or because of slack law enforcement. Currently, this exists for migrants who illegally enter the United States to find illegal employment, or who enter Europe (most importantly) to apply for asylum. When these strong incentives exist, walls cannot keep all migrants out. Furthermore, if the incentives did not exist, walls and border controls would probably be quite superfluous. If Western countries did not provide real opportunities to earn a living for migrants they do not want, these would stop coming, with or without walls.

For the same reason, there is also probably little warrant for the common beliefs that two particular types of migration are set to increase considerably in the future. One fairly common belief is that as climate change destroys the livelihoods of an increasing number of people around the world, Western countries should expect large numbers of climate refugees to arrive in the future just as war refugees have done for a long time. Yet this expectation overlooks the difference in incentives between these two groups. Refugees of war and persecution have a legal right to asylum if they get into a country. This gives them a strong incentive to travel. Climate refugees do not. These could only live illegally in Western countries, as long as these countries do not voluntarily decide to make climate refuge a condition for legal immigration.

With this in mind, it is more likely that in the future we will see most climate refugees in the same places as we see them today. That is in the larger cities in the regions they come from, and sometimes, in the most dire situations, in camps in the same regions where they can receive humanitarian aid. In the latest decades, hundreds of millions of poor people in difficult situations in rural areas have moved to nearby cities. This is the major opportunity that has been open to them. And that does not change, economically or legally, depending on whether their situation is due to climate change or not. In this sense, climate refuge is not something new. It is just more of poor people's same age-old struggles.

A second common belief is that, while the aging of Latin American and Asian population may decrease illegal migration to the United States, the fast-growing and sustained youth of the African population may bring a sharp future increase in illegal migration to Europe (which does not involve crossing the Atlantic). Yet as long as European countries keep up their mostly effective monitoring of illegal employment, incentives to migrate there illegally from Africa will remain weak.

The global quest for talent

While attempting to limit the inflow of those migrants of which they do not want too many, Western countries also devote increasing efforts to attract more of those potential migrants of which they all want more. In the last decades, productivity differences within high-income countries have increased. High-tech and knowledge-intensive production generates higher economic values per worker than more traditional industry. The countries that succeed best in attracting this production will thereby increase their GDP, their average income and their potential tax revenues. To do this, they need among other things to attract the people with the necessary skills to work in this industry, and not least to spur new innovations and technological development. These people come from all over the world, they face a global labor market, and countries fight over them more and more intensely.

Several European countries engage in this fight by allowing foreign workers in certain important positions to pay lower taxes than natives. Yet the three countries that may reasonably be seen as the most active in this global quest for talent are probably the United States, Canada and Australia. This section builds on a study that has already been referred to in Chapter 4, and which compares policies for the immigration of skilled workers in these countries and which migrants they manage to attract.[8]

The United States stepped up its efforts to attract highly productive migrants in its Immigration Act from 1990. The number of annual H1-B visas was then strongly increased (see Chapter 2) and it kept increasing throughout the 1990s. After that, less has changed. H1-B visas are given to highly skilled workers, mostly in science and technology, who already have job offers in the United States. These migrants are thus guaranteed employment from their first day in the country, often at very productive positions. The H1-B visas are commonly seen as having been very successful in attracting highly productive migrants.

Before 1990, when US immigration was determined by family connections to an even larger extent than what is the case today, immigration policies in Canada and Australia were in comparison considerably more geared toward

---

[8] Clarke, Ferrer and Skuterud (2019).

attracting more skilled migrants. Immigration for economic reasons was, since 1967 in Canada and 1979 in Australia, determined through points systems where points were awarded, for example, for education and language skills.

These points systems have become very well known. They have inspired much discussion in several European countries, most of all in Germany and the United Kingdom, where many have wanted to implement copies of them as means to better enter into the quest for talent. Yet in Canada and Australia they have been less universally hailed. Their constructions guarantee that they are effective in ensuring, for example, that immigrants are mostly highly educated. Still, many of these highly educated immigrants have performed quite weakly on these countries' labor markets. Figure 4.5 showed that young men with college degrees who immigrated in 1986–90 had on average much larger negative entry wage gaps to similarly old native college graduates in these two countries compared with in the United States, in spite of the less selective immigration policies in the United States. The gap was 30 percent in Australia and 20 percent in Canada but only 1 percent in the United States.

A central conclusion that was drawn in Canada and Australia from immigrants not performing more strongly on the labor market in this period was that general qualifications such as college degrees are easy to measure, and award points, yet do not provide satisfying measures of a person's potential on a country's labor market. Therefore, both countries have since moved toward giving employers greater roles in determining who is allowed to immigrate, just like the United States has done by its increase in the number of H1-B visas.

Australia introduced employment visas in 1996 that made it easier for employers to hire highly skilled foreign workers. Like the H1-B visas, these were temporary but also offered paths to permanent residence permits later. Thus the share of the country's immigrants that had first been evaluated by employers increased, as did the share of permanent permits given to people whose skills had by then been tested at the country's labor market. Canada introduced similar, yet more limited changes in 2007. All in all, the study argues that policies for attracting highly skilled workers in the three countries, which were quite different before 1990, have been quite similar since 2007.

The study also tries to correlate these policy changes with changes in immigrants' entry wages. Ascribing wage changes to specific immigration policy changes is of course risky, because other important things may have happened at the same time. Yet in any case, the pattern of changes in entry wages that was shown in Figure 4.5 does lend itself fairly well to being possibly explained by these policy changes and their timing.

In the United States, the entry wages of newly arrived college graduates compared with similarly aged natives have been higher for those who arrived in 1996–2000 and onward compared with for earlier arrivals. This corresponds well to the increase in the share of H1-B visas in 1990 and thereafter. In Australia, we can observe a gradual increase in relative wages over the whole period between 1986–90 and 2001–5. This corresponds to the fact that policies changed during this period, although it is difficult to claim that wages would have increased more right after the policy change. On the other hand, Australian immigrants' entry wages were again lower among 2006–10 arrivals. The study explains this by an increase in the share of immigrants arriving as students, that is, without first being evaluated by employers. In Canada, immigrants' entry wages moved little between 1986–90 and 2001–5. Yet they were considerably higher in the 2006–10 group, which is consistent with the policy change in 2007.

It is thus possible to interpret the patterns in Figure 4.5 as the changes in all three countries having led to more effective selection of more productive migrants, although it is a fairly generous interpretation. It leads to the conclusion that relying to a high degree on employers is a comparably effective strategy for attracting immigrants who will really perform well on the labor market.

At the same time, the figure also shows what was discussed in Chapter 4. Throughout the entire period, college-educated immigrants' entry wages have been higher in the United States than in the other two countries. In the period 2006–10, when the study argues that policies were not much different, these wages, expressed as shares of those of similarly aged native college graduates, were a full 25–27 percentage points higher in the United States than in Australia and Canada. And the difference was approximately as high in 1986–90 when policies were more selective in the latter two.

Most likely, this is much due to the part of migrant selection that happens not in the form of the receiving country's policies, but of the self-selection of migrants depending on their income prospects in different countries. For the very most gifted and productive potential migrants, there is nowhere else in the world where their gifts may earn them as high wages as in the United States (see Chapter 4). Therefore, these people have particularly strong reasons to move to that particular country.

Hence, while the study concludes that immigration policy can do much, it also concludes that there is much it cannot do. It cannot compensate very much for which jobs and salaries are offered on the labor market in a country. And this is of course most evident in comparisons that involve the United States, which is so clearly world leading in much of the most knowledge-intensive production, and where income inequality is so high.

Self-regulating legal migration

This account from the United States, Canada and Australia appears to show that selecting immigrants through administrative systems has important limitations, and that leaving the task more to employers may bring considerable benefits. Recent European experiences also indicate a more far-reaching conclusion in the same direction, that is, that even regulating the total volume of legal immigration can be left to market forces to a considerable extent.

The recent eastward expansion of the EU was a unique event in modern history. There exists nothing similar in the way of allowing workers to migrate freely between countries with so different income levels, and between which it is so cheap and simple to travel—and even to visit family members at home over the weekend. The only legal condition that limits the flow of migrants in this case is that migration is only allowed for those who have a job offer that follows the relevant regulations in the receiving country, such as minimum wage levels set by legislation or collective bargaining.

I do not think it has been fully appreciated how radical this has been, and how much we may learn from how smoothly it has worked (apart from its likely contribution to the Brexit vote). In the short run, that is, in the first few years after the EU expansion, the ensuing migration was quite concentrated to sectors with labor shortages.[9] This is not much surprising. In the short run, wage floors were mostly fixed. The scope for immigrants to compete with other workers by accepting lower wages was limited, and hence it is not surprising that migration mostly happened where jobs were already available at the going wages.

But now, more than 15 years ahead, a more profound and less obvious insight is that the vast pool of *potential* migrants that remain in Eastern Europe has not had much impact on wage-setting in richer countries in Western Europe. Several million workers have moved from East to West (see Chapter 2). Yet far above 90 percent of all Eastern European citizens are still in Eastern Europe. With all likelihood, many millions more of them would move too if they were offered jobs in Western Europe, even if so at wages that were considerably below current Western levels. This could still be considerably above what most people earn in Eastern Europe.

In other words, if employers in Western Europe had the ability to lower wages to the point where their native employees started quitting, many of them would most likely be able to replace those workers quite swiftly, and legally, by increasing immigration from Eastern Europe. However for more than 15 years, we have not seen this happening. The institutions that determine

---

[9] Kahanec and Zimmermann (eds.) (2010).

wages appear to be safeguarding effectively against it. Legal minimum wages continue to be set prioritizing domestic workers. Collective bargaining is done between employers and employees, with little concern even for the non-employed domestic workforce, and even less for non-employed in other countries.

Hence, by and large, experiences from the EU enlargement appear to show not only that effective monitoring of the labor market can replace border controls to stem illegal immigration, but also that strong wage-setting institutions can replace numerical limits as a means of regulating legal immigration. The fundamental insight in this is—again—that economic migrants are not attracted to high-income countries as such. They are attracted to income opportunities for themselves. In most instances in history, countries have regulated their economic immigration at the point of entry into the country and not at the point of entry into employment. Yet in regulating its internal migration, the EU has chosen a different strategy, where migration is in effect regulated not at the border but in wage-setting and monitoring of the labor market. So far, this mostly appears to have worked really well, with the additional benefits of more effective matching of workers to jobs, less administration and bureaucracy, and more individual freedoms.

There also exists a narrower but more far-reaching similar success story. Since 2008, Sweden has what probably deserves being (and often is) called the most liberal labor immigration policy in the Western world. Any Swedish employer that has advertised yet not been able to fill a vacancy with a domestic (or EU) worker, has the right to instead employ a person from anywhere in the world, as long as collective agreements are followed and total monthly pay exceeds a certain (very low) threshold. Even in this example, where potential migrants who would certainly be willing to work also at wages considerably below those currently specified in the collective agreements are probably counted in hundreds of millions, that is, many times the size of the Swedish workforce, there has been no obvious feedback on the wage-setting process. Wage increases over time have not been obviously smaller because this vast pool of potential migrants exists. The number of migrants admitted has also remained fairly low.

Final words—really

Migration creates many strong feelings and cause difficult political controversies across the Western world today. The aim of this book has been to provide a basic knowledge foundation about the causes and consequences of migration, and hence to hopefully also make a contribution to better discussions on the matter.

Migration often brings considerable benefits to the migrants themselves. For some of them, it is necessary for their survival, or for being able to live together with their partner. And according to the rough estimate from Chapter 7, the average migrant from the rest of the world has increased their annual income by more than US$10,000 by migrating to the West. This, everyone may probably agree, is something very positive. Yet weighing against it are the potential negative consequences of migration for other people and societies. Without doubt, migration even has a theoretical potential to undermine the entire current social model. This model, with countries and citizenships as the basic foundations for political decision-making and public economics, is built on the basic premise that not too many move between countries too often. If, for example, one-fifth of countries' populations were replaced each year through in- and out-migration, we would certainly have had a different model.

Yet in practice we have never seen migration on a scale that has challenged the foundations of this model. In the Western countries that have had the highest immigration per capita over the last half century, that is, Switzerland and Australia, around 30 percent of current populations are immigrants. This has not forced these countries to adopt any very different social models than other Western countries where immigration has been much lower. And they still remain among the best-functioning societies on the globe.

This, and the contents most of all of Chapters 5 and 6, indicate that any negative consequences for receiving societies of immigration, at levels that we have seen anywhere so far, are at least limited and manageable. Yet we have also seen that migration that could hardly be described as manageable, or consistent with the current social model, is possible. In the autumn of 2015, Sweden, with a population of 10 million, had an inflow of 10,000 asylum seekers per week. This inflow showed no sign of decreasing by itself, before the Swedish government introduced measures to stop asylum seekers from crossing the bridge into the country from Denmark. An inflow of that size of people with mostly weak prospects for surviving without public support could not have been sustained for a long period of time without considerable changes to welfare systems, and would most likely have been very harmful for the country's social cohesion. And if it had not been actively prevented, it could have happened.

Considering all of this together, the strong resistance to immigration among many citizens of Western countries may feel partly well motivated and partly not. It should perhaps not be much of a surprise that people react to the clear inability to manage and control immigration that has been put on display with the high illegal immigration in the United States in the last decades, and even more with the European refugee crisis of 2015. These situations have created uncertainty about what the future may bring in ways that few other political issues do. It is then quite logical if the topic receives high priority for many voters.

Yet also far from these more exceptional situations, indeed almost irrespectively of time and place, there seems to be a clear dominance among Western populations of preferences for reduced immigration (see Chapter 6). This is perhaps more difficult to give a rational explanation for, and could perhaps be interpreted as at least to some extent due to ignorance. From what we know about the mostly limited consequences of migration for receiving economies and societies, it appears difficult to explain this rather compact wish for less of it. It may be easier to explain it as due to people believing that consequences are more negative than what they actually are. If so, I hope that this book may contribute to a somewhat less-concerned outlook on migration such as it looks, or at least has looked so far, in most—although not all—cases.

However, to reduce public concerns over immigration, it is probably central to bring it more under control in those cases where it currently is not and which have caused such particularly strong negative reactions. If we can succeed with this, and hence with giving ourselves less reason to worry about future migration becoming much higher than we intend, perhaps we may then also allow ourselves to be more generous. It is easier to be generous when one is in control. If we can create a situation where we feel that we are in control, per-haps we may then also give the opportunity to more people to get a chance to experience the substantial increases in living standards that migration to our part of the world may bring.

Increasing control is likely to be possible, yet not by building even higher walls (physical or virtual) but by removing the incentives to climb them. Economically motivated migration is probably best controlled by controlling illegal employments. And refugee migration is probably best controlled by removing the link between border crossing and right to asylum, and replacing it with more resettlement of refugees from the countries that border the con-flict zones and to which almost all refugees first escape.

If migration is under control, and one wants to create a regulatory frame-work that gives the opportunity to migrate to as many as possible, yet without causing too important negative consequences or too much resistance from the resident population, the basic framework for immigration to the United States may be a good example to follow. Its stable and predictable annual quotas show clearly that the country is in control (over its legal immigration) and minimizes any negative consequences on the labor market. Maybe the frame-work could be further improved in the latter respect, if the annual immigra-tion quota was made automatically dependent on the national unemployment rate, so that more immigration was allowed when unemployment was low than when it was high.

If one wants to create a framework that as efficiently as possible enables the immigration that is demanded on the labor market, the current Swedish framework appears to be a good example to follow. The experiences from the Canadian and Australian points systems appear to have shown that it is difficult to use bureaucratic systems to determine which migrants are actually in demand. These two countries and the United States together appear to have shown that employers can do this better with highly educated migrants on highly productive jobs. And the Swedish experience has shown that it is possible to hand the task over to employers also for other labor immigration. With firm wage-setting institutions, such as in Sweden, it has been possible to control immigration through the simple condition that employers must first have failed to find a suitable worker to hire within the country (or the EU).

Migration to the West has given many people the opportunity to improve their living conditions, and will certainly keep doing this in the future. Yet among those who have benefited from this so far in recent history, few have come from the poorest sections of the Earth's population. This is both because of the skill requirements on Western countries' labor markets and in their immigration laws, and because the very poorest cannot afford long-distance travel. In consequence, it is also seldom the poorest that benefit from migrants' remittances.

This is likely to remain the case also in the future. And it is probably good to leave it like that. Allowing more immigration as a means of raising living standards among people born in low- and middle-income countries can only be a good idea if the migrants can earn their incomes on the labor market by their own means. In the advanced Western economies this mostly takes quite skillful migrants. The currently existing migrants who did not migrate because of their income opportunities, that is, refugees, typically face considerable difficulties on the labor market. Migration thus probably best remains a tool for creating income increases mostly among the more educated and skillful, who have the best prospects to create those income increases on their own if they are only allowed to. Other tools are likely to be more appropriate for fighting severe global poverty.

REFERENCES

Abrams, Kerry (2005), "Polygamy, prostitution, and the federalization of immigration law," *Columbia Law Review*, 105(3): 641–716.

Acemoglu, Daron, and James A. Robinson (2012), *Why Nations Fail: The Origins of Power, Prosperity and Poverty*, London: Profile Books.

Ahlerup, Pelle, and Ola Olsson (2007), "The roots of ethnic diversity," Working Papers in Economics no. 281, Department of Economics, Gothenburg University.

――― (2012), "The roots of ethnic diversity," *Journal of Economic Growth*, 17(2): 71–102.

Alba, Richard, and Nancy Foner (2015), *Strangers No More*, Princeton, NJ: Princeton University Press.

Alesina, Alberto, and Eliana La Ferrara (2005), "Ethnic diversity and economic performance," *Journal of Economic Literature*, 43(3): 762–800.

Alesina, Alberto, Stelios Michalopoulos and Elias Papaioannou (2016), "Ethnic inequality," *Journal of Political Economy*, 124(2): 428–88.

Andersson, Ruben (2014), *Illegality, Inc.*, Oakland: University of California Press.

Aydemir, Abdurrahman, and Murat Kirdar (2017), "Quasi-experimental impact estimates of immigrant labor supply shocks: The role of treatment and comparison group matching and relative skill composition," *European Economic Review*, 98: 282–315.

Banting, Keith, and Will Kymlicka (eds.) (2017), *The Strains of Commitment: The Political Sources of Solidarity in Diverse Societies*, Oxford: Oxford University Press.

Barnett, Laura (2002), "Global governance and the evolution of the international refugee regime," *International Journal of Refugee Law*, 14(2–3): 238–62.

Barro, Robert, and Jong-Wha Lee (2013), "A new data set of educational attainment in the world 1950–2010," *Journal of Development Economics*, 104: 184–98.

Bartel, Ann (1989), "Where do the new U.S. immigrants live?" *Journal of Labor Economics*, 7(4): 371–91.

Beine, Michel, Fréderic Docquier and Hillel Rapoport (2008), "Brain drain and human capital formation in developing countries: Winners and losers," *Economic Journal*, 118(528): 631–52.

Belot, Michèle, and Timothy Hatton (2012), "Immigrant selection in the OECD," *Scandinavian Journal of Economics*, 114(4): 1105–28.

Bertoli, Simone, Herbert Brücker and Jesús Fernández-Huertas Moraga (2016), "The European crisis and migration to Germany," *Regional Science and Urban Economics*, 60: 61–72.

Bijwaard, Govert, and Jackline Wahba (2014), "Do high-income or low-income immigrants leave faster?" *Journal of Development Economics*, 108: 54–68.

Bollard, Albert, David McKenzie, Melanie Morten and Hillel Rapoport (2011), "Remittances and the brain drain revisited: The microdata show that more educated migrants remit more," *World Bank Economic Review*, 25(1): 132–56.

Borjas, George (1985), "Assimilation, changes in cohort quality, and the earnings of immigrants," *Journal of Labor Economics*, 3(4): 463–89.

––––––– (1987), "Self-selection and the earnings of immigrants," *American Economic Review*, 77(4): 531–53.

––––––– (1992), "Ethnic capital and intergenerational mobility," *Quarterly Journal of Economics*, 107(1): 123–50.

––––––– (1993), "The intergenerational mobility of immigrants," *Journal of Labor Economics*, 11(1): 113–35.

––––––– (1994), "Long-run convergence of ethnic skill differentials: The children and grand-children of the great migration," *Industrial and Labor Relations Review*, 47(4): 553–73.

––––––– (1995), "Assimilation and changes in cohort quality revisited: What happened to immigrant earnings in the 1980s?" *Journal of Labor Economics*, 13(2): 201–45.

––––––– (1999), "The economic analysis of immigration," in Orley Ashenfelter and David Card (eds.), *Handbook of Labor Economics*, Vol. 3A, 1697–760, Amsterdam: Elsevier.

––––––– (2001), "Does immigration grease the wheels of the labor market?" *Brookings Papers on Economic Activity*, 32(1): 69–119.

––––––– (2016), *We Wanted Workers: Unraveling the Immigration Narrative*, New York: W. W. Norton.

––––––– (2017), "The wage impact of the *Marielitos*: A reappraisal," *Industrial and Labor Relations Review*, 70(5): 1077–10.

Borjas, George, and Bernt Bratsberg (1996), "Who leaves? The outmigration of the foreign-born," *Review of Economics and Statistics*, 78(1): 165–76.

Brücker, Herbert, Stella Capuano and Abdeslam Marfouk (2013), *Education, Gender and International Migration: Insights from a Panel-Dataset 1980–2010*, mimeo.

Card, David (1990), "The impact of the Mariel boatlift on the Miami labor market," *Industrial and Labor Relations Review*, 43(2): 245–57.

––––––– (2001), "Immigrant inflows, native outflows, and the local labor market impacts of higher immigration," *Journal of Labor Economics*, 19(1): 22–64.

Castles, Stephen, Hein De Haas and Mark Miller (2013), *The Age of Migration: International Population Movements in the Modern World*, 5th ed., London: Palgrave Macmillan.

Chiswick, Barry (1978), "The effect of Americanization on the earnings of foreign-born men," *Journal of Political Economy*, 86(5): 897–921.

Chiswick, Barry, and Timothy Hatton (2003), "International migration and the integration of labor markets," in Michael Bordo, Alan Taylor and Jeffrey Williamson (eds.), *Globalization in Historical Perspective*, 65–120. Chicago: University of Chicago Press.

Clark, Ximena, Timothy Hatton and Jeffrey Williamson (2007), "Explaining U.S. immigration, 1971–1998," *Review of Economics and Statistics*, 89(2): 359–73.

Clarke, Andrew, Ana Ferrer and Mikal Skuterud (2019), "A comparative analysis of the labor market performance of university-educated immigrants in Australia, Canada, and the United States: Does policy matter?" *Journal of Labor Economics*, 52(S2): 443–90.

Clemens, Michael (2007), "Do visas kill? Health effects of African health professional emigration," Working Paper no. 114, Center for Global Development.

––––––– (2013), "What do we know about skilled migration and development?" Policy Brief no. 3, Migration Policy Institute.

Clemens, Michael, and Jennifer Hunt (2019), "The labor market effects of refugee waves: Reconciling conflicting results," *Industrial and Labor Relations Review*, 72(4): 818–57.

Clemens, Michael, and Gunilla Pettersson (2006), "Medical leave: A new database of health professional emigration from Africa," Working Paper no. 95, Center for Global Development.

Clemens, Michael, and Lant Pritchett (2008), "Income per natural: Measuring development for people rather than places," *Population and Development Review*, 34(3): 395–434.

Collier, Paul (2013), *Exodus: Immigration and Multiculturalism in the 21st Century*, London: Allen Lane.

Corak, Miles (2006), "Do poor children become poor adults? Lessons from a cross-country comparison in generational earnings mobility," 143–88 in John Creedy and Guyonne Kalb (eds.), *Dynamics of Inequality and Poverty*, Bingley: Emerald Group.

Dustmann, Christian, Maria Casanova, Michael Fertig, Ian Preston and Christoph M. Schmidt (2003), *The Impact of EU Enlargement on Migration Flows*, UK Home Office, Online Report 25/03, London: UK Home Office.

Dustmann, Christian, Tommaso Frattini and Caroline Halls (2010), "Assessing the fiscal costs and benefits of A8 migration to the UK," *Fiscal Studies*, 31(1): 1–41.

Dustmann, Christian, and Joseph-Simon Görlach (2016), "The economics of temporary migrations," *Journal of Economic Literature*, 54(1): 98–136.

Dustmann, Christian, Uta Schönberg and Jan Stuhler (2016), "The impact of immigration: Why do studies reach such different results?" *Journal of Economic Perspectives*, 30(4): 31–56.

Dustmann, Christian, Uta Schönberg and Jan Stuhler (2017), "Labor supply shocks, native wages, and the adjustment of local employment," *Quarterly Journal of Economics*, 132(1): 435–83.

Edin, Per-Anders, Robert LaLonde and Olof Åslund (2000), "Emigration of immigrants and measures of immigrant assimilation: Evidence from Sweden," *Swedish Economic Policy Review*, 7: 163–204.

Edo, Anthony (2020), "The impact of immigration on wage dynamics: Evidence from the Algerian independence war," *Journal of the European Economic Association*, 18(6): 3210–60.

Eltis, David (1983), "Free and coerced transatlantic migrations: Some comparisons," *American Historical Review*, 88(22): 251–80.

Fasani, Francesco, Tommaso Frattini and Luigi Minale (2018), "(The struggle for) refugee integration into the labour market: Evidence from Europe," Discussion Paper no. 11333, IZA.

Fauri, Francesca (2014), "European migrants after the second world war," in Francesca Fauri (eds.), *The History of Migration in Europe: Perspectives from Economics, Politics and Sociology*, 103–25. Abingdon: Routledge.

Frattini, Tommaso (2017), "Integration of immigrants in host countries. What we know and what works," *Revue d'Economie du Développement*, 25(1): 105–34.

Gibney, Matthew J. (2004), *The Ethics and Politics of Asylum: Liberal Democracy and the Response to Refugees*, Cambridge: Cambridge University Press.

Gibson, John, and David McKenzie (2011), "Eight questions about brain drain," *Journal of Economic Perspectives*, 25(3): 107–28.

——— (2012), "The economic consequences of 'brain drain' of the best and brightest: Microeconomic evidence from five countries," *Economic Journal*, 122(560): 339–75.

Goldin, Ian, Geoffrey Cameron and Meera Balarajan (2011), *Exceptional People: How Migration Shaped Our World and Will Define Our Future*, Princeton, NJ: Princeton University Press.

Gould, John (1979), "European inter-continental emigration 1815–1914: Patterns and causes," *Journal of European Economic History*, 8(3): 593–679.

Grogger, Jeffrey, and Gordon Hanson (2011), "Income maximization and the selection and sorting of international migrants," *Journal of Development Economics*, 95(1): 42–57.

Hall, Peter A. (2017), "The political sources of social solidarity," in Keith Banting and Will Kymlicka (eds.), *The Strains of Commitment: The Political Sources of Solidarity in Diverse Societies*, Oxford: Oxford University Press.

Hällsten, Martin, Ryszard Szulkin and Jerzy Sarnecki (2013), "Crime as a price of inequality? The gap in registered crime between childhood immigrants, children of immigrants and children of native Swedes," *British Journal of Criminology*, 53(3): 456–81.

Hamel, Christelle, Doreen Huschek, Nadja Milewski and Helga de Valk (2012), "Union formation and partner choice," in Maurice Crul, Jens Schneider and Frans Lelie (eds.), *The European Second Generation Compared: Does the Integration Context Matter?* 225–84. Amsterdam: Amsterdam University Press.

Hanson, Gordon, and Craig McIntosh (2012), "Birth rates and border crossings: Latin American migration to the US, Canada, Spain and the UK," *Economic Journal*, 122(561): 707–26.

——— (2016), "Is the Mediterranean the new Rio Grande? US and EU immigration pressures in the long run," *Journal of Economic Perspectives*, 30(4): 57–81.

Hanson, Gordon, Chen Liu and Craig McIntosh (2017), "The rise and fall of U.S. low-skilled immigration," *Brookings Papers on Economic Activity*, (1): 83–168.

Hatton, Timothy J. (2015), "United States immigration policy: The 1965 Act and its consequences," *Scandinavian Journal of Economics*, 117(2): 347–68.

Hatton, Timothy J., and Jeffrey G. Williamson (1998), *The Age of Mass Migration: Causes and Economic Impact*, Oxford: Oxford University Press.

——— (2005), *Global Migration and the World Economy: Two Centuries of Policy and Performance*, Cambridge, MA: MIT Press.

Hunt, Jennifer (1992), "The impact of the 1962 repatriates from Algeria on the French labor market," *Industrial and Labor Relations Review*, 45(3): 556–72.

International Monetary Fund (2009), *Balance of Payments and International Investment Position Manual, Sixth Edition (BPM6)*.

Jasso, Guillermina, Douglas Massey, Mark Rosenzweig and James Smith (2000), "The New Immigrant Survey Pilot (NIS-P): Overview and new findings about U.S. legal immigrants at admission," *Demography*, 37(1): 127–38.

Kahanec, Martin (2013), "Labor mobility in an enlarged European Union," in Amelie F. Constant and Klaus F. Zimmermann (eds.), *International Handbook on the Economics of Migration*, 137–52. Cheltenham: Edward Elgar.

Kahanec, Martin, and Klaus F. Zimmermann (eds.) (2010), *EU Labor Markets after Post-Enlargement Migration*, Berlin: Springer.

Kanazawa, Mark (2005), "Immigration, exclusion, and taxation: Anti-Chinese legislation in gold rush California," *Journal of Economic History*, 65(3): 779–805.

Kerr, Sari Pekkala, William Kerr, Çağlar Özden and Christopher Parsons (2017), "High-skilled migration and agglomeration," *Annual Review of Economics*, 9: 201–34.

Kovacheva, Vesela, and Dita Vogel (2009), "The size of the irregular foreign resident population in the European Union in 2002, 2005, and 2008: Aggregated estimates," Working Paper no. 4/2009, Database on Irregular Migration, Hamburg Institute of International Economics.

Krogstad, Jens Manuel, Jeffrey S. Passel and D'Vera Cohn (2019), "5 facts about illegal immigration in the U.S.," Pew Research Center.

McGregor, Russell (2016), *Environment, Race, and Nationhood in Australia: Revisiting the Empty North*, New York: Palgrave Macmillan.

McKenzie, David, John Gibson and Steven Stillman (2010), "How important is selection? Experimental vs. non-experimental measures of the income gains from migration," *Journal of the European Economic Association*, 8(4): 913–45.

Miller, David (1995), *On Nationality*, Oxford: Clarendon Press.

——— (2017), "Solidarity and its sources," in Keith Banting and Will Kymlicka (eds.), *The Strains of Commitment: The Political Sources of Solidarity in Diverse Societies*, 61–79. Oxford: Oxford University Press.

Munshi, Kaivan (2003), "Networks in the modern economy: Mexican migrants in the U.S. labor market," *Quarterly Journal of Economics*, 118(2): 549–99.

National Academies of Sciences, Engineering, and Medicine (2017), *The Economic and Fiscal Consequences of Immigration*, Washington, DC: National Academies Press.

Olzak, Susan (1983), "Contemporary ethnic mobilization," *Annual Review of Sociology*, 9: 355–74.

Pedersen, Peder, Mariola Pytlikova and Nina Smith (2008), "Selection and network effects—Migration flows into OECD countries 1990–2000," *European Economic Review*, 52(7): 1160–186.

Peri, Giovanni, and Vasil Yasenov (2019), "The labor market effects of a refugee wave: Synthetic control meets the Mariel Boatlift," *Journal of Human Resources*, 54(2): 267–309.

Pinotti, Paolo (2016), "Immigrants and crime," in Francesco Fasani (eds.), *Refugees and Economic Migrants: Facts, Policies and Challenges*, 115–24. CEPR Press. Available at: https://voxeu.org/content/refugees-and-economic-migrants-facts-policies-and-challenges.

Preston, Ian (2014), "The effect of immigration on public finances," *Economic Journal*, 124(580): F569–F592.

Price, Charles (1981), "Immigration policies and refugees in Australia," *International Migration Review*, 15(1–2): 99–108.

Pripp, Oscar (2001), *Företagande i minoritet: om etnicitet, strategier and resurser bland assyrier and syrianer i Södertälje*, Tumba: Mångkulturellt Centrum.

Rothstein, Bo (2017), "Solidarity, diversity, and the quality of government," in Keith Banting and Will Kymlicka (eds.), *The Strains of Commitment: The Political Sources of Solidarity in Diverse Societies*, 300–26. Oxford: Oxford University Press.

Rothstein, Bo, and Eric Uslaner (2005), "All for all: Equality, corruption, and social trust," *World Politics*, 58(1): 41–72.

Rowthorn, Robert (2008), "The fiscal impact of immigration on the advanced economies," *Oxford Review of Economic Policy*, 24(3): 560–80.

Ruggles, Steven, Katie Genadek, Ronald Goeken, Josiah Grover and Matthew Sobek (2015), *Integrated Public Use Microdata Series: Version 6.0 (dataset)*, University of Minnesota.

Ruist, Joakim (2014), "Free immigration and welfare access: The Swedish experience," *Fiscal Studies*, 35(1): 19–39.

——— (2017a), "Outmigration and income assimilation during the first post-EU-enlargement migrants' first decade in Sweden," Working Papers in Economics no. 696, Department of Economics, Gothenburg University.

——— (2017b), "Long live the American Dream: Self-selection and inequality-persistence among American immigrants," Discussion Paper no. 1714, Centre for Research and Analysis of Migration (CReAM).

———— (2018a), *Tid för integration—en ESO-rapport om flyktingars bakgrund and arbetsmarknadsetablering*, Rapport till Expertgruppen för studier i offentlig ekonomi 2018:3, Stockholm: Regeringskansliet, Finansdepartementet.

———— (2018b), "The prosperity gap and the free movement of workers," in Ulf Bernitz, Moa Mårtensson, Lars Oxelheim and Thomas Persson (eds.), *Bridging the Prosperity Gap in the EU – the social challenge ahead*, 85–101. Cheltenham: Edward Elgar.

———— (2020), "The fiscal aspect of the refugee crisis," *International Tax and Public Finance*, 27(2): 478–92.

Schwartz, Ada (1973), "Interpreting the effect of distance on migration," *Journal of Political Economy*, 81(5): 1153–169.

Sjaastad, Larry (1962), "The costs and returns of human migration," *Journal of Political Economy*, 70(5, part 2): 80–93.

Solon, Gary (2014), "Theoretical models of inequality transmission across multiple generations," *Research in Social Stratification and Mobility*, 35: 13–18.

Statistics Denmark (2018), *Invandrere i Danmark 2018*, Statistics Denmark.

Statistics Netherlands (2018), *Jaarrapport integratie 2018*. Summary in English at: https://www.cbs.nl/en-gb/news/2018/48/younger-turkish-moroccan-2nd-generation-marrying-later (accessed on December 21, 2018).

Stichnoth, Holger, and Karine Van der Straeten (2013), "Ethnic diversity, public spending, and individual support for the welfare state: A review of the empirical literature," *Journal of Economic Surveys*, 27(2): 364–89.

Storesletten, Kjetil (2000), "Sustaining fiscal policy through immigration," *Journal of Political Economy*, 108(2): 300–23.

UNHCR (2000), *The State of the World's Refugees 2000: Fifty Years of Humanitarian Action.*

U.S. Department of Homeland Security (2016), *Yearbook of Immigration Statistics: 2015*. Washington, DC: U.S. Department of Homeland Security, Office of Immigration Statistics.

Van der Meer, Tom, and Jandem Tolsma (2014), "Ethnic diversity and its effects on social cohesion," *Annual Review of Sociology*, 40: 459–78.

Waters, Mary, and Tomás Jiménez (2015), "Assessing immigrant assimilation: New empirical and theoretical challenges," *Annual Review of Sociology*, 31: 105–25.

Wegge, Simone (1998), "Chain migration and information networks: Evidence from nineteenth-century Hesse-Cassel," *Journal of Economic History*, 58(4): 957–86.

Yang, Dean (2008), "International migration, remittances and household investment: Evidence from Philippine migrants' exchange rate shocks," *Economic Journal*, 118(528): 591–630.

———— (2011), "Migrant remittances," *Journal of Economic Perspectives*, 25(3): 129–52.

Yang, Dean, and HwaJung Choi (2007), "Are remittances insurance? Evidence from rainfall shocks in the Philippines," *World Bank Economic Review*, 21(2): 219–48.

Zimmermann, Andreas, Jonas Dörschner and Felix Machts (eds.) (2011), *The 1951 Convention Relating to the Status of Refugees and Its 1967 Protocol: A Commentary*, Oxford: Oxford University Press.

INDEX